Doing Research on
Sensitive Topics

Doing Research
on
Sensitive Topics

Raymond M. Lee

SAGE Publications
London • Thousand Oaks • New Delhi

First published 1993
Reprinted 1995

 SAGE Publications Ltd
6 Bonhill Street
London EC2A 4PU

SAGE Publications Inc
2455 Teller Road
Thousand Oaks, California 91320

SAGE Publications India Pvt Ltd
32, M-Block Market
Greater Kailash – I
New Delhi 110 048

British Library Cataloguing in Publication Data

Lee, Raymond M.
  Doing Research on Sensitive Topics
  I. Title
  300.72

  ISBN 0–8039–8860–5
  ISBN 0–8039–88861–3 (pbk)

Library of Congress catalog card number 92–056616

Typeset by Photoprint, Torquay, Devon
Printed and bound in Great Britain by
Biddles Ltd, Guildford and King's Lynn

To Christopher, Julia and Paul

Contents

Acknowledgements

A number of people have helped me during the production of this book. In particular I would like to thank Nigel Fielding and Claire Renzetti for their comments on various drafts and Sara Arber, Janet Finch and Jennifer Platt for commenting on individual chapters. I am also grateful to Anne Akeroyd, Eileen Barker, Jon Bing, Ben Bowling and Gary Marx for providing me with information about a variety of topics. I first grappled with some of the issues discussed in the book on research projects directed by Mike Hornsby-Smith and Chris Harris. I am grateful to both of them for their help and support over the years and for their indulgence of some of my more recondite methodological enthusiasms. Colleagues in the Department of Social Policy and Social Science at Royal Holloway University of London and, earlier, at St Mary's College, Twickenham, have been generous with encouragement while the book was being written and my thanks go to them. More specifically, I would like to thank colleagues and students on the MSc in Sociology with Special Reference to Medicine at Royal Holloway. A number of the ideas in this book have been elaborated in the seminar on Theory and Methods of Social Research on the MSc. Finally, at Sage, I am grateful for the encouragement of Sara Miller McCune when the book was in its formative stages and to Stephen Barr for his continuing support and help.

1

Introduction

In September 1989 Margaret Thatcher, the then British Prime Minister, used a little known power to veto the public funding of a large-scale survey of sexual behaviour. She apparently felt that the study would be intrusive and would fail – given its subject matter – to produce reliable information. In making her decision Mrs Thatcher set aside the importance of the survey to an understanding of the factors involved in the transmission of HIV infection, a topic of demonstrable public concern. She also apparently ignored the results of a detailed pilot study which confirmed that reliable and' valid data could be produced, and that there was virtually no sign of public anxiety or hostility to the research (Jowell and Field, 1989). Two years later, in not dissimilar circumstances, Louis Sullivan, the US Secretary of Health and Human Services, cancelled a large scale federally-funded survey of American teenagers. Dr Sullivan's action, which followed a campaign by conservative politicians, was prompted by the inclusion on the proposed survey of questions about sexual behaviour.[1]

Encapsulated in these episodes are a number of the problems and issues which form the subject of this book. Studies of 'sensitive' topics like sexual behaviour raise questions, for example, about the kinds of research regarded as permissible in society, the extent to which research may encroach upon people's lives, the problems of ensuring data quality in dealing with certain kinds of topics and the ability of the powerful to control the research process. This book is intended to give guidance to those who are beginning or have embarked on research in a sensitive area. 'Sensitivity' potentially affects almost every stage of the research process from the formulation of a research problem, through the design and implementation of a study, to the dissemination and application of the findings (Lee and Renzetti, 1990; Brewer, 1990a; Sieber and Stanley, 1988; Siegel and Bauman, 1986). The problems and issues that arise at each stage take a variety of forms. They may be methodological, technical, ethical, political or legal. Sensitive research often also has potential effects on the personal life, and sometimes on the personal security, of the researcher (Plummer, 1983; Brewer, 1990a).

Clearly the 'sensitivity' of a topic is not a measure of either its social or its theoretical significance. Yet, frequently, research on sensitive topics 'addresses some of society's most pressing social issues and policy questions' (Sieber and Stanley, 1988, 55). Sensitive research is important too precisely because it illuminates the darker corners of society. As Rock puts it, 'The taboo, the proscribed and the unusual all promote distancing experiences' (1973, 25). Studies involving sensitive topics may therefore aid theory-building because they challenge taken-for-granted ways of seeing the world. In addition, sensitive topics tax the methodological ingenuity of social scientists.

Investigating sensitive topics usually introduces into the research process contingencies less commonly found in other kinds of study. Because of the threat they pose, sensitive topics raise difficult methodological and technical problems (Lee and Renzetti, 1990). Access is often problematic. The adequate conceptualization of particular topics is sometimes inhibited (Hertzberger, 1990). Where research is threatening, the relationship between the researcher and the researched is likely to become hedged about with mistrust, concealment and dissimulation. This affects the availability and quality of data with usually adverse consequences for levels of reliability and validity. In response to the technical problems generated by sensitive topics researchers have produced a range of methodological innovations (Caplan, 1982). However, much of the relevant material is either buried in the methodological literature, or else is spread across a range of substantive fields. One goal of the book is therefore to make such methodological developments more widely known, and to assess their effectiveness.

Sensitive topics also raise wider issues related to the ethics, politics and legal aspects of research. Issues of this kind impinge on all research, whatever its character. They may impinge more compellingly, however, in the case of research on sensitive topics. Those researching sensitive topics may need to be more acutely aware of their ethical responsibilities to research participants than would be the case with the study of a more innocuous topic. In addition, the issues raised by sensitive research point in a wider sense to the factors, both legitimate and illegitimate, which shape and determine the permissible boundaries of inquiry. In many cases neither the problems raised by studying sensitive topics, nor the wider issues involved, can be dealt with in any simple way. The relationship between methodological or technical decisions in research and ethical, legal or political considerations is often complex and reciprocal. A second goal of the book is, therefore, to examine the ethical, political and legal contexts within which socially sensitive research is carried out, and to understand their impact on research practice in a sociologically informed way.

Defining sensitive research

One difficulty in talking about 'sensitive topics' is that the phrase is often used in the literature as if it were self-explanatory. The term, in other words, is treated in a common-sense way without being defined (Lee and Renzetti, 1990). One exception is the definition proposed by Sieber and Stanley. Sieber and Stanley define 'socially sensitive research' as:

> studies in which there are potential consequences or implications, either directly for the participants in the research or for the class of individuals represented by the research. For example, a study that examines the relative merits of day care for infants against full-time care by the mother can have broad social implications and thus can be considered socially sensitive. Similarly, studies aimed at examining the relation between gender and mathematical ability also have significant social implications. (1988, 49)

An advantage of defining sensitive research in this way is that it broadens the scope of the definition to include topics which might not ordinarily be thought of as 'sensitive', and alerts researchers to the wider implications of their work. Given the ethical and professional issues which form the primary focus of Sieber and Stanley's article this is entirely appropriate. The difficulty is that Sieber and Stanley do not specify the scope or nature of the kinds of consequences or implications they have in mind. Their definition, therefore, logically encompasses research which is consequential in any way. This would presumably include almost any kind of applied research, even where it had limited scope or was wholly beneficial. In addition, while the importance of ethical issues should not be diminished, it needs also to be remembered that research on sensitive topics raises a whole range of problems including those of a more specifically technical and methodological kind. Sieber and Stanley's definition tends to direct attention away from these problems.

While Sieber and Stanley focus on the consequences of research, Farberow (1963) equates sensitive topics with those areas of social life surrounded by taboo. Farberow's discussion is based in a rather eclectic way on a range of anthropological and psychoanalytic sources. On the basis of this material Farberow regards taboo topics as those which are laden with emotion or which inspire feelings of awe or dread. It is not difficult to see such topics – Farberow apparently has in mind matters relating to sex or death – as being 'sensitive'. The problem with this approach is that it is much too narrow. It does not allow for the possibility that research may have a sensitive character for situational reasons (Brewer, 1990a) or because it is located within a particular socio-political context (Rostocki, 1986). At the same time studies of deviant behaviour, an area often regarded by researchers as sensitive, do not easily fit with Farberow's definition. To add to the confusion Farberow also includes under the heading of taboo topics research on areas like graphology or parapsychology which have a disputed scientific status.

An alternative approach would be to start from the observation that insofar as there is a common thread in the literature it lies in the implicit assumption that some kinds of topics potentially involve a level of threat or risk to those studied which renders problematic the collection, holding and/or dissemination of research data (Lee and Renzetti, 1990). A simple definition of sensitive research would therefore be 'research which potentially poses a substantial threat to those who are or have been involved in it'. Another way to put this is to say that sensitive topics present problems because research into them involves potential costs to those involved in the research, including, on occasion, the researcher. It is true, of course, that all research has some cost to those involved, if only in terms of time and possible inconvenience. While there are cases where research makes demands on participants which are quite substantial, the potential costs in the case of sensitive topics go beyond the incidental or the merely onerous.

Research as threat

From the scattered literature on sensitive topics one would most expect research to be threatening within three broad areas. The first is where the research poses an 'intrusive threat', dealing with areas which are private, stressful or sacred. The second relates to the study of deviance and social control and involves the possibility that information may be revealed which is stigmatizing or incriminating in some way. Finally, research is often problematic when it impinges on political alignments, if 'political' is taken in its widest sense to refer to the vested interests of powerful persons or institutions, or the exercise of coercion or domination. In these situations researchers often trespass into areas which are controversial or involve social conflict.

Obviously, a particular study may encompass any or all of these aspects of sensitivity. What needs to be stressed, however, is that the kind of threat posed by a particular piece of research, as well as its level, is a highly contextual matter. In other words, the sensitive character of a piece of research seemingly inheres less in the specific topic and more in the relationship between that topic and the social context – defined both broadly and narrowly – within which the research is conducted. It is not unusual, for example, for the sensitive nature of an apparently innocuous topic to become apparent once research is under way, nor for a researcher to approach a topic with caution only to find initial fears about its 'sensitivity' have been misplaced. In a similar way, just as Goyder (1987) has hypothesized that different social groups attribute different meanings to requests for participation in research, it may well be that a study seen as threatening by one group will be thought innocuous by another. One consequence of this is that, although the term 'sensitive topic' is a convenient one to use, it does not seem useful to try to develop a comprehensive list of sensitive topics. Instead a more fruitful approach is to look at the conditions under which 'sensitivity' arises within the research process. A further important point to make is that while the threat posed by research most obviously affects research participants it may also have an impact on others. These include the researcher, but also the family members and associates of those studied, the social groups to which they belong, the wider community, research institutions and society at large (Sieber and Stanley, 1988; see also Lee and Renzetti, 1990; Bailey, 1988).

Intrusive threat

Although it might seem obvious that research which intrudes into the private sphere is likely to have a sensitive character, this is not inevitably the case. Following a careful review of the available literature, Day (1985) has concluded that there is no fixed private sphere. Topics and activities regarded as private vary cross-culturally and situationally. Nevertheless, more than other topics, survey respondents record misgivings or unease about questions directed towards their finances or sexual behaviour (Goyder, 1987, 143; Bradburn and Sudman, 1979). The threatening character of interviews on relatively intimate matters may also be gauged from reports of interviewees lapsing into embarrassed silence (George, 1983) or needing to use alcohol as a prop while being interviewed (Brannen, 1988). In part, disclosing private information in interviews is likely to be problematic because privacy itself produces pluralistic ignorance. That is, because individuals only know about their own behaviour, it is difficult for them to judge how 'normal' that behaviour is compared to other people. This may lead to additional threat in research situations since the researcher may be presumed to know how one stands in relation to others (Richardson et al., 1965, 72).

Other areas of personal experience, such as bereavement, are not so much private as emotionally charged. Research into such areas may be threatening to those studied because of the levels of stress which it may induce. An additional problem here, which also affects research into the private sphere, has to do with maintaining an appropriate demeanour in face-to-face contact with the researcher. Although it may be difficult to remain composed in trying circumstances, the ability to do so is socially prized (Goffman, 1957; Scheff, 1988). Doubts that one can maintain proper standards of poise when asked about sensitive matters may therefore make matters even more threatening. Of course, this is also frequently true for the researcher as well, who may have to share with those researched feelings of unease, discomfort or emotional pain.

In Western societies the sphere of the sacred has become increasingly diminished. Social scientists are therefore unlikely to face the kinds of problems anthropologists have sometimes encountered in non-Western societies in relation to sacred artefacts or objects (Barnes, 1979). Even so, the values and beliefs of some groups can still be threatened in a fundamental way by research. The old-time Pentacostalists studied by Homan (1978; but see more particularly Homan and Bulmer, 1982) devalue worldly knowledge in favour of divine revelation. As a result they reject education and scholarship, and stigmatize sociologists in particular as communists or atheists. Research for some groups in other words is quite literally an anathema.

Threat of sanction
The presence of a researcher is sometimes feared because it produces a possibility that deviant activities will be revealed. As Becker (1964) points out, even in relatively innocuous situations a sociologist will often point to activities and practices which may be deviant but which are tacitly accepted as long as no-one draws attention to them. In addition, in many, particularly organizational, situations 'fear of scrutiny' (Payne et al., 1980) is common. The researcher is therefore frequently identified as someone explicitly seeking discreditable information. Thus, John Johnson (1975), on entering the social work agency he had chosen to study, was openly accused by one of the social workers of being a spy for the state governor's office. Accusations of spying are presumably most common in situations of conflict or tension. Warren (1988) notes that, not uncommonly, American anthropologists working in Third

World countries have faced accusations of spying for the Central Intelligence Agency. After an initial period in which researchers were welcomed, research in certain areas in Northern Ireland became much more difficult. As Rupert Taylor (1988) points out, some researchers were forced into hiding or had to leave Northern Ireland altogether as fears arose in some communities that research materials were finding their way to the security forces.

Research which might bring to light that which was formerly hidden can also be unwelcome. One example of this is seen in the difficulty involved in studying a group of individuals who worked in the hidden economy (Lee, 1986b). In this case the initial contact was a 'ghost worker' whose existence was completely unknown to the tax authorities. Apparently following Simmel's dictum that, 'Of all protective measures, the most radical is to make oneself invisible' (Wolff, 1950), he was unwilling to compromise his invisibility or that of his co-workers by being studied.

Where the members of some group to be studied are powerless or disadvantaged, they may fear exploitation or derogation, or be sceptical about research. Thus, Josephson (1970) found it impossible to proceed with an adolescent health survey in Harlem after a local action group initiated a campaign against the study, charging that the data collected would be used for social control purposes (see also Vargus, 1971; Goudy and Richards, 1973). The group of Black, unemployed young people studied by Ullah (1987) were initially hostile to him. They felt not only that no tangible benefit would result from the study, but also that the research itself was completely futile. This was so, they reasoned, because it hardly needed research to reveal that being unemployed was an unpleasant experience. 'You see a man on the road', said one of Ullah's (1987, 117) informants, 'and he's been stabbed a hundred times. You don't go up to him and say, "How does it feel?".'

Political threat
Since research settings invariably exist inside a wider social, economic and political environment, that context may have repercussions inside the setting. This is particularly true where the external environment is conflictual, producing fears that the results of the research may favour one faction rather than another (Record, 1967), or that it might upset moves to resolve the conflict (Sjoberg and Nett, 1968). Brewer's (1990b) study of routine policing in Northern Ireland provides a good example of a study which was threatening to both participants and researchers due to the nature of the external social environment. Given the violent social conflict in Northern Ireland, police officers feared that their physical safety

could be compromised should there be a leakage of information from the project (Brewer, 1990a).[2]

Even in less overtly conflictual situations research which seems to threaten the alignments or interests of those being studied is frequently seen as having a sensitive character. This is particularly so where a study touches on the exercise of power or on extremes of wealth and status. 'Historically', says Beynon, 'the rich and powerful have encouraged hagiography, not critical investigation' (1988, 23). As a result there has been a tendency for social scientists to study 'down' rather than 'up'; directing their attention towards the relatively powerless rather than at élites, powerful organizations or the state apparatus (Rainwater and Pittman, 1967; Galliher, 1980; Schensul, 1980; Nader, 1972). To some extent the difficulties involved in studying élites may be exaggerated. Élite groups may share values with researchers concerning the importance of research, as Moyser and Wagstaffe (1987, 158) point out. They may also presume that a study will be objective, unbiased and useful to the formulation of policy. Winckler notes, too, that a central feature of élite psychology, which was helpful to him, is the desire to know how one stands in relation to others. Some of those he studied allowed him access because they were curious to know 'what it was like for the others and how they rated alongside the famous' (1987, 137).

Hoffman (1980), reflecting on her own research on élite group members, suggests that there may even be a self-fulfilling prophecy at work. Research is not even attempted on powerful groups in the first place because it is assumed that they will be difficult to study. However, some of the force of Hoffman's argument is blunted by the fact that her research was partly possible because she herself was an insider, a member of a family that was itself part of the élite she was trying to study. Other researchers have been less fortunate. Indeed Cassell (1988) implies that élites may in some cases actually feel demeaned by being studied by those of lower status, while Punch has commented ruefully on the difficulties of studying 'literate, articulate, self-conscious people with the power, resources and expertise to protect their reputation' (1986, 77).

In some settings the interests of those who hold positions of power lie in maintaining quiescence. Wood (1980) reports, for example, that he was denied access to redundancy situations on a number of occasions by managers who felt that the workforce remaining needed to 'settle down' and to 'put the redundancies behind them'. As one manager rather graphically put it, to permit the research would be 'like taking the plaster off and looking at the wound, running the risk of reopening it when things were getting back to normal'. More broadly, within bureaucratic structures especially, 'the researcher is a relatively uncontrollable element in an otherwise highly controlled system' (Spencer, 1973, 93). In this situation, research can be perceived as threatening to the careers of those who might have to take responsibility if the study subsequently reveals information unfavourable to the organization. Spencer also argues that researchers may pose an implicit threat to the culture of an organization. This is particularly true in organizations like the military where a strongly embedded internal normative order provides a source of identity for its members. Outsiders whose values are thought to be unsympathetic, or even just different, may be feared or greeted with suspicion.

Where power is capable of being used corruptly or in an illegitimate manner researchers are an obvious liability to be excluded or hindered in their work (Braithwaite, 1985; Punch, 1989). Even where this is not the case, élites, powerful organizations and governments are often sensitive to the way in which their image is portrayed. As a result in an attempt to forestall what they regard as negative criticism they may be led to impugn a researcher's motives, methods and credibility (Beynon, 1988; see also Cohen and Taylor, 1977).

Threats to the researcher

Where deviant groups or individuals are being studied research can become problematic for the researcher. This seems to be true in particular for researchers on human sexuality, who have not infrequently remarked on their stigmatization by colleagues, university administrators and students (Plummer, 1981; Troiden, 1987; Weinberg and Williams, 1972). According to Troiden (1987) the 'occupational stigma' which attaches to research (or teaching) on sexual behaviour produces personal and professional risks. Such risks arise, Troiden suggests, because of the stereotypical expectations social audiences have of those who research sexual matters. On the one hand researchers may find their work being trivialized or treated in a joking manner. On the other, they may be viewed as undermining what is 'natural' or sacred, of subverting traditional values or of being advocates for particular sexual practices.

Researchers on sexual deviance seem often to suffer 'stigma contagion' (Kirby and Corzine, 1981), coming to share the stigma attached to those being studied. It is apparently not unusual, for example, for those who study homosexual behaviour to be assumed themselves to be homosexual. Alternatively, as Troiden (1987) notes, others often assume that an interest in researching sexual behaviour derives from psychological disturbance or is a sign of either sexual prowess or ineptitude. Troiden suggests that those who research sexual behaviour face professional risks in the form of career disadvantage. Jobs or promotion may be closed to them because administrators fear difficulty or controversy. In addition, sex research may by its nature make career progression difficult. It often involves interdisciplinary work, and can become highly specialized. Both these factors may displace a researcher out of the mainstream of a discipline where career advantage is most likely to be assured and towards the margins where promotion can be inhibited.

Troiden points to a range of strategies which those who research sexual behaviour may use for coping with occupational stigmatization. Researchers may withdraw from the area altogether or may try to conceal their 'stigma' by selectively revealing their research interests only to potentially sympathetic social audiences. Other strategies include retreating into the field itself, treating as a primary reference group only those doing work of a similar kind, or redefining one's professional role as that, for instance, of counsellor or educator. Negative attitudes can also seemingly become assuaged through external changes. Silverman (1989) notes, for instance, that the flow of funding into AIDS research has had beneficial consequences for genito-urinary medicine, a previously low-status specialty, although whether the same is also true of hitherto deprecated social science specialisms is not entirely clear.

Although the topic is not pursued here in detail,[3] researchers often face as a further threat to their activities the physical danger inherent in situations of violent social conflict or among groups within which violence is common. Yancey and Rainwater (1970) distinguish between two kinds of danger that may arise during the research process: the 'presentational' and the 'anonymous'. (Similar distinctions have been proposed by Brewer [1990a] and Sluka [1990].) Presentational danger arises when the researcher's presence or actions evoke aggression, hostility or violence from those within the setting (see, e.g., Carey, 1972; Bourgois, 1989). Anonymous danger arises when the researcher is exposed to otherwise avoidable dangers simply from having to be in a dangerous setting for the research to be carried out. A study of routine policing in Northern Ireland, for example, involved accompanying police officers in situations where they were potential targets for armed attack (Brewer 1990a).

The possible dangers involved do not, of course, totally preclude research in violent settings. Researchers may, if need be, fall back on secondary sources of data where they are available. However, even this may not be necessary. As a number of writers have found, somewhat to their surprise, *bona fide* researchers may be welcome in a factionalized and violent situation (R.H. Wax, 1971; Migdal, 1979; Gilmore, 1991). A principal reason for this is the perception that the researcher provides an audience and a voice for the factions involved. Despite this, there seems little doubt that the dangers inherent in some research settings have deterred researchers from entering them. It is noticeable, for instance, that (relatively peaceful) rural communities in Northern Ireland have been more commonly studied by ethnographers than those based in conflict-ridden urban areas. (On the rural ethnographies, see McFarlane, 1986. Urban ethnographies include those by Burton [1978] and by Jenkins [1983].) In a similar way anthropological research in certain areas of Peru showed a marked decline following armed insurrection by Shining Path guerrillas. Graduate students who might formerly have worked in these areas now apparently opt to carry out fieldwork in Ecuador or Bolivia (Starn, 1991).

Sociology and research on sensitive topics

Systematic enquiry into existing social conditions predates academic sociology. However, as Oberschall (1972) points out, research of the kind undertaken, for example, by nineteenth-century statistical societies in Britain was episodic and non-cumulative. Promising research techniques were invented, forgotten and then reinvented elsewhere. It was only when sociology emerged as an academic speciality in its own right, and when academic sociologists, most notably at the University of Chicago in the 1920s, began to treat social research as a legitimate and important component of their academic role, that social research became institutionalized.[4]

Many of the topics studied by the Chicago sociologists would today be regarded as 'sensitive'. The Chicagoans granted 'primacy to the primary', as Lofland (1983) puts it. Much of their attention was focused on groups based around the primary ties of family, friendship or neighbourhood, any of which might implicitly involve intrusion into the private sphere. They also had an abiding interest in the study of deviance (Matza, 1969; Downes and Rock, 1988).[5] The Chicagoans clearly recognized some of the problems involved in asking questions which might yield incriminating information, and the potential difficulties in gaining access to research sites. They even had some awareness of the need to match the race of interviewers and respondents on surveys, as well as the importance of maintaining confidentiality (Bulmer, 1984, 78, 169). By and large, however, as Bulmer (1984, 90) points out, the Chicagoans were relatively unselfconscious about their methods, something which in part may have allowed them to sidestep the methodological and ethical issues raised by the study of sensitive topics.

Chicago sociologists in effect minimized the threatening aspects of research to those studied through the use of nonreactive methods involving documents and case records, their reliance on professional informants such as social workers, and by means of covert interviewing and observation (Bulmer, 1984). Only in life-history research can the beginnings of a discussion be found about the effects of threatening questions on the reliability and validity of the data gathered. Ernest Burgess (1932), in his discussion of Clifford Shaw's life-history of the rapist 'Sydney', attempted to assess the reliability and validity of Sydney's account of his crimes, and developed a preliminary typology of interviewing situations and relationships (see also Palmer, 1928). This work seems not to have been developed further, however, presumably in part because the life-history method fell into disuse with the advent of more quantitative research strategies.

The Chicagoans were also trapped by their own reformist leanings. On the one hand, they had little incentive to study 'upwards', if this meant directing their attention towards local élites. Even if sociologists sometimes stressed the need to redress social and economic inequalities more than their reformist patrons would have liked (Carey, 1975), a portion of this élite provided funding for research. In any case local reformers and the Chicago sociologists had similar perceptions concerning the social and physical location of the city's problems. On the other hand, those among the locally powerful who felt themselves to be the target of reformist zeal resisted study. The political machine and powerful trade unions were scarcely sympathetic to outside scrutiny (D. Smith, 1988). Even the businessmen who owned the taxi-dance halls would not co-operate in Cressey's study, and in some instances were directly hostile to it. As a result, those who lacked power were more often the subject of study by Chicago sociologists than those who possessed it (D. Smith, 1988).

Following the intellectual decline of the Chicago school, American sociology, by mid-century, had become dominated by what Bryant (1985) calls 'instrumental positivism'. Premised on an essentially individualistic conception of society, this approach emphasized quantification and statistical sophistication, and relied heavily on the sample survey as a means of gathering data.[6] Moreover, in their attempt to establish sociology's scientific respectability, American sociologists increasingly shifted their attention away from the low-life concerns of the Chicago sociologists. Studies of trends in journal publication in the post-war period suggest an increasing emphasis on research in professional and bureaucratic spheres and in the public realm (Brown and Gilmartin, 1969; Simpson, 1961; Tibbitts, 1962; Presser, 1984). Such studies also show that, as the survey gained dominance, the study of attitudes, the investigation of which was less threatening to respondents, began to take precedence over the study of behaviour (Presser, 1984). In addition, sociologists of this period seem rather readily to have accepted the demarcation lines implicit in existing, often medicalized, definitions of areas such as family violence, alcoholism, mental illness and sexual deviance (Gelles, 1973; Gold, 1977; Plummer, 1975).

This situation was not, however, to remain. The social transformations of the 1960s and 1970s had a profound effect on social research both in the United States and in other countries, like Britain, where the development of sociology had only recently become institutionalized. For a variety of reasons, both internal and external to sociology, research agendas widened, often to encompass topics which had previously been ignored or left under-researched because of their perceived 'sensitivity'. In the United States, an increasing amount of research funded by federal government and private foundations began to be directed at the ills of racism, poverty, violence and crime (Hill, 1983). As Hill points out, an important catalyst to this development was the use of social science expertise by the US Supreme Court in its landmark school desegregation ruling in 1954. Social research in the United States also had an organizational structure which allowed social scientists to respond readily to these new demands. Academic survey researchers were increasingly located in research organizations, which often took the form of semi-independent research units attached to universities (Hill, 1983; Lazarsfeld, 1962; Converse, 1987; Bryant, 1985; and, for a rather more jaundiced view, Mills, 1959). Such researchers, Hill argues, had to develop a client-oriented, contract-based style of research to maintain their existence, and sometimes used commercial funding indirectly to further methodological and substantive interests.

The importance of this in relation to sensitive topics lay in the impetus it gave to methodological development. Traditionally, survey practitioners were not entirely averse to researching sensitive topics. Early opinion pollsters, according to Converse, had displayed 'a curious mixture of daring and caution' (1987, 402–3). They were wary of asking respondents about their educational attainment, for example, but included questions on venereal disease and birth control in their questionnaires. Researchers now had to deal on a much more routine basis with 'special' populations who were often too difficult to contact by usual means, not necessarily co-operative, and from whom threatening information of various kinds had to be elicited. This in turn led to the development of methodo-logical innovations of a largely technical kind relating, for example, to the asking of sensitive questions on surveys or methods for protecting the confidentiality of research data (see, e.g., Boruch and Cecil, 1979; Bradburn and Sudman, 1979). (In Britain, by contrast, there was relatively little of this kind of development. The presence of the commercial market research sector inhibited aca-demic survey research, while for a long time little public funding was directed towards applied social research [Hoinville, 1985].)

The 1960s and 1970s were also notable for a series of challenges to traditional orthodoxies which emerged from within the discipline itself. Younger sociologists, shaped by the counterculture and, in the United States, by radical political action in the struggle for civil rights and against the Vietnam war, attacked what they saw as the pretensions and hypocrisies of the discipline. Sociology's search for scientific respectability, its attempts to provide knowledge useful to policy-makers and its proclaimed value neutrality were seen, at best, to have conservative implications and, at worst, to be directly exploitative. The radical critique, although wide-ranging, was some-what programmatic. Moreover, since social research could be seen as a distraction from or substitute for radical political action, the relationship between research and radical politics was by no means an unproblematic one (Becker and Horowitz, 1972). One solution to this problem was to emulate investigative journalism and especially the earlier muckraking tradition in American journalism which at the turn of the century had sought out and exposed municipal corruption. Indeed, some sociologists appropriated the term 'muckraking sociology' to describe a research style which had an 'exposé, sacred cow-smashing, anti-establishment, counter-intuitive, even subversive quality' (Marx, 1972, 3); an approach which was designed to sustain social criticism and facilitate radical social change. As the name implies, muckraking sociology sought to uncover what the powerful, for their own ends, wanted to keep hidden. Such research was therefore intrinsically sensitive and might even depend on the use of unconventional 'investigative' methods (J.D. Douglas, 1976; Galliher, 1980).

If muckraking research was intended to uncover the misdeeds of the powerful, the 1960s and 1970s also saw the emergence of what Gouldner (1962; 1968) has described as 'underdog sociology'. Associated with writers like Howard Becker and Edwin Lemert, this strand of writing within the sociology of deviance had an affinity with muckraking sociology, but flowed more directly from a theoretical reworking of traditional Chicago themes. Described by some as a sociology of 'nuts, sluts and perverts' (Liazos, 1972), underdog sociology has sometimes, as Gouldner points out, romanticized those it studies. Be that as it may, research in this tradition has typically required involvement in and a detailed observation of the worlds of confidence tricksters, prostitutes, drug addicts, hustlers and others of similar ilk. Not surprisingly writing in the area is methodologically preoccupied with the problematics of access to stigmatized and derogated groups, ways of managing field relations, and the dilemmas which arise from possessing 'guilty knowledge' of deviant activities.

A third strand which emerged, though somewhat later, out of the radical milieu of the 1960s was feminist research. Here, too, a tension exists between feminism as a form of radical politics and as a sociological perspective. As a result, there is disagreement about the nature and scope of a specifically feminist methodology (Gelsthorpe and Morris, 1988). Despite these differences feminist researchers tend to share a set of commitments to ways of researching the position of women in society. Methodologically, there is an emphasis on establishing non-hierarchical forms of relationship between researcher and researched (Oakley, 1981; Finch, 1984). Substantively, feminist researchers have sought to overcome the traditional invisibility of women in social research (Eichler, 1988), and to explicate patterns of power, domination and disadvantage in gender relations. In so doing they have made the world of private experience a focus for study. Persistent themes in feminist research include the study of sexuality and the breaking down of taboos surrounding abusive, violent and victimizing behaviour directed towards women (Dobash and Dobash, 1979; Kennedy-Bergen, 1992).

It seems likely that in the future social scientists are more rather than less likely to have to face the problems and issues which surround research on sensitive topics. Berardo and Shehan (1984), reviewing research in one particular area, family sociology, have pointed to substantive shifts in research in the direction of potentially sensitive topics like marital breakdown, single-parent families, adolescent pregnancy, cohabitation and family violence. They point out that, among other factors, this widening of research agendas can be linked to the proliferation of social research, and to the diversification of researchers' social characteristics and involvements. As they observe, unintended consequences of researchers' increasingly diversified backgrounds and their involvements in social movements include opportunities for access to research populations, exposure to researchable problems as well as challenges to the conventional wisdom which have often produced reformulations of research topics. In addition to this, muckraking sociology, underdog sociology and feminist research in their various ways resurrected the methodological and ethical problems the Chicago sociologists had evaded and their post-war descendants had by and large disdained. Such criticism has encouraged the study of sociology as a social phenomenon in its own right and turned attention towards the relationship between sociologists and those they study.

In recent years the ethical, political and legal aspects of research have also become increasingly salient. One instance of this is the growing concern in many countries for the rights of individuals and social groups affected by social research. Trends of this kind are likely to intensify as researchers move towards more complex research designs (Kimmel, 1988), and a greater involvement in applied research (Bailey, 1988). More generally, there seems to have been a shift in the area of policy research. The research agendas of the post-war period were shaped in many respects by issues such as housing, employment and education which had a public, institutional and taken-for-granted character. Increasingly, however, major social problems take on a global character. Problems like the scourges of AIDS, drug use and child abuse defy solution in the absence of increasing knowledge, but require for their understanding entry into private and/or deviant worlds.

Sieber and Stanley (1988) observe that some researchers have dealt with the problematic aspects of studying sensitive topics by opting out of researching such areas altogether. This kind of approach they argue, while personally convenient, is in effect an evasion of responsibility. If they are not to opt out, researchers need to find ways of dealing with the problems and issues raised by research on sensitive topics. The threats which research poses to research participants, to the researcher and to others need to be minimized, managed or mitigated, but without compromising the research itself or limiting the overall scope of research to address important features of contemporary society.

Notes

1. See Sieber (1992). Details of the congressional debate sparked by this decision can be found in *ASA Footnotes*, 19(7), September 1991.

2. On the problems of carrying out research in Northern Ireland more generally, see Burton (1978); R.M. Lee (1981); R. Taylor (1988).

3. A more detailed presentation of the issues raised by research in dangerous social settings is in preparation.

4. Quite obviously, the following account of how institutionalized social research has dealt with sensitive topics is a sketch rather than a detailed history.

5. Downes and Rock (1988) suggest that the development of the sociology of deviance was not an 'express ambition' of the Chicago sociologists, since deviant populations 'formed but one segment of the city and they were no more engaging than any other'. It reflected instead the availability of funds from local reform-minded organizations, as well as a desire to demonstrate the practical relevance of sociology. Furthermore, deviant populations tended to be located in the 'zone of transition'. This area of the city not only held an important theoretical significance in Chicago sociology (Saunders, 1981), it also provided, as Downes and Rock point out, a visible and accessible resource for research by graduate students.

6. For a discussion of the variety of factors, both internal and external, which produced the decline of the case study methods typical of the Chicago school and the advent of more quantitative approaches, see Platt (1992).

2
Limits on Inquiry

Alasdair MacIntyre has observed that:

> Our culture has one idiosyncratic feature that distinguishes it from most and perhaps all other cultures. It is a culture in which there is a general desire to make social life translucent, to remove opacity, to reveal the hidden, to unmask. . . . A secret in our culture has become something to be told. And social science research cannot hope to avoid being in part an expression of this same tendency. (1982, 182–3)

To say that society is 'translucent' does not, of course, imply that it is transparent. The notion of a 'sensitive topic' itself implies otherwise. It is not difficult, however, to point to some of what MacIntyre presumably has in mind. Gary Marx (1984) has described a number of factors, such as the trend in recent times towards open government legislation of various kinds, which have increased accessibility to information previously hidden from view. As he observes, this trend owes much to the activities of special-interest groups. Righteous indignation, which in earlier times fuelled moral crusades directed at the evils of drinking or gambling, now fuels consumer-oriented or environmental campaigns. Such campaigns, as Marx notes, produce a market for hidden information, as well as a body of knowledge among journalists, reformers and researchers about how such information can be acquired and used. Another, perhaps less edifying, illustration of the increasing frankness of social life lies in what might be called the 'commodification of scandal'. Some elements of the mass media in their search for titillating detail are voracious consumers and producers of stories relating to deviance, especially where they relate to crime, sex and violence.

The contribution of the social sciences to the tendency MacIntyre describes has sometimes been driven by simple curiosity or by the lure of the bizarre, the exotic, or the Gothic (Rock, 1979). For some, research in 'sensitive' or 'difficult' areas has the appeal of a controlled adventure. As Thorne suggests,

> this is a recurring phenomenon: sociologists and anthropologists venturing into exciting, taboo, dangerous, perhaps enticing social circumstances; getting the flavor of participation, living out moments of high drama; but in some ultimate way having a cop-out, a built-in escape, a

point of outside leverage that full participants lack. The sociologist can have an adventure, but usually takes it in a controlled and managed way. (1983, 225)

More generally, however, a 'desire to make social life translucent' is embedded deep in the intellectual roots of the social sciences in general, and sociology in particular. First of all, an important tradition in Western thought, most obviously associated with Marx, Nietzsche and Freud, stresses the distorting and obscuring character of surface appearance (Bendix, 1951; Ricoeur, 1970), and the need to strip that appearance away to reveal a deeper, elemental and more clearly seen reality underneath. It can be argued that sociology forms part of that tradition. Indeed Berger and Kellner suggest that a defining feature of sociology is precisely what they call 'a certain debunking angle of vision' (1981, 11) – a frame of reference which looks beyond the visible and the obvious to what is latent, hidden or obscured.

A second strand which encourages social scientists to reveal that which is hidden is encapsulated in the wry comment by Shils that:

> Just as the craft of dentistry is concerned with cavities and malformations and pays little attention to sound teeth, so social science disregards that which is not morally problematic. (1980, 277)

The social sciences have often in their history allied themselves to liberal reformist concerns. The character of that alliance has varied over time and has differed in the United States and Britain in ways which have been crucial in both countries to the development of sociology. Behind such an association has often been a desire to demonstrate that sociology in the form of an 'applied social research' can be useful to those who formulate and implement social policy (Bulmer, 1987; Gouldner, 1970). Applied social research by its nature concerns itself, therefore, with social problems, focusing its attention on the deviant, the problematic or the marginal.

Finally, a fundamental, though often unnoticed, source of social science's contribution to the translucency of modern society is a conception of data which is 'open' or 'democratic' rather than 'closed' (Gouldner, 1973). Gouldner has argued that a democratic conception of data is central to the social sciences, and has traced its roots to the German Romantic tradition. Faced with the disappearance of peasant culture under the impact of industrialization, writers in this tradition undertook direct observation of rural life. As a result, according to Gouldner:

> Despite the common view of Romanticism as politically conservative (if not reactionary), Romantic pluralism actually contributed importantly to the 'democratization' of the concept of data. Specifically, Romantic pluralism undermined the Classical metaphysics which had ordered

reality hierarchically and which in consequence had, overtly or tacitly, conceived of some portions of reality as being 'high' or worthy of emulation and attention, and of others *as 'low', indecorously deviant, and worthy only either of contempt or neglect.* (1973, 351; emphasis added)

Insofar as a democratic conception of data implies that nothing social is beyond the purview of sociology, the discipline can hardly escape the study of topics which are 'sensitive' in the ways described earlier. If, as Gouldner (1970) asserts, the democratization of data has triumphed in modern social science over Classical metaphysics, traces of a closed conception of data can still be found. Sometimes this takes the form of an implicit cultural aversion to the study of certain topics. More frequently, however, research is embedded in institutional contexts which shape and limit research agendas. This chapter looks at a variety of those contexts by exploring in turn the cultural, financial, legal, political and professional limits which exist on social inquiry.

Cultural inhibitions

Traditionally in Western societies, the back-regions associated with sex, reproduction and death have been marked off by strong physical, symbolic and moral boundaries. The existence of such boundaries does not, of course, preclude – indeed has been implicated in – a loquacious and differentiated preoccupation with matters relating to sex (Foucault, 1981). At the level of research practice, however, fear of offending sensibilities by trespassing in restricted areas has often had a constraining influence on research. Anderson, for example, argues that for a long time the sociology of the family was inhibited in its development because cultural definitions stressed the intimate and personal character of family life. As a result, conducting research into the family ran the risk of seeming like 'the worst kind of nosey-parkerism' (1971, 9). Humphreys (1970) remarks that few would regard topics like sex, religion and suicide as being illegitimate areas of study within the social sciences. Yet people commented to him that his study of impersonal sex in public restrooms would, because of its sensitivity, have been better left undone.

Despite an apparently growing concern about privacy (Goyder, 1987), it would be difficult to assert that such inhibitions remain as strong as they were. Some writers feel, however, that in this movement to greater openness something has been lost. According to MacIntyre, protective boundaries need to be retained around certain areas of personal and social life. As he puts it:

The study of taboos by anthropologists and of privacy by sociologists show how important it is for a culture that certain areas of personal and social life should be specially protected. Intimacy cannot exist where everything is disclosed, sanctuary cannot be sought where no place is inviolate, integrity cannot be seen to be maintained – and therefore cannot in certain cases be maintained – without protection from illegitimate pressures. (1982, 188)

For MacIntyre, to violate those sanctuaries is to do a wrong to those one studies. MacIntyre acknowledges that research into the areas of human life he would like to protect – bereavement, for example – would lead to substantial good in terms of increasing knowledge. He insists, however, that, despite the benefits, it cannot be right to do a wrong to anyone. MacIntyre's position is open to a number of objections. First of all, MacIntyre formulates his position on the basis of empirical research on privacy, at least some elements of which might be themselves unethical from his point of view (Lee and Renzetti, 1990). Second, research on sensitive topics often reveals a desire by research participants for catharsis rather than sanctuary (Kübler-Ross, 1970; R.M. Lee, 1981). Third, it is by no means clear how the generalized disclosures produced by social science affect the intimate character of relations between particular individuals. Personal secrets are not precluded by the existence of social science knowledge. Finally, MacIntyre ignores how far the kind of restricted social sphere he would like to see may serve the interests of some within it more than others. Families, for instance, harbour not just sanctuary but abuse.

Forbidden research terrains

Fuller (1988) has drawn attention to the role of the state in creating and maintaining what she calls 'forbidden research terrains'. These are 'whole areas of possible investigation, which may be geographically, intellectually or institutionally defined, where social scientists are strongly discouraged from pursuing research' (1988, 99).[1] Fuller coined the term in relation to the considerable difficulties she faced as a US citizen in carrying out research in Cuba. According to Fuller, the US government has created and maintained Cuba as a forbidden research terrain as part of an all-embracing anti-Cuban policy. This policy, which reflects a range of economic, military and geo-political interests, attempts to isolate the island economically, politically and ideologically. Interdictions imposed by the US government make communication between the United States and Cuba difficult. Contact with the island by telephone or letter is time-consuming and unreliable, and travel back and forth to the United

States is subject to restriction. Fuller notes that researchers returning from Cuba may be subject to surveillance and harassment and that Cuban publications may be impounded by customs. (She suggests, as does Peritore [1990], that similar difficulties may have affected research on Nicaragua during the Sandinista period.)

The existence of forbidden research terrains means that even where research is carried out on those terrains, difficulties remain. In the Cuban case, Fuller argues, funding agencies are loath to support work by US citizens. The island's isolation has eroded professional and institutional contacts between US and Cuban scholars. All of this makes access difficult and produces suspicion and distrust of American researchers who do visit the island. Beyond this, forbidden research terrains have more insidious consequences. Fuller suggests that where independent research is carried out in a forbidden terrain it is greeted with suspicion and can become subject to a double-bind. The restrictions which surround the topic make it difficult to produce research to the kind of methodological standard found in open research situations. These difficulties are rarely taken into account, however, in assessing the research which may be criticized for its methodological inadequacies. At the same time, because only a relatively narrow range of information about Cuba is available, government officials become de facto 'experts' on the Cuban situation. It is these officials who then shape important aspects of the political and media agenda surrounding US–Cuban relations. By shaping knowledge production about Cuba in this way, government sources, Fuller argues, reinforce US state power.

In the United Kingdom, research on the state apparatus is hampered by restrictive legislation. In particular, the Official Secrets Act, 1911, which was passed in order to govern unauthorized disclosure or 'leaking' by civil servants, has been a particular *bête noire* of journalists. For social scientists, the 1911 Act was important because it placed limits on the disclosure and dissemination of material gathered during research on or about government agencies (including the police). Bridges (1989), for example, carried out a rather innocuous piece of research in which case studies of ordinary policing were used as the basis for developing police training materials. Before being allowed access to the police force involved he was required to sign a declaration designed for 'non-civil servants on first being given access to Government information' which contained the following clauses:

> I am aware that I should not divulge any information gained by me as a result of my appointment to any unauthorized person, either orally or in writing, without the previous official sanction in writing of the Depart-

ment appointing me. . . . I understand also that I am liable to be prosecuted if I publish without official sanction any information I may acquire in the course of my tenure of an official appointment. . . . (1989, 152–4)

In fact, Bridges and some other researchers (see, e.g., Raab, 1987) have seen the 1911 Act in a not entirely negative light. They admit that the requirements of the Act were irksome and that it precluded access by other researchers to their raw data. Bridges points out, however, that his having signed the Act (to which he was subject anyway as a citizen) did not inhibit the pedagogical goals which lay behind his study. At the same time it had some positive benefit. Senior officers in the police force being studied were reassured about the research because Bridges had signed the declaration. Cohen and Taylor (1977), on the other hand, were embroiled in a long-running disagreement with civil servants over their plans for a study of long-term prisoners. They clearly regard the Act, which was invoked at various points in the dispute, as one of a range of tools used by officials to frustrate research on topics which they clearly regarded as sensitive.

The Official Secrets Act, 1911, was amended in 1989. On the face of things, the Act became more liberal. One estimate is that the notorious 'catch-all' Section 2 of the 1911 Act created 2,000 separate offences (Robertson and Nicol, 1984). This is no longer the case. However, those areas of officially protected information that remain are subject to even tighter control. As Rosamund Thomas puts it, 'even though a more *limited* amount of official information is protected by the new Official Secrets Act 1911, it will be a sharper tool to treat unauthorized leakages' (emphasis in original) (1991, 213). The impact of the new Act on researchers in the United Kingdom remains to be seen.

Apparently forbidden terrains may, of course, prove much more accessible than they appear at first sight. One obvious example here is MacKenzie's (1990) research on the history of guidance systems for strategic missiles. MacKenzie found that studying this 'secret technology' was much less difficult than he had anticipated. The chief restriction on his study flowed from the security classifications which surround the topic. MacKenzie notes, however, that these precluded investigation of the actual performance of the guidance systems. They did not hinder the interviewing of research scientists and defence analysts about the technical and social processes involved in the design of missile guidance systems. It is also possible, as Lock Johnson indicates in his (1989) study of the Central Intelligence Agency's relations with academics, for researchers in some circumstances to gain direct – though far from unconditional – access to forbidden terrains. The CIA draws on academic expertise through research contracts, consultancy and a scholars-in-residence programme. Over the years, and partly as a response to public and academic disquiet at past CIA practices, the CIA has published guidelines for its relations with universities and individual academics. These guidelines permit, for example, material based on classified information to be published subject to prior Agency review of those portions of the manuscript which draw on the classified material. As Johnson points out, however, the guidelines are unacceptably vague in places and provide inadequate safeguards against researchers being drawn into clandestine activities.

Fuller (1988) suggests that researchers should deal with the existence of forbidden research terrains by organizing collectively. By exposing and protesting against the existence of forbidden research terrains, Fuller argues that it may be possible to provide a counterbalance to official definitions. She also calls on scholars to use whatever power they may have over funding sources to channel funding towards forbidden research terrains. How far organizational strategies of this kind are likely to be effective is open to question. In general, those who have not been deterred altogether by the presence of forbidden research terrains have opted instead for methodological innovation. This has sometimes had a rather improvisatory character, as in the former Soviet Union where researchers developed a variety of means to circumvent some of the restrictions they faced. They asked, for example, about related but non-sensitive topics or used indirect indicators of various kinds. Preferences for certain kinds of material published in literary magazines might stand, say, as an indication of ideological position (Shlapentokh, 1987). Soviet sociologists also apparently used clandestine research methods on occasion (Zaslavsky and 'Z', 1981). In other settings, writers like Marx (1984) and T.R. Young (1971; Lehmann and Young, 1974) have encouraged social scientists to adapt to their own purposes the wider processes of discovery current in society (see Chapter 8).

Pre-emptive barriers to research

Radical sociologists in the 1970s advanced a critique of the institutional organization of social research. According to this critique, those who commissioned and/or funded research, and especially research relevant to policy, did so in a way which precluded the study of powerful groups in society or topics which they might judge to be sensitive or detrimental to their interest. Alongside this critique of funding gatekeepers has also been set criticism of the institutional context within which researchers are directly located. Countervailing pressures against powerful interests are feeble, it is argued, since universities and research institutes dislike offending local élites or putting in jeopardy sources of possible funding (J. Moore, 1973; Record, 1967; Broadhead and Rist, 1976). According to these arguments, funding agencies – whether private or governmental – set agendas which define as worthy of financial support only certain kinds of study. The agendas themselves arise as the by-product of a set of preferences by funding gatekeepers for research having a particular character. These preferences include: (a) utility, defined in an essentially technocratic way as relevance to the policy-making process (Abrams, 1981; Sjoberg and Nett, 1968); (b) modes of theoretical understanding which are individualistic, or which stress pathological rather than structural explanations (Hanmer and Leonard, 1984; Galliher and McCartney, 1973); and (c) research which is quantitative or positivistic in its methodology (Ditton and Williams, 1981; Broadhead and Rist, 1976). In sum, the radical critique of the 'funding process asserts that, as Bell and Encel ⸱ succinctly put it, 'Sociology is done *on* the relatively powerless *for* the relatively powerful' (emphasis in original) (1978, 25). By default, research on powerful groups comes to be pre-emptively denied as a result of their ability to wield unobtrusive power (Lukes, 1974; Hardy, 1985).

Galliher and McCartney (1973) argue that the emergence in the late 1950s of increased funding from government and foundation sources for juvenile delinquency research enhanced a tendency towards a positivistic style of research based around hypothesis testing, and the use of 'simplistic and politically appealing theories such as Opportunity Theory which still stresses [*sic*] the individual as the locus of the problem' (Galliher and McCartney, 1973, 86). A further research area which seems to illustrate these processes well is that relating to the study of redundancy, lay-offs and plant closures. A great deal of the research which looks at the impact of these events has been informed by policy considerations aimed at making the labour market more efficient (R.M. Lee, 1986a). Much of it, therefore, tends to be concerned with the methods and strategies used by individual workers to find new jobs, and relies very heavily on the use of sample surveys. By contrast, the class context of collective dismissal, the way corporate disinvestment decisions are made, and the inability of workers to challenge those decisions are all topics which remain relatively little studied (Fryer, 1981; Rothstein, 1986).

Purely as an account of the funding process itself the kind of critique just outlined faces a number of difficulties. One is that the arguments advanced deal only with the demand side of the funding 'market', but not with supply. Bell, who in his earlier writing (1978) argued strongly for sociologists to study the powerful, has subsequently suggested (1984) that the lack of funding for particular types of research is partly the product of a self-fulfilling prophecy. According to Bell, the principal source of funds for social scientific research in Britain, the Economic and Social Research Council (formerly the Social Science Research Council), has had little opportunity to fund studies which are critical or which are qualitative in their methodology, because such projects have not been presented to it. Again, the results of Galliher and McCartney's (1973) study are somewhat less clear-cut than they initially appear. The funded research projects they examined made more use of multiple data-gathering methods than did unfunded studies. This may in turn imply that these projects were larger in scale and had a more complex division of labour. In other words, smaller, more qualitatively oriented projects may have less need of funding than large-scale surveys. One can further question the contention that academic institutions are inevitably subservient to powerful outside interests. Gouldner (1970) notes, for example, that the development of critical sociologies in the United States stemmed from the ability of younger researchers to obtain federal funds which allowed them more successfully to resist local pressures. The importance of policy relevance to research funding is also belied somewhat if one looks directly at the way those who make policy actually utilize research. It is clear, for example, that policy-makers use research in a number of different ways which extend beyond the directly instrumental (Pelz, 1978). Furthermore, some policy-makers, for professional reasons, welcome research which at least challenges, even if it does not subvert, prevailing orthodoxies (Weiss and Bucuvalas, 1980).

If the processes surrounding the social organization of research funding are more complicated than the radical critique would allow, it still remains difficult to argue that funding policies have reversed the direction of research attention towards the powerful or that élite groups are not insulated to some extent from sociological study. As Cox et al.'s (1978) account of research carried out for an incoming Labor administration in Australia in the early 1970s makes clear, even situations which are very favourable from the point of view of the social researcher in terms of increased funding and sympathetic policy-makers can still be problematic where researchers wish to broach sensitive topics. Moreover, pressures to fund research that is individualistically focused, narrowly policy relevant and positivistic in its methodology have clearly increased in the 1980s with the advent of 'New Right' governments in both Britain and the United States (for examples of the narrowing of funding criteria in the United States in the early days of the first Reagan administration, see Chubin and McCartney, 1982; see also Flather, 1987; R.B. Miller, 1987).

The legal regulation of research

Research is regulated by the law in a variety of ways. In some countries the state regulates the relationship researchers have to those they study by stipulating, for example, that research involving human subjects meets proper standards of informed consent. In a similar way, the protection of data held on computers – and in some cases in manual record systems – has now become a legal requirement in many countries (Akeroyd, 1988). It is likely that most social scientists are sympathetic to the principles underlying legislation of this kind. Conflict between researchers and regulators has arisen, however, over the *form* regulation should take. For present purposes, the structures which regulate research can be regarded as being of one of two types (see also Bennett, 1986, chap. 5). One is the *proactive* where researchers are required to comply with certain standards and conditions before they begin their research. The other is a *reactive* structure. Here, an agency or authority takes on an ombudsman role, examining research practices after the fact with a view to judging their adequacy or legality, and to reconciling conflicting interests. Often reactive measures follow a complaint of some kind.[2] Proactive systems of regulation seem to provide most difficulties for researchers who study topics of a 'sensitive' kind.

Legal regulation and research on sensitive topics
Legal regulation causes greatest difficulty to researchers in the social sciences where they are required to submit details of their proposed research for prior review by a body charged with ensuring compliance with the law. This has happened most obviously in the case of the US regulations relating to the protection of human subjects in research, as well as being required by the data protection laws in some countries. The activities of social researchers in the United States were strenuously governed for a time by the Department of Health, Education and Welfare's regulations on human subject research which operated between 1974 and 1981.[3] The regulatory structure produced by these regulations depended on the establishment of local Institutional Review Boards (IRBs) at insti-

tutions receiving federal funds. Research, whether biomedical or social, which involved human subjects had to be reviewed by an IRB which had to analyse the balance of risks and benefits arising from participation in the proposed research (Reynolds, 1982). IRBs were also charged with ensuring that proposals embodied adequate procedures for the securing of informed consent from those being studied. That consent had ordinarily to be obtained in writing before human subjects participated in a study (Gray, 1979; 1982). The DHEW set down minimum standards. Local IRBs could set more stringent standards if they wished.

In the United Kingdom most research in medical settings, including research by social scientists, is subject to prior ethical review. The UK Department of Health and Social Security issued an advisory circular in 1975 drawing the attention of medical researchers to recommendations made by the Royal College of Physicians concerning the establishment of medical ethics committees. There is, however, no *statutory* obligation on medical bodies to do so (Nicholson, 1986). In practice, social scientists involved in medical research rarely escape ethical review since funding agencies generally insist that proposals should have been cleared by an ethics committee before being submitted for possible funding.[4]

The most notable example of a system of prior review mandated under national data protection laws was that set up in Sweden with the passing of the Swedish Data Act in 1973. There, anyone wishing to set up a personal data file had first to obtain permission from the Data Inspection Board. As Freese (1985) records, for the Board to grant a permit allowing the file to come into existence, it had to be satisfied that there was no risk of privacy being infringed. To that end, the Board was empowered to lay down detailed stipulations relating, for example, to the information which could be collected or the security measures to be adopted in order to ensure confidentiality. The Data Inspection Board would only grant permission to create files containing 'sensitive' information, to do, for example, with previous convictions or religious or political views, in exceptional circumstances (although such circumstances might include for the purposes of research).

One argument against prior review is that it is likely to distort the research enterprise. It can produce a form of censorship in which research on particular topics is likely to be inhibited or sanitized. Qualitative researchers can face particular difficulties from prior review (Øyen and Olaussen, 1985; Akeroyd, 1988, 1991). Such a system implies that the topic of the research can be specified before it begins. Typically, however, field researchers do not know what they are going to find until they have actually entered the field, and it is common in field research for the focus of the research to emerge only after data collection has actually begun.

There has been a fairly widespread perception among researchers in the United States that research in certain areas was suppressed because of difficulties in negotiating proposals past IRBs. In this context, Reiss (1979, 85) speaks of a double standard which made research on deviance more difficult to carry out than in other, less sensitive areas. Murray Wax, in a similar vein, comments that 'even casual observation yields the impression that some types of valuable research are being discontinued and other radically redesigned' (1977, 321; see also Olensen, 1979). Surveys of those involved in the institutional review process in the United States suggest that prior review does have some inhibiting effect on research. Just over half of a sample of social and behavioural researchers asked about the impact of IRBs in their institution felt that the 'review procedure has impeded the progress of research done at this institution' (Gray, 1979). Seiler and Murtha (1980) sampled the chairs of IRBs in colleges and universities having graduate departments of sociology. A quarter of those in the sample responded affirmatively to a questionnaire item which asked whether their committee had ever denied permission for a survey research project because the questionnaire or interview schedule contained items of a sensitive nature. A number of experimental studies (Hessler and Galliher, 1983; Ceci et al., 1985) also point to the general conclusion that IRBs look with disfavour on research in areas which are potentially controversial. (For a critique of Hessler and Galliher's research, see Reynolds, 1983).

It has sometimes been charged that the review process opens up research to pressure from powerful interests (Seiler and Murtha, 1980; Øyen, 1974). Although it is not clear how far this has been the case in the United States, the practice is apparently institutionalized in Sweden (Hammar, 1976; Janson, 1979). In accordance with general practice the Swedish Data Inspection Board consulted a variety of agencies and organizations about a proposed study of the political attitudes of immigrants (Janson, 1979; Flaherty, 1979). A number of questions which were central to the research, but which were judged to be sensitive, were ordered to be deleted from the questionnaire.

Prior clearance of a research project by the data protection authorities can have a beneficial effect on survey response rates. Respondents may be reassured about the uses to which personal data held about them will be put. Procedures for obtaining informed consent in social science research, on the other hand, can be reactive, particularly where research is being carried out on sensitive topics. In a careful experiment Eleanor Singer (1978; 1983) has explored the effects of informed consent procedures on responses to a range of survey questions on matters generally regarded as sensitive. She found that asking for a signature to confirm that the interviewee had given consent to be interviewed depressed the response rate, though only by a relatively small amount. In addition, respondents who had signed the consent form before the interview gave lower reports of socially undesirable behaviour than those who were asked to sign the form after the interview had finished.

Systems of prior review have an effect both on social scientists' trust of the regulatory system, and on the extent to which those studied are able, legitimately, to trust the researchers. That sociologists in the United States were not necessarily hostile to informed consent as a principle is clear from the Code of Ethics formulated by the American Sociological Association in 1963, which embodied notions of informed consent in a number of ways (Galliher, 1973). In spite of this, however, the DHEW regulations were deeply unpopular with social scientists. Indeed, Wax and Cassell go so far as to describe the imposition of the regulations on social researchers as 'traumatic' (1981, 224). (For collections of articles debating the issues raised by the regulations, see Wax and Cassell, 1979a; Klockars and O'Connor, 1979; Beauchamp et al., 1982.) A survey of the workings of the IRB system (see Gray, 1982) showed that social and behavioural scientists were rather more likely than biomedical researchers to have negative attitudes to the boards. Long and Dorn's (1983) survey of sociologists' attitudes to ethical issues also recorded a very sizeable majority opposed to the regulation of research by official bodies.

Some of the unpopularity of the regulations derived from what was perceived to be their all-embracing character. They applied not just to research directly funded by the federal government. *All* research on human subjects, whether social or biomedical, carried out in institutions receiving federal funds had to be subject to review. In addition, an institution's use of review procedures was taken as a criterion for deciding whether it was deemed fit to receive federal funding. There was therefore a strong suspicion that, as Seiler and Murtha put it,

> the federal government and members of such powerful professions as law and medicine, formulated ethical principles for the politically weaker and unrepresented social sciences. (1980, 149)

It also seems that the Swedish data protection legislation has been unpopular with researchers (Flaherty, 1979; Janson, 1979). This unpopularity is related to perceptions of the care already taken to ensure the confidentiality of data, a lack of demonstrable harm caused to human subjects by social research, and feelings that the arguments put by researchers have not been listened to. Reiss (1979) argues from a sociology of deviance perspective that where regulatory systems lack legitimacy patterned evasions of the regulations become increasingly likely. Such evasions might include disguising research as consultancy or therapeutic practice, or as research which is merely exploratory. Alternatively, researchers might engage in selective disclosure of their research plans, package their proposals in standardized ways which conform to review committee expectations, or keep selective or misleading records. Where control is vested locally rather than with a central government bureaucracy, as in the IRB system in the United States, informal ties and contacts can also be utilized to ensure sympathetic treatment or inside knowledge of committee requirements. Even outside systems of prior review evasion might be possible. As Akeroyd (1988) argues, some researchers might opt out of compliance with data protection laws in Britain simply to avoid inconvenience.

How far do prior review procedures allow those studied to trust researchers? One difficulty with the obtaining of prior informed consent is that, once given, the burden of liability shifts from the investigator to the subject should something in fact go wrong (Reiss, 1979).[5] Procedures which require informed consent to be obtained prior to the research and to be documented may also threaten those engaged in deviant activity. This is so because the procedures used actually provide physical evidence of an informant's identity in the form of a signature (Bond, 1978). Further, as Reiss (1979) again points out, in situations where there is cause for complaint, individuals involved in deviant activity may not come forward since to do so is to expose their deviance. Finally, even if informed consent may protect subjects, it does not protect investigators. This is particularly so in the United States where there is little protection, as will be seen in a later chapter, against having data subpoenaed by a court.

The changing climate of regulation
The legal regulation of social research has not generally sprung from a widespread public perception of abuses by social scientists. Although there has been some disagreement among social scientists about the potential harm social research poses to its subjects (Hessler and Galliher, 1983; Reynolds, 1983), the activities of social

researchers have excited little public concern. As Barnes (1979, 182) points out, criticism of social researchers figures hardly at all in a number of works popular in the 1970s which decry threats to privacy and the development of computer data banks. Social research probably has a relatively low level of visibility in the public consciousness. It is also the case that individuals can exercise direct informal control over research in ways they cannot where the state or large corporations are involved. They can refuse to participate in research (as apparently increasing numbers do when asked to respond on surveys [Goyder, 1987]) and in some cases, as an earlier discussion made clear, local communities can be mobilized to resist the attentions of researchers. In fact, the regulation of social research has generally emerged as an incidental or unintended consequence of attempts to control wider social abuses. Social scientists become subject to regulation because of bureaucratic unwillingness to draw the boundaries of control narrowly rather than widely.

In a similar vein, both Øyen (1974) and Janson (1979) note that in Scandinavia the development of data protection laws arose for the most part out of public concern over the governmental and commercial use of personal data stored on computers. Despite some controversy over a large-scale longitudinal study, Project Metropolitan (Øyen, 1974; Akeroyd, 1988), the activities of social researchers were largely absent from the debate. In Britain, it is now generally accepted that Data Protection legislation emerged largely from the need to ratify the Council of Europe Convention (1981), and to bring domestic law into line with it. Far from seeking to deal with abuse, passage of the data protection Act was prompted rather by the threat posed to British commercial interests by the increasing harmonization of data protection laws elsewhere in Europe (Pearce, 1988; see also Akeroyd, 1988).

Simitis (who is not only an academic lawyer, but also the Data Protection Commissioner for the State of Hessen in Germany) has examined (1981) the relationship between data protection legislation and research. He acknowledges that there may be a conflict between data protection legislation and the acquisition of scientific knowledge through research. However, he argues that the conflict must be resolved in favour of the law. The first reason he gives for this is that self-regulation through the adherence of researchers to professional codes of ethics provides insufficient safeguard to the rights of individuals. This is because there is no real assurance that voluntary codes will in fact be followed, and because difficulties arise from the variety of research methods and kinds of research carried out by social scientists. The second reason seems to be that exceptions or exemptions from laws should be kept to a minimum. This seems to be reflected in the general reluctance in many countries to extend specific privileges to researchers. Research, in other words, is almost always bound by the same basic rules as other activities which involve the use of personal data. As Simitis puts it:

> the reaction of the professionals is carefully taken into consideration, but is in the end no more than an important element in a regulation prepared by an external agency. Thus, administrative action remains necessary. It may be completed but not replaced by self-regulation. (1981, 587)

Faden and Beauchamp's (1986) discussion of the origins of the human subject regulations in the United States suggests that considerations similar to those outlined by Simitis were in operation there. They note that at various points, while the regulations were under development, government officials blurred the distinctions between social and biomedical research in order to produce a consistent national policy. Indeed, according to Faden and Beauchamp, the establishment of the IRB system was designed in part to allow the national policy to remain intact by permitting diversity of research practice to be dealt with at the local level.

In 1981 a set of revised regulations was issued by the Department of Health and Human Services (DHHS), the successor to the DHEW. The changes led to 'dramatic reductions in the scope of projects that must be submitted to full committee review' (Reynolds, 1982, 103–12). Research activities such as secondary analysis, educational testing, 'routine' surveys and interviews and 'routine' field observations were made exempt from prior review. Social research was liable to review in studies where subjects had to be identified, where the research could be damaging or where it dealt with sensitive topics, but only if *all* of the conditions existed. Secondary analysis was also permitted provided the data contained no identifiers. Although the existence of IRBs was still considered to be evidence of an institution's suitability for receiving federal funds, the regulations apply only to research funded by the DHHS. Prior review of non-federally funded research was no longer required.

National data protection laws have also had to be adapted to changing circumstances. Some 'first generation laws' (Flaherty, 1984) have been amended on the basis of experience, and signs exist in a number of countries of accommodation between researchers and regulatory bodies. In Norway, the Norwegian Research Council for Science and the Humanities, possibly with the Swedish experience in mind, established a Secretariat for Data Protection Affairs which performs a central co-ordinating and brokerage role for researchers *vis-à-vis* the national Data Inspectorate (Øyen and Olaussen, 1985). Simitis (1981) argues that the data protection authorities in Hessen have been mindful of the dangers of censoring research. As a result they have attempted increasingly to avoid adjudicating on the social scientific worth of research by putting the weight of their requirements on ensuring that the necessary steps are taken for the security and protection of the data. 'The expectations of researchers are accepted but compensated by adequate security measures' (Simitis, 1981, 594). A somewhat simplified procedure has also been in operation in Sweden since 1982. This procedure involves only the registration of routine personal data files (Bennett, 1986). In cases where a file containing sensitive information is to be collected or where data files are to be linked in some ways, the prior permission of the Data Inspection Board is still required.

By and large, changes in the legal regulation of research are possible because regulatory agencies have responsibility for monitoring and reviewing the working of legislation. To the extent that data protection norms diffuse among research practitioners (Øyen and Olaussen, 1985), and given the relative lack of harm occasioned to data subjects by social research, moves, particularly towards the simplification of procedures, are possible.

Chilling

Chilling occurs when researchers, anticipating hostile reactions from colleagues, are deterred from producing or disseminating research on a particular topic (Sieber and Stanley, 1988). In recent years, writers of a conservative bent, particularly in the United States, have criticized what they regard as insidious pressures towards 'political correctness' in academic life. Such pressures, they argue, have chilled research which challenges dominant social science perspectives on the formation and implementation of public policy, especially in areas relating to race. Lynch (1989) has argued, for example, that there is a dearth of sociological studies directed at the effects of affirmative action policies in the United States on white males (see also Beer, 1987; 1988). Speaking of a 'new McCarthyism', Lynch asserts that sociology's liberal sympathies have produced 'an ideologically induced blindness and defensiveness' (1989, 128). In consequence, he goes on, 'Sociologists have not been keen on looking at either the state of their discipline or the effects of pet social reforms such as affirmative action.'

Critics of what they see as a dominant left-leaning political consensus in social research argue that those who step outside that consensus face marginalization, negative labelling or sanction. They must cope, it is argued, with hostile professional opinion, reduced opportunities for publication, promotion or funding, and even, in some cases, orchestrated public protest directed at their research. Although for critics the existence of such sanctions and their effects are self-evident, claims of this kind are notoriously difficult to evaluate. The deterrent effect of chilling has, by definition, no visible outcome. Its extent, therefore, is difficult to measure. Neither can one take the fact that research studies are absent from a particular area as evidence of chilling. Research agendas are shaped by many different factors and one cannot readily say what form a particular field of research would have taken in different circumstances. Accusations that research has been chilled also have a powerful rhetorical function. They provide a means by which those on opposing sides of a debate can accuse each other of abandoning reasoned argument and trying to impose their views by extra-intellectual means. As a result, when matters are controversial, disagreements emerge not just about the substantive issues involved but also about the tenor of debate and/or the way it is organized or conducted. In these cases those embroiled in a controversy may well magnify anecdotal evidence (Collins and Pinch, 1979). They may also tend to overestimate the extent of hostility directed towards their position or the degree of unanimity among their opponents.

A number of specific claims concerning the chilling of 'politically incorrect' research are evaluated below. The first is that research standing outside the presumed liberal consensus in the social sciences is difficult to publish. Second, attention is directed towards the hypothesis that research in certain areas is governed by a 'spiral of silence'. Finally, the efficacy of public protest directed against research deemed to have unwelcome political implications is assessed. This evaluation draws on a number of empirical studies. Not all of these were formulated to address directly the issue of chilling. Given the methodological difficulties just outlined, this may be, however, an advantage. Indications that research has or has not been suppressed in particular areas may be more difficult to dismiss if produced by those whose immediate concerns lie elsewhere.

Publishing difficulties
Sociologists like Gordon (1980) contend that researchers whose work challenges the dominant liberal assumptions in the discipline have difficulty publishing in professional journals. Claims of this sort are again difficult to evaluate. The rejection of manuscripts for publication in itself may say relatively little. Social science journals

in general have relatively high rejection rates (Zuckerman and Merton, 1971). For example, only 9 per cent of peer-reviewed manuscripts submitted to the *American Sociological Review* between 1977 and 1981 were unconditionally accepted; 63 per cent received an unqualified rejection (Bakanic et al., 1987, 634). Bakanic et al. (1987; 1989) have examined referees' comments on a sample of manuscripts submitted to the *ASR*, as well as complaints to the journal's editors from authors who had a manuscript rejected for publication (Simon et al., 1986). Bakanic et al. note that, while referees were critical even of articles they recommended for publication, *ad hominem* remarks or negative comments directed towards the topic of the research were relatively uncommon. Neither is there much evidence that research in particular substantive areas is published more easily than in others. (In the *ASR*, at any rate, publication preferences are methodological rather than substantive. Qualitative studies are rather less likely to be published than quantitative ones.) The prevalence of 'split' reviews in which · referees had divergent views about whether the paper should be accepted suggests, according to Bakanic et al. (1987), that editors do not funnel papers directly to uniformly sympathetic or hostile referees. Turning to letters of complaint, Simon et al. (1986) found that demography and sociology of science were the disciplinary subfields most overrepresented relative to a random sample of submissions about which no complaint had been made. In justifying their complaints, authors most often accused reviewers of incompetence or arbitrariness. Some 16 per cent of them attributed rejection to bias or prejudice on the part of reviewers. For the most part, however, they alleged that bias was directed towards the type of data or the method used rather than the topic of the research or the conclusions reached. None of these patterns precludes, of course, the consistent rejection of papers espousing particular unpopular positions. Neither do they suggest, however, that such rejection is inevitable.

The 'spiral of silence'

Lynch (1989) argues that research on affirmative action is affected by the process Noelle-Neuman (1984) describes as the 'spiral of silence'. According to Noelle-Neuman, individuals, fearing social isolation, refrain from expressing opinions out of step with the general climate of opinion. A spiral of silence occurs because remaining silent in this way reinforces the impression of unanimity in public opinion which, in turn, increases pressure on those holding minority views. Lynch describes in some detail various negative responses to his own work on affirmative action. However, he does not convincingly demonstrate in more general terms how the operation of a spiral of silence hinders affirmative action research. As he admits (Lynch, 1989, 122), critics are likely to see much of the evidence he uses as anecdotal.

From Lynch's point of view, legal disputes surrounding contentious social issues might provide a more useful context within which to test the spiral of silence hypothesis. Increasingly in the United States social scientists have been recruited to act as expert witnesses in litigation surrounding public policy decisions. The public and adversarial character of the legal process makes it difficult for individuals recruited in this way to avoid taking an explicit position. Moreover, litigation produces pressures for protagonists to present a united front and creates a stake in obtaining a successful outcome. Burstein (1991) has pointed out that litigation surrounding allegations of 'reverse discrimination' is surprisingly lacking in the United States. Fortunately, however, the use of social science evidence in litigation surrounding another highly contentious topic, school desegregation, has been well studied (Chesler et al., 1988). Social science research had an important bearing on the US Supreme Court's ruling in the landmark *Brown v. Board of Education of Topeka* school desegregation case. Since then, the National Association for the Advancement of Colored People (NAACP) has repeatedly drawn on the expert testimony of social scientists in challenges directed at segregated school boards in the United States (Chesler et al., 1988). More recently, local school boards fighting desegregation plans have themselves sought testimony from social scientists in order to rebut social scientific evidence put before the court.

In interviews with witnesses and lawyers Chesler et al. (1988) found rather clear evidence of social scientists being reluctant to appear on behalf of defendants in school desegregation cases. Chesler et al. note that fear of being sanctioned by colleagues was stronger for those of their respondents who were based in disciplines such as sociology, political science or psychology. By contrast, respondents based in schools of education expressed rather less concern about the possible negative consequences of their giving testimony. Chesler et al. argue that this pattern is related to two aspects of the experts' professional environment. First, in contrast to fields like sociology which endorse predominantly academic activities such as journal publication, disciplines such as education expect and reward involvement in applied settings. Second, in the United States at least, the overall political stance of disciplines such as sociology is to the left of that of education (Chesler et al., 1988, 170; Ladd and Lipset, 1975). As a result, for some of those interviewed by Chesler et al., testifying on behalf of a school board resisting desegregation was regarded by colleagues as a betrayal of liberal principles.

A not insubstantial number of the expert witnesses Chesler et al. interviewed reported experiencing various kinds of cognitive, professional or ideological dissonance arising from the need to align themselves for or against particular political groups or in relation to dominant professional opinion. However, those who testified for school boards were able in various ways to resolve these dilemmas. In some cases they appealed to their presumed professional obligations to disseminate data neutrally, or to use relevant data to inform the public policy process even where those data failed to coincide with their own personal value preferences. Others particularized the situation; supporting school desegregation in general but adducing reasons for testifying on behalf of a particular school board. Chesler et al. also note that over time testifying on behalf of school boards has become easier. Some of the political heat has gone out of the school desegregation issue while research on the issue has revealed a variety of complexities.

Chesler et al. were unable to document specific instances of sanctions being applied to those testifying on behalf of school boards. They remain convinced, however, that 'professional sanctioning of some scholars occurred' (1988, 170). At the same time, their research does not lend strong support to the spiral of silence hypothesis. As Price and Allen (1990) point out, spiral of silence theory is based on three assumptions: that individuals fear isolation, that they scan public opinion before expressing their viewpoint and that the climate of opinion is highly consonant. Despite the climate of opinion, researchers were not completely deterred from testifying on behalf of school boards. Fear of isolation, where it exists, can apparently be overcome as witnesses find ways to justify their decision to testify. This suggests, in line with a number of other assessments of Noelle-Neuman's work (Kennamer, 1990; D.G. Taylor, 1982), that the initiation of a spiral of silence is a highly contingent matter. Perceptions of dominant opinion need not necessarily be converted into the silencing of minority opinion.[6]

Public protests against scientific research
For a number of writers whose work produced controversy in the 1970s (Jensen 1969, 1972; Herrnstein, 1973; Gordon, 1980; L.J. West, 1986), chilling effects arose from what they perceived as an intimidatory climate surrounding research on particular topics. Attacks on their work, they charged, were motivated and orchestrated by groups of political radicals with the acquiescence or even

possibly the connivance of liberal academics. For example, Jensen's (1969) article in the *Harvard Educational Review* challenging the effectiveness of compensatory education programmes sparked a lengthy and acrimonious debate between those stressing the hereditability of IQ differences and opponents who argued that intelligence is predominantly defined by environmental factors (Harwood, 1982). Those adopting the hereditarian position frequently complained of harassment by their opponents. In particular, they pointed to incidents where radical students disrupted lectures or meetings given by hereditarians and occasions on which supporters where warned about the negative consequences of their sympathies by colleagues (see variously Jensen, 1972; Herrnstein, 1973; Harwood, 1982). Jensen in particular made much of the fact that a number of colleagues supported his view in private but were afraid to side with him in public.

In a comprehensive and dispassionate examination of this controversy, the British sociologist Jonathan Harwood (1982) has concluded that those on the hereditarian side of the debate did indeed face difficulties promoting their case. Proponents of the environmentalist position, by contrast, had few corresponding pressures exerted on them. On the other hand, writers like Powledge (1981) and Nelkin and Swazey (1981), who have studied a number of controversies surrounding research on violent behaviour, have been rather more sceptical about the efficacy of attempts to mobilize opinion against particular areas of research. These writers stress the legitimacy of protest, the conditions under which it occurs and the organizational limits on the mobilization and co-ordination of protest activities.

Nelkin and Swazey (1981) argue that protests against research on the psychological and biological bases of violent or aggressive behaviour grew out of the shifting social and political climate of the 1960s and 1970s. Concerns grew during this period over the possible use of social science research to provide ever more effective tools for social control. Many, distrustful of science and technology, came to emphasize instead the rights of those potentially affected by research to accountability, participation and choice. According to Nelkin and Swazey, those concerned about such issues have tended to see existing institutional mechanisms such as peer review or ethics committees as serving the interests of professional groups. In other words, those potentially affected by research have no legitimate institutional forum – apart from public protest – within which they can voice their concerns. (Interestingly, this last point has also been made by Coleman [1984], who was himself subjected to rather virulent criticism in the school desegregation controversy.)

Powledge (1981; 1986) studied in some depth three controversial research projects on violent behaviour, each of which was abandoned after sustained protest. Powledge argues that it is misleading to attribute the fate of these projects to the success of the protest campaigns against them. The ability decisively to influence events lay in each case not with the protest movement itself but elsewhere. She concludes, for example, that the demise of a centre for the study of violent behaviour at UCLA owed more to the hostility of funding and legislative bodies than it did to the activities of protesters (Powledge, 1986). In a similar way, in a controversy over research involving the screening of children with XYY chromosomes, the abandonment of the project reflected the protest movement's *inability* fully to control the actions of all of its supporters (see also Nelkin and Swazey, 1981). Both sides apparently accepted that the group which co-ordinated most of the opposition to the study had tried explicitly to avoid *ad hominen* attacks. The project director was plagued, however, by anonymous threatening phone calls apparently from some other source which were instrumental in encouraging him to give up the research (Powledge, 1981). According to Powledge, the targeting of research for protest depends on a study's location, its visibility and on the local political environment. The projects and their associated protest groups were based at large, prestigious and highly politicized institutions. In this kind of situation, protest groups emerged out of existing *ad hoc* arrangements or were based around loose coalitions of disparate constituencies. Where these conditions have not been met, however, work has proceeded unhindered. Research similar to that which was terminated has in each case subsequently been carried out elsewhere, sometimes with the same researchers being involved but using different funding sources, often in less visible settings and under less obviously threatening rubrics (Powledge, 1981).

Although they do not explicitly acknowledge it as such, Powledge and Nelkin and Swazey adopt an implicit resource mobilization perspective. From this point of view, the ability of a movement to attain its ends depends on the web of support and constraint – social, financial and organizational – which surrounds it (McCarthy and Zald, 1977). Interestingly, accounts by those targeted for protest in the controversy over the hereditability of IQ differences offer some indirect support for this position. Herrnstein estimated, for example, that those fomenting protest against him at Harvard comprised 'fewer than a dozen active radicals and perhaps another dozen part-time participants, not all of whom were Harvard students' (1973, 166). He stresses also that he received considerable institutional support from Harvard. At Berkeley, the main radical group opposing Jensen's work, Students for a Democratic Society (SDS), had been infiltrated (Jensen, 1972, 52–3). A source privy to the inner workings of the movement told him that SDS considered their campaign against him a failure. Apparently, its stridency had alienated students and university staff. This last instance suggests that universities frequently find ways to contain or deflect protest within their walls. Jensen seems often to have been forewarned about his opponents' activities and was thus able to thwart them. Indeed, it is rather noticeable that where speakers like Jensen and Herrnstein were prevented from speaking by demonstrations, it was at universities other than their own.

Attempts have sometimes been made to mobilize professional opinion in support of those opposing research on a particular topic. These efforts have usually involved the circulation of petitions, the passing of resolutions at meetings of professional associations or the making of public statements expressing the views of the association (see, e.g., Karmen, 1980). In some instances steps are taken to have professional sanctions applied to individuals. Calls were made to have Arthur Jensen censured or expelled from the American Psychological Association (Jensen, 1972). In a similar way, the then president of the American Sociological Association, Alfred McClung Lee, attempted to have the ASA Council and its Committee on Professional Ethics take action against James Coleman. Lee (1978) alleged that, in the controversy over school desegregation and 'white flight', Coleman had acted unethically by presenting his personal opinions as verified scientific findings. Episodes of this kind are probably better seen as having a symbolic character rather than a punitive one. Resolutions passed by professional associations typically reiterate the right of scholars to free inquiry, while pointing to possible deleterious consequences from pursuing a particular research agenda (Karmen, 1980). Appeals to ethics committees have also generally been unsuccessful. After acrimonious debate, the ASA Council rejected Lee's recommendation (A.M. Lee, 1978; M. Hunt, 1985, 90). Jensen not only remained in the APA but had one of his opponents successfully censured by its ethics committee (Jensen, 1972).

Chilling: an assessment

The work of writers like Lynch and Gordon (see also Snyderman and Rothman, 1990) forms part of a wider neo-conservative challenge to the intellectual underpinnings of welfare-state liberalism. Criticism, particularly of sociology's affinity to collectivist and redistributive social policies, is not new. Early on, Gouldner (1968;

1970) drew attention to the tendency for sociologists induced by their liberal sympathies to romanticize those in underdog positions, and to critique society at the level of intermediate functionaries rather than the very powerful. More recently, writers like Lieberson (1988) and Felson (1991) have cautioned social scientists against being more ready to evaluate favourably research findings in line with their political sympathies than those which are not. To speak of a 'new McCarthyism', however, is to exaggerate. Clearly, there are some risks in espousing positions politically unpopular in one's discipline. However, the consequences of voicing unpopular opinion are often both less serious and more manageable than writers like Lynch assume. Indeed, as Rainwater and Yancey (1967, 307) suggest, where research is focused on important public issues, having to cope with robust criticism is a routine occupational hazard.

Conclusion

Researchers in countries like Britain and the United States do not face restrictions on their research of the kind seen, for example, in the former Soviet Union. Nevertheless, direct and officially sanctioned barriers to research of the kind experienced by Fuller do exist to a degree. In Western countries control is informal and indirect. Often it arises as an unintended consequence of funding decisions or, as in the case of legal regulation, from commendable efforts to balance 'the need to know and the right to remain unknown' (Barnes, 1979, 187). While the extent to which limits are placed on inquiry is sometimes exaggerated and can be circumvented, researchers still need to bear in mind Sieber and Stanley's comment. 'Although there is nothing that forbids research on sensitive topics, there are powerful forces against the conduct of such research' (1988, 49).

Notes

1. Political changes have made clearer the nature and extent of forbidden research terrains in countries like the former Soviet Union. (On how the organization, agenda and conduct of social research in the Soviet Union were controlled before *glasnost*, see, variously, Beliaev and Butorin, 1982; Shalin, 1990; Shlapentokh, 1987; Weinberg, 1992; Zaslavskaya, 1988.) (For the People's Republic of China see, e.g., Wong, 1975, and, in the post-Tiananmen period, Curran and Cook, 1992.)

2. Not discussed here are the reactive structures often built into professional codes of ethics. The concern here is only with regulatory systems which have some statutory authority.

3. The regulation of human subject research in the United States had its origins in the 1960s. During that period the US Public Health Service developed internal

procedures for control of federally funded research involving human subjects. Initially, however, these procedures had little impact on social researchers (Gray, 1982; Faden and Beauchamp, 1986). In the early 1970s, a series of scandals involving medical experiments on human subjects came to light (Pattullo, 1982). These scandals, with their uncomfortable echoes of experimentation on concentration camp victims in Nazi Germany, aided the passage through Congress of the National Research Act (Faden and Beauchamp, 1986; Tropp, 1982). The Act contained a provision for setting up a commission to deal with the protection of human subjects in research. Senator Edward Kennedy, who had been pushing for a commission with regulatory powers, withdrew his proposal in favour of an advisory commission if the DHEW would publish appropriate regulations.

4. See, for example, Cannon (1992).

5. Ironically, there are difficulties in using empirical research to document the effects of prior review procedures. These difficulties arise out of what Reiss (1979) refers to as the 'paradox of presumption'. Reiss argues that the US human subject regulations were based on presumptions of fact concerning abuses caused by unregulated social research. However, the regulations effectively bar any attempt to test the impact of the regulations experimentally, since such experiments would almost inevitably involve deception and the absence thereby of informed consent.

6. It is interesting to note that a relatively new kind of chilling may have emerged out of the growing involvement of social scientists in the legal process: the 'decredentializing' of rival experts. Thus, scholars in the psychology and sociology of religion and in religious studies have presented *amicus curiae* briefs in cases before the California Supreme Court involving litigation against new religious movements. In these briefs, the *amici* have tried to discredit testimony concerning the mental health outcomes of participation in the movements given in lower courts by clinical psychologists. The briefs argue that these expert witnesses fail to meet both legal and scientific standards for the admissibility of scientific expert testimony, for example, by failing to acknowledge the methodological weaknesses underlying research suggesting 'brainwashing' as a method of recruitment into the movements (see Barker, 1984; Beckford, 1985).

3

Estimating the Size of Hidden Populations

Social scientists often want to estimate rates of prevalence for deviant activities or to make judgements about the size of deviant groups. Sensitivity surrounds the production of such estimates since, often, those concerned feel threatened by disclosing their membership of a particular group or their participation in some particular activity. This chapter concentrates on how estimates of this kind may be produced using available data derived from official or administrative sources, or existing survey data.[1] In particular, much of what follows focuses on methods for estimating the extent of so-called 'invisible' or 'complaintless' crimes. Crimes of this kind do not, of course, exhaust the range of hidden populations one might want to estimate. Other examples might include activities which, though not illegal, are rare, transitory or normatively suspect, for example, intermarriage in divided societies, or participation in an apparently bizarre religious cult. Invisible crime, however, well illustrates many of the problems involved in using available data.

Mark Moore (1983) has distinguished a number of different kinds of invisible crime. These include crimes without victims, white-collar crime, and crimes of victimization in which complaints by the victim are repressed in various ways. Victimless crimes typically involve, according to Schur, 'the willing exchange, among adults, of strongly demanded but legally proscribed goods and services' (1965, 169). Victimless crimes frequently remain hidden from view because the willing exchange involved means that there is no complainant to bring them to public attention. White-collar crime, like fraud, tax evasion and computer crime, is also frequently invisible. Those who commit such crimes can typically hide what they are doing, and it is often not clear who in fact is being victimized. Those who lose as a result of such crimes may be part of a diffuse group such as shareholders, and in some cases the crime is only discovered long after it has taken place (Braithwaite et al., 1987). Other invisible crimes involve direct victimization. However, crimes like blackmail or protection rackets remain invisible because, although the victims know they are being victimized, they are usually afraid to come forward (Hepworth, 1971). A lack of complaint is also a feature of exploitative crimes such as sexual abuse. Such crimes often take place in the context of an existing relationship in which there is a marked disparity of power, one result of which is to ensure the silence of the victim.

Invisible crime and official statistics

One ostensible advantage of official statistics is their availability.[2] Where, as is often the case in studying sensitive topics, there are difficulties in obtaining first-hand information, the use of available statistics may seem like an attractive option. There are, however, well-known problems surrounding the use of official statistics on deviance. The production of official statistics by bureaucratic agencies results in a 'dark figure': that part of what the statistics purport to measure which goes unreported or unrecorded. Official statistics therefore notoriously underestimate the size of hidden populations and the extent of deviant activities. Both criminal statistics, the amount of crime recorded by the police, and judicial statistics, which relate to cases processed by the courts, provide a very imperfect measure of underlying rates of crime. This is particularly so in the case of judicial statistics, for while crimes may be reported, they may not be solved, nor the perpetrator(s) apprehended. Even if an apparent lawbreaker can be found, the case may be disposed of in a variety of ways which do not show up in the statistics, for example, by caution or through acquittal (Downes and Rock, 1988; Box, 1981).[3] La Fontaine (1990) has described some of the difficulties which arise when judicial statistics are used to estimate the extent of child sexual abuse. In England and Wales, she points out, statistics are given for offences and convictions, but not for offenders. One cannot tell from this, therefore, the number of individuals who have committed sexual offences against children. Particular individuals may have been counted more than once by virtue of having been charged with multiple offences, while charges may relate to the same or a number of different victims. Furthermore, in cases of child sexual abuse obtaining convictions can be difficult. The nature of the crime means that some kinds of evidence, for example, testimony from very young children, may be inadmissible, and corroborative evidence may also be lacking. In addition, La Fontaine points to the possibility that plea bargaining may take place. This will, of course, increase the apparent number of less serious offences while underestimating more serious crimes.

Quite obviously, the size of prevalence estimates depends on how researchers choose to define what it is that they are measuring. A number of commentators (see, e.g., Peters et al., 1986; Hertzberger, 1990) have noted, for example, that prevalence estimates for child abuse are extremely variable. Much of this variability (though by no means all) can be traced to differences in the definitions of abuse used. Thus, the estimates produced vary depending on whether what is being measured includes both contact abuse and non-contact abuse, whether abuse by peers is counted as well as abuse by adults (Peters et al., 1986), or whether one focuses on the perpetrator's act alone or on the antecedents and consequences of those acts as well (Hertzberger, 1990). In some cases estimates are based on broad definitions which in fact group together heterogeneous phenomena. For example, Best (1989), who is severely critical of figures which have been published for the number of children abducted by strangers in the United States, argues that some estimates include runaway children, missing adults, and children taken by non-custodial parents.

It is also important to distinguish clearly between the measurement of incidence and the measurement of prevalence, that is, between the number of new cases coming to notice in a specific population over a given period as opposed to the total number of cases in a specific population over a given period.[4] A further difficulty is that what should be regarded as a case when counting instances of some phenomenon is not always self-evident. As La Fontaine (1990) points out, this can be a particular problem in the study of child abuse where there is sometimes ambiguity about whether the case refers to the individual children involved or to their families. She notes, for example, that in the notorious Cleveland case in the United Kingdom the number of children taken into care was 160, but the number of families involved was only 44. Quite different perceptions of the problem might arise depending on which figure one takes.

Whether a particular crime finds its way into the criminal statistics depends on its reportability, visibility and recordability (J. Scott, 1990, 91). Reportability refers to the likelihood of a given crime being brought to the attention of the police. A number of factors serve to inhibit reporting. An offence may not be reported because it is perceived not to be serious. The difficulty or inconvenience of making a report may outweigh an individual's inclination to do so. In some instances, instead of reporting the matter to the appropriate authorities, an aggrieved party might make an informal response to a particular act. Most relevant in the present context is the disincentive to reporting produced because disclosure is potentially threatening. Reports may not be made because to do so is potentially to risk embarrassment, intimidation or publicity. Computer fraud apparently goes undisclosed because financial institutions affected by it fear the embarrassment of admitting they have been defrauded. In a similar way, a very different crime, child sexual abuse, often remains unreported because it is accompanied by threats which seek to forestall discovery. Victims may also experience feelings of fear or guilt which inhibit disclosure (La Fontaine, 1990; S. Taylor, 1989).

The extent to which data are available derives in part, however, from the varying degrees of 'recordability' (J. Scott, 1990) which surround different areas of social life. To take one example, the extensive literature on estimating the size of the underground economy partly reflects the fact that the scale and scope of economic measurement is extensive relative to other areas of social life (Miles and Irvine, 1979). In many other instances data on a particular hidden population may simply not exist at all.[5] John Scott (1990) notes that reportability is often linked to the visibility of deviant activities. The social organization of deviance provides varying opportunities for concealment or disclosure (Best and Luckenbill, 1980). Some kinds of deviant behaviour are multifaceted in ways which leave multiple traces. Thus, even if they do not provide a reliable basis for measurement, drug abuse may be tracked to some extent through rates of notification of viral hepatitis, drug seizure statistics and so on (Hartnoll et al., 1985b). On the other hand, activities which take place in secret may come to light only rarely, if at all. Child sexual abuse is again an obvious example.

Recordability is affected by administrative routines. In the case of crime, as Scott (1990) points out, the law is enforced in a discretionary way.[6] What is recorded as crime reflects the policies and priorities of local forces. The police may not record an offence or may record only the most serious of a number of related offences. The contingencies which surround the policing of invisible crimes means that, often, they receive a specialist response. If the issue has been medicalized this may take the form of specialized diagnostic or treatment agencies. Alternatively, activities may be targeted by specialist units involved in proactive policing (Marx, 1980; Braithwaite et al., 1987). As with official statistics, reliance on figures based on the case records of particular agencies can be hazardous. Figures for the number of cases referred to specialist agencies represent those which have become known to professionals and exclude those which remain hidden. Agency cases are usually therefore unrepresentative, making difficult not only estimation but also bivariate analysis (La Fontaine, 1990). Those cases which do come to light often reflect the character of the referral process. In a detailed study of cases referred to a specialized hospital unit dealing with the diagnosis and treatment of child sexual abuse, La Fontaine (1990) noted, for example, an increase in the number of cases referred between 1981 and 1984 as a result of greater awareness of the extent of the problem. However, this increase in its turn had consequences for the character of cases accepted. On the one hand, because of increased pressure on resources fewer cases of a purely diagnostic character were seen. On the other hand, increased awareness of the problem also meant that alternative sources of assessment and treatment were now available elsewhere, again changing the character of referrals to the agency studied. Routine record-keeping procedures within non-specialist agencies can also often militate against the disclosure of potentially embarrassing information. Macintyre (1978) notes that nurses and midwives in the antenatal clinic she studied were embarrassed to ask pregnant women questions about nervous or genetic disorders. They therefore phrased questions about these topics in vague or leading ways which tended to produce socially acceptable answers. Yet the responses to these questions formed the basis for official medical records.

To the extent that specialist surveillance units are used to police invisible crimes, their procedures will affect the estimates derived. Every year the US Internal Revenue Service intensively examines a random sample of tax returns on approximately 50,000 individuals. Despite these efforts the ability of IRS investigators to uncover evidence of non-compliance partly depends on the resources available to them. As Mattera puts it: 'This measurement technique thus has the peculiarity that its efficacy is a function of IRS budgetary decisions' (1985, 52; see also Weigand, 1987). Moreover, it depends on the existence of a paper trail capable of being followed by an IRS investigator; 'income which is entirely off the books – unreported by both the payer and the recipient – will escape detection' (Mattera, 1985, 52).

In the eyes of some writers official statistics are irrevocably compromised by the existence of the dark figure. Those who take this view argue that official statistics reflect the organizational contingencies embedded in their production more clearly than they do the behaviours they are alleged to measure. Or, as Kitsuse and Cicourel put it, the rates presented in statistical tables 'can be viewed as indices of organizational processes rather than as indices of certain forms of behavior' (1963, 137). Other writers have suggested that this view is much too austere. While conceding that the use of official statistics may be problematic, they suggest that criticisms have been exaggerated and that the problems raised are in many cases tractable (for a defence of this view, see, e.g., Bulmer, 1980). Since the debate is by now of sufficient duration and hardiness to have become a staple of undergraduate textbooks (see, e.g., Eglin, 1987), the arguments on either side will not be reprised here in any detail. Instead, the remainder of this chapter will focus on two broad areas. The first of these looks at attempts to side-step the problem of the dark figure through a variety of strategies: the use of traces, imputation from case-based data, and what are called here 'implicative methods'. The second area of discussion relates to statistical estimates of the size of hidden populations produced and disseminated, not by bureaucracies, but by social *movements* or by those wishing to advance moral, political or policy claims in contentious areas. The issue here, to paraphrase Kitsuse and Cicourel (1963, 137), is how far estimates of the dark figure may be taken as indices of *political* processes rather than as indices of behaviour.

Traces: the measurement of inadvertence

Webb et al. (1966; 1981) have suggested that researchers should add to their repertoire of methods a range of 'unobtrusive' or 'non-reactive' measures. As the term implies, the major feature of such measures is that they do not intrude into the research situation (Sechrest and Phillips, 1979). As a result, they help offset the tendency of research participants to change their behaviour or to give socially desirable responses because they know they are being studied. Webb et al. place great stress on the opportunistic exploitation of available data. They also celebrate the role of imagination and serendipity in the data collection process. For them, the use of unobtrusive measures often requires an imaginative leap by which the researcher comes to see mundane, unpromising or inconspicuous sources of information as appropriate data.

Webb et al. describe a wide range of possible measures including those based on various kinds of archival sources, covert observational methods, and the use of what they call 'traces'.[7] Dabbs (1982) has distinguished between lasting traces and ephemeral traces. Lasting traces include physical traces produced by the erosion of the environment or by accretion to it (Webb et al., 1966, 36–46). Wear on floor tiles, for example, is an erosion measure which may denote the frequency of use of particular areas. The amount of litter left behind in a particular area is, on the other hand, an accretion measure. Ephemeral traces reflect 'much of the ordinary behavior of people and organizations, but unless someone or something is there to make a record, the ephemeral trace is lost' (Dabbs, 1982, 35). Ephemeral traces might include representations, photographs, film, video and the like; material objects, including what Scott calls 'circulatory devices' (1990, 13), coins, stamps, tickets and so on; and 'collateral outcomes' where a trace appears as an unanticipated consequence of an unrelated activity, as, for example, when someone acquires a notifiable disease, viral hepatitis, from intravenous drug use (Hartnoll et al., 1985b).

Ephemeral traces have occasionally been used to estimate the size of hidden populations. According to Mattera (1985), US economists in the late 1960s became puzzled by the unusually high amount of currency in circulation despite the rapid spread of financial innovations such as credit cards. A further curious feature of this situation was that a substantial amount of the currency in circulation was accounted for by large denomination bills. Subsequently, Mattera notes, it became fashionable to suggest that the use of such bills reflected in some way the extent of tax evasion, and could provide a basis for estimating the size of the 'underground economy'.

One difficulty with unobtrusive measures is that, beyond the injunction to be imaginative, it is difficult to know how best they might be generated. There have been several attempts to produce a generative taxonomy of such measures which would aid researchers systematically to develop new measures (Sechrest and Phillips, 1979; Bouchard, 1976; Webb et al., 1981, 287–306), but so far no entirely satisfactory schema has emerged. This is hardly surprising since, from a substantive rather than a methodological point of view, what Webb et al. have actually produced is a sociology of the inadvertent. Unobtrusive measures are also 'inferentially weak' (Bouchard, 1976). This can be illustrated, according to Bouchard, with reference to a classic example of an unobtrusive measure, the use of floor wear to measure frequency of use. Differential wear may result from the location of facilities such as bathrooms or water fountains. Passage across the floor may be constrained by the arrangement of furniture. Wear is also related to the physical properties of the floor-covering itself. In the case of the underground economy in the United States, Tanzi (1982) has pointed out that using the amount of large denomination notes in circulation as a measure is substantially affected by large amounts of US currency held outside the United States. Because of their inferential weakness, Webb et al. stress that unobtrusive measures are best used alongside other methods. Alternatively they may be appropriate for tracking changes in the magnitude of some activity even if the level of the activity itself can not be adequately measured.

Imputation from case-based data

In some instances controlled procedures can be used for imputing the number or characteristics of those not referred to an agency from those who are found in its case-records. Procedures of this kind seem to have been most well developed in studies which attempt to estimate levels of drug abuse in local areas. Hartnoll and his colleagues (1985a; 1985b) have used a number of techniques for estimating the size of non-agency populations in their study of drug use in two inner-London boroughs. The imputive methods used by Hartnoll et al. include capture–recapture procedures and the use of nomination techniques. Capture–recapture methods derive from those originally developed in biology for estimating animal populations in the wild. Nomination techniques use information about nominated others provided by agency attenders. As will be seen elsewhere, nomination techniques can also be used in conjunction with random samples of the population. In the kind of 'case-based' nomination techniques described by Hartnoll et al. the 'seed' for the nominated sample is provided by the case records of some agency. The nominated sample, in other words, is linked to a 'found' base rather than a random one.

Capture–recapture methods
Capture–recapture methods are based on procedures developed by ethologists for estimating the size of a population of animals in their natural habitat. (For a detailed review see Blower et al., 1981.) This involves capturing a sample of animals, marking them in some way and releasing them back into the wild. Sometime later a second sample is taken and the number of marked animals from the first sample within it is noted. The following assumptions also have to be met: marked and unmarked animals must be similar in their behaviour and they must intermingle freely; furthermore, there should be no addition to the population between the time points at which the two samples were taken.

Provided the two samples are independent random samples of the total population, the size of that population can be derived from the following equation (Blower et al., 1981, 29):

$$P_i = \frac{n_i \, n_{i+1}}{m_{i+1}}$$

where:
P_i = the population size at time *i*
n_i = animals captured, marked, released at time *i*
n_{i+1} = number of animals in sample taken at time *i* + 1
m_{i+1} = number of recaptured marked animals in second sample.

Obviously, for ethical as well as operational reasons, one cannot proceed in this way with human populations. Hartnoll et al. (1985a, b) note, however, that samples of cases from any pair of sources can be substituted into the formula provided the samples are independent of each other and that they are comparable in terms of case definitions, time periods and the population from which the samples are drawn. For example, in their research, the clientele of two different agencies were used.

The difficulties with using capture–recapture methods in social research arise from the problems of ensuring that the assumptions underlying the method can be met. In agency studies it often cannot be guaranteed that the samples used are independent, while there may be problems of ensuring data are collected over the same period. In human populations the method relies on individuals being identified and therefore may produce problems of confidentiality. Particularly in studying an area like drug abuse, the assumption that the population is in a steady state over the study period may be untenable. Biologists have apparently extended the range of the original method to allow some of the underlying assumptions to be relaxed, in order to study more complex population dynamics (Blower et al., 1981). It is unlikely, however, that these more elaborate procedures could easily be applied to human populations.

Nomination techniques
In the study of drug abuse attempts have also been made to use nomination techniques to estimate the size and character of the user population not known to therapeutic agencies (Hartnoll et al., 1985a,b; Blumberg and Dronfield, 1976). In these studies clinic attenders are interviewed by a fieldworker and asked to nominate in an anonymous fashion friends who are regular drug users and to indicate whether these friends have attended a clinic in the past year. Because of the possibility of the same nominated user being double-counted, one cannot simply sum the number of nominated users to estimate the number of non-clinic attenders. It is, however, possible to produce an estimate of the ratio of treated to untreated users.

The use of case-based methods can be valuable. Comparisons of the various estimates Hartnoll et al. (1985b) produced for opioid users who are not in the treatment population show them to be of a comparable order. In addition, as might be expected, these estimates were also considerably higher than official estimates based on the number of registered addicts. Estimates imputed from case-based data may indicate the kind of correction which may need to be applied to official estimates at the national level. It should be clear, however, that case-based methods are most reliable where they are used on relatively small areas. Their direct use at the national level would appear to be difficult.

Implicative methods

The term 'implicative methods' is used to refer to those methods for estimating the size of hidden populations based on the notion that measurement of one aspect of a population has implications for the level of another. Methods of this kind assume it is possible to produce estimates where one has (a) data relating to a range of variables and (b) a theory which accounts for the relationship between them. These conditions are much more likely to be met in areas like demography and economics, than in disciplines such as sociology and anthropology.[8]

Multiplier methods

Multiplier methods depend on the assumption that the portion of a population which can be measured stands in a fixed ratio to that which cannot. For example, it seems that those having the surname Cohen form a relatively constant proportion of the Jewish population (Waterman and Kosmin, 1986). This constant can be derived empirically by noting the proportion of Cohens recorded in birth and death notices in Jewish newspapers. Waterman and Kosmin were able to estimate the size of the Jewish population in London by counting the number of Cohens found in telephone directories and, much more usefully, on the electoral roll and applying the relevant multiplier. Multiplier techniques have also been used in the study of drug abuse (Hartnoll et al., 1985a). It has been assumed that there is a direct relationship between the number of drug-related deaths and the prevalence of drug abuse. If the death rate for users is known or can be reliably estimated, the number of deaths in a given year multiplied by the annual morality rate can be used to give an annual period prevalence. This particular method has a number of obvious shortcomings. There may be difficulties in reliably identifying user deaths from mortality data. It is plausible to suggest that rates of mortality are different for known addicts and for those who have hidden their drug use. Changes in the way drugs are used – for example, a shift from injection of the drug to smoking – can also affect mortality rates, as can variations in purity.

Discrepancy methods

In theory, estimates of the size of a population derived from different measures should coincide. Where they do not, the discrepancy between two measures can be used as an estimate for the hidden portion of some population. Brendan Walsh (1971), for example, estimated the extent of religious intermarriage in the Republic of Ireland by assuming that such marriages accounted for discrepancies between rates of marriage performed under the auspices of various denominations and the proportion of members of those denominations recorded as ever-married in the Census. Dilnot and Morris (1981) used a discrepancy method to estimate the extent of tax evasion and social security abuse in Britain using data from the 1977 Family Expenditure Survey. They inspected (anonymized) data for households in the FES where expenditure exceeded reported income, but where the income–expenditure discrepancy could not be due to factors such as the run-down of existing wealth.

Discrepancy measures tend, like unobtrusive measures, to be inferentially weak. The difficulty is that one is always dealing with an 'unexplained residual' (Frey and Pommerehne, 1982), that which is assumed to be left over when all other factors have been taken into account. As Frey and Pommerehne go on to point out, in cases where direct measurement is impossible use of the residual may well be reasonable. But in many cases its size is likely to be affected by a variety of factors, not all of them obvious or directly measurable. To be confident that the unexplained residual contains only what one is interested in requires both good data and a sound underlying theoretical model. Research on the size of the hidden economy is perhaps a good example of a field where both have been lacking. J.J. Thomas (1990) has criticized much of the work in the area for being based on 'measurement without theory'. Neither has the calibre of the data used been impressive, for, if sociologists can be accused of being too sceptical of official statistics (Bulmer, 1980), economists can be chided for caring little about the basic quality of their data (Morgenstern, 1963; Reuter, 1982, 182; Jacob, 1984; J.J Thomas, 1988; 1990).

Soft-modelling

Again in relation to the underground economy, writers like Frey and Weck (1983) and Button (1984) have adopted a rather more complex approach known as 'soft-modelling'. Soft-modelling is unconcerned with the absolute size of the underground economy but deals with comparisons between countries and regions. The argument soft modellers make is that the scale of activity in the underground economy is for all intents and purposes unknown. They suggest, however, that it remains reasonable to examine the relative importance of factors which may be assumed *a priori* to produce variations in levels of informal economic activity. Provided one can specify a range of variables likely to encourage participation in the hidden economy and making the entirely plausible assumption that the pressures towards participation are not spatially uniform, then a sensitivity analysis based around the relative weights in a regression model can be used to rank countries or regions. Frey and Weck (1983) have produced a ranking of 17 OECD countries in terms of the likely size of their hidden economy by examining the impact at national level of factors such as taxation rates, the degree of legal regulation, attitudes towards paying taxes, labour market variables and so on. Button (1984) has performed a somewhat similar exercise for regions in Great Britain. Soft-modelling tries to compare areas by looking at their propensity to produce economic activities outside the formal sphere (assuming, of course, that one can in fact delineate the formal from the informal [see Harding and Jenkins, 1989]). It can be argued in favour of the approach that this is often more useful to know than is a global figure, say for 'underground GNP'. On the other hand, there is no way to validate the patterns found. There are also difficulties in finding appropriate data, selecting the variables to be entered into the analysis, assuring their comparability and developing a cogent theoretical framework to account for their effects.

Advocacy estimates

Attempts to estimate prevalence often follow the emergence or recognition of a phenomenon which is regarded as being socially problematic or contentious. After all, as Best (1989) points out, in such circumstances numerical estimates help to fix the dimensions of a social problem. Academic researchers tend to assume that producing reliable estimates of prevalence in such circumstances is vitally important, especially in making policy decisions. The production of such estimates, however, may bring them into conflict with those taking advocacy positions around the issue concerned.

As Nathan Keyfitz has observed: 'Numbers provide the rhetoric of our age' (1987, 235). Advocacy groups presumably use numerical estimates because they are assumed to have persuasive power. Large estimates suggest a sizeable problem which demands urgent attention; they perform a consciousness-raising role (Rossi, 1987). Large numbers are newsworthy and therefore more likely to attract media attention. Although the media will sometimes question the size of estimates, Best (1989) points out that this is unusual. Usually their reliability will remain unquestioned provided the figures used can at least be attributed to an apparently knowledgeable source. Because those who bring a topic to public attention often appear to be better-informed about it than everyone else, their views are taken as authoritative even where, Best argues, they are only based on guesswork or unreliable data. (For some examples of media distortions of prevalence estimates relating to tranquillizer dependence, see Gabe and Bury, 1988.)

The 'statistical conflicts of interest' (Biderman and Reiss, 1967) which sometimes surround differences between academic and advocacy estimates arise in a number of different ways. Rossi (1987), for example, found the size and composition of the homeless population in Chicago to be roughly 10 times *smaller* than estimates produced by housing activists. As he reports in an article sardonically entitled 'No good applied social research goes unpunished' (1987), the findings of the study were bitterly attacked by advocates for the homeless, and he found himself being repeatedly shunned at conferences on homelessness. Opponents argued that his definition of the problem was too narrow, and that the study had damaged the cause of the homeless by potentially allowing the problem to be dismissed as trivial.

Social scientists may also undermine advocacy estimates in less direct ways. In recent years statistical exegeses aimed at professional, lay and advocacy audiences have begun to appear on the use, and more particularly the misuse, of statistics relating to a range of sensitive topics. (La Fontaine [1990] and Steve Taylor [1989], both writing about child sexual abuse, are good examples of this genre.) It is true, of course, that such writing can serve advocacy needs. Some groups have apparently assimilated sociological critiques of official statistics and used them in their campaigns to call for improved reporting of particular crimes (Best, 1989). However, by rehearsing the complexities of using statistics, whatever their provenance, the cumulative effect of such exegeses may be to undermine advocacy claims even if it is not the intention of the authors concerned to do so.

A third situation is where researchers set out explicitly to debunk advocacy claims, as does Best (1989) in his work on stranger abductions in the United States. According to Best:

> it is apparent that the missing children crusaders' initial claims greatly exaggerated the extent of the problem. There is simply no evidence to support claims of 50,000 stranger abductions annually, of 40,000 permanently missing victims, 5000 abduction-related homicides, or 5000 unidentified juvenile corpses. (1989, 30)

Those who have drawn attention to the discrepancies between academic estimates and advocacy estimates tend implicitly to invoke a market model of advocacy. Advocacy groups work in a competitive environment in terms of public attention, media coverage and the availability of funding (on the media especially, see Nelson, 1984). A purely market model of advocacy may explain why advocacy groups propagate high estimates. It does not, however, explain how such estimates are arrived at, nor how their plausibility is maintained even when they are undermined by academic estimates. Unlike the routines by which statistics are produced in bureaucracies, the processes which lead to the production of advocacy estimates are generally not accessible to researchers. Indeed, it may be difficult even to establish the source of a particular estimate. According to Rossi (1987), for example, local housing activists in Chicago told him that their estimates of the number of homeless in the city came from a report produced by a Federal agency. The authors of the report, however, told him that these estimates had been obtained from local activists in Chicago.

One reason for large estimates may lie in the fact that newly recognized social problems are often triggered by traumatic events and situations. Paradoxically, the singularity of particular cases reinforces their apparent ubiquity. Nisbett and Ross (1980) suggest that, cognitively, information which is vivid and tangible is weighed much more heavily, and has much greater influence, than that which is pallid and abstract. Information is vivid where it has emotional interest, is concrete and image producing, and is temporally and spatially close (1980, 44–6). The social processes which bring novel and undesirable events and situations to widespread attention are likely to reinforce this sense of vividness. Best (1987) notes that examples of new problems which are used to grab public attention are often chosen for their horrific nature. These are then taken as basic referents around which the problem as a whole is subsequently defined. In particular, such examples may specifically trade on the invocation of negative emotions (see, e.g., J.M. Johnson, 1989), and may utilize images which are immediate and compelling (see, e.g., Nelson, 1984). Growing social concern about problematic groups, events or activities also often involves a process of what Cohen (1972) calls 'sensitization'. A perception develops that the novel social phenomenon causing concern is not an isolated instance but is in reality all around. This in turn can produce a self-fulfilling prophecy by encouraging investigative action which might not otherwise have taken place. Subsequently, as cases are uncovered the apparent rate of growth of the problem seems alarming because the numbers are starting from a small base. All of these factors do little to discourage the view that the problem is a substantial one.[9] (To say this is not to assume that any particular problem is in fact insubstantial.)

How do the differences between academic and advocacy estimates affect the relationship between social scientists and activists? Best (1989) notes that when estimates for the number of stranger abductions in the US were challenged activists responded that even one child abducted is one too many. This comment can validly be taken as a criticism of the tendency for human suffering to fade from view in the process of sociological abstraction (see, e.g., R.K. Merton, 1972, on 'sociological sadism'; Killian, 1981). (Best, for example, is largely silent about the ethical implications of his work.) On the other hand, activists may wish through the 'one is too many' argument to exempt their estimates from critical scrutiny. For the researcher to accept this position, however, is to give in to the logic of the market place. In the long run, without critical scrutiny, it is likely to be those with the largest estimates or the most horrific examples who win attention and resources, perhaps at the expense of other, more deserving issues.

Some researchers, because of their own personal commitment to a particular cause, try to minimize the distance between their own findings and advocacy estimates. Rossi was unwilling for his research findings to be used in ways which might affect the collective interests of the homeless. (On this issue, which is discussed more widely in a later chapter, see, e.g., Becker, 1967; Finch, 1984; Felson, 1991.) In publicizing his research he tried unsuccessfully to present the findings in a way which put more stress on the social and material circumstances of the homeless rather than on their numbers. He also records that he has actively resisted attempts to use his research in support of those politically unsympathetic to the homeless. However, there are a number of problems with adopting the kind of minimization strategy attempted by Rossi. It is probably difficult to carry out where the discrepancy between academic and advocacy estimates is very wide. Furthermore, minimization depends on the researcher being fully in control of the research findings. This, however, can be difficult, especially with a large-scale study in which many people are involved. Advocacy groups had already heard of Rossi's results, and had begun to attack them even before publication, while, despite his efforts, the local press still chose to concentrate on the numerical estimates rather than the study's other findings.

It seems likely that social researchers will be unable to avoid being drawn into disputes surrounding the size of hidden populations. In some cases, of course, this outcome may be an ironic one given the support social research has lent in recent decades to the claims particularly of disadvantaged groups. However, as Guillemin and Horowitz contend, many groups, having successfully mobilized, no longer need research by academics to bolster their case.

By the early 1970s . . . it was patently obvious that once marginal groups could generate their own framework for organization on which to base entitlement, they could make a strong bid for government recognition, representation and support quite without sociological advocates. The initial mobilization of ethnic groups, drug users, homosexuals, prisoners, women and the aged may have required the legitimating participation of social scientists; but the broadening of channels of appeal appeared to eliminate the necessity for scholarly validation. (1983, 198)

Indeed, as Rossi (1987) points out, as overall levels of funding shrink, researchers may actually find themselves competing with advocacy groups for scarce funding resources. One pessimistic conclusion is therefore that the scene is being set for increasing conflict between researchers and advocacy groups.

Notes

1. In many cases, of course, existing statistics are simply not available. The researcher may be forced, therefore, to rely on guesswork. Mosteller (1977) discusses some of the factors affecting the accuracy of guesstimates, as well as procedures for improving conjectural methods.

2. On the development of statistical systems and on the changing role of statistical information in society, see Starr (1987).

3. For some rich ethnographic detail on the social production of criminal statistics, see M. Young (1991).

4. For a good example of misleading claims based on confusing incidence and prevalence, see Bibby and Maus's (1974) study of the 'outcome measures' used by skid road missions in Seattle.

5. They can, though, materialize occasionally from unexpected sources. For example, figures for the yearly incidence of Catholic–Protestant intermarriage in Northern Ireland withheld from social scientists emerged as a by-product of research by a geneticist (Masterson, 1970) on cousin marriage in Ireland (R.M. Lee, 1981).

6. See, for example, D.J. Smith (1983).

7. To this list might be added the secondary analysis of existing survey data. One advantage of secondary analysis in studying sensitive topics arises from what, paradoxically, has often been seen as one of its drawbacks, the discrepancy between the conceptual framework used by the original data collector and the secondary analyst (Bulmer, 1980). Data used for a purpose for which they were not collected may be 'nonreactive' in the sense of being less subject to response biases caused because the original data collector's purposes and intentions were transparent enough to respondents to affect the measurement process. (On secondary analysis in general see Hyman, 1972; Hakim, 1982; Dale et al., 1988.)

8. Again, for a number of useful illustrations, see Mosteller (1977).

9. Although the focus here is on numerical estimation, from the social control point of view what is being discussed here is, of course, the process of 'deviance amplification' (Jock Young, 1971).

4

Sampling Rare or Deviant Populations

This chapter focuses on sampling, in other words, the selection of people, places or activities (Spradley, 1980) suitable for study.[1] In addition, indirect methods of gathering information where sampling or access prove impossible will also be discussed briefly. Put rather baldly, the aim of sampling is to select elements for study in a way which adequately represents a population of interest (though see Patton, 1987), both in relation to the purpose of the research, and at reasonable cost. In many situations, there are well-developed strategies for realizing these twin aims of representativeness and cost-effectiveness. Neither, however, may be easy to obtain where the topic under investigation is a sensitive one. First, other things being equal, sampling becomes more difficult the more sensitive the topic under investigation, since potential informants will have more incentive to conceal their activities. Second, and related to this, the less visible an activity is the harder it is to sample. Deviant worlds are often melded to or shielded from conventional worlds (Rock, 1973, 79–83) in ways which may induce failures even to recognize as deviant those capable of being so defined. Third, obtaining sample elements which are rare is more difficult, in the sense of being more costly, than is obtaining them for some behaviour which occurs frequently. Finally, while obtaining respondents over a widely dispersed geographical area is likely to improve representativeness, dispersal also drives up cost.

Systematic treatments of sampling issues related to deviant populations can be found in Becker (1970) and for rare populations in Sudman and Kalton (1986) and Kish (1965). Interestingly, although the emphases are quite different the range of strategies outlined by Becker are rather similar to those described by Sudman and Kalton, and by Kish. Becker's article, in particular, celebrates the ingenuity of researchers in finding 'pathways to data', and represents an accumulation of lore and practice concerning access to deviant groups (see also Spradley, 1980, 46–52).[2] It is important to stress, however, that sampling is always a theoretical matter before it is a technical one. In other words, as well as substantive knowledge and technical judgement, the selection of a research site or the specification of a sampling procedure requires reflection on the theoretical purposes to which the data collected by means of the sample will be put (R.G. Burgess, 1984; Biernacki and Waldorf, 1981; Galtung, 1967). In the case of sensitive topics, however, adequate reflection of this kind is not always possible. Available knowledge can be limited, while levels of sensitivity, visibility, frequency and dispersal are often the product of complex patterns of social organization (Best and Luckenbill, 1980) which may not be obvious to the researcher *before* the research has begun.

A further aspect of this is that in some situations sampling can also become a political issue. As Gillespie and Leffler (1987) point out, the scientific legitimacy of an emerging social problem – the example they use is sexual harassment – often depends on the methods used to study it. Yet, it is precisely at the point where a social problem is not yet widely acknowledged that researchers will usually lack the means to generate statistically adequate samples. A reliance on convenience or other kinds of non-probability samples often means that the issue is not taken seriously. However, until the issue is taken seriously, it may not be possible to fund detailed and comprehensive studies.[3]

Sampling strategies

The major strategies which can be used, singly or in combination, for sampling 'special' populations which are rare and/or deviant in some way are as follows:

1 List sampling.
2 Multi-purposing.
3 Screening.
4 Networking.
5 Outcropping.
6 Advertising.
7 Servicing.

List sampling

Rarely available for deviant populations, lists have on occasion been used to sample rare populations. Thornes and Collard (1979), for example, were able to obtain a sample of the recently divorced using local newspapers which, in some parts of Britain, make a practice of listing petitioners for divorce after every sitting of the local divorce court. Unfortunately, this kind of fortuitous availability is in itself likely to be a fairly rare occurrence. In many instances the researcher may not even know that a suitable list exists. Furthermore, even where the existence of lists is known, access to them may remain closed. Thus, while Lopata (1980) was able to have a sample of widows drawn from lists of social security beneficiaries kept by the US Social Security Administration, her access to these lists was facilitated by her being under contract to the Administration. By contrast, in a similar study in Britain, Marris (1958) was unable to generate a sample of widows using death registration records held by local registrars. At the same time, Marris's research nicely illustrates the point that a sampling frame not available from one source may be available from another. He subsequently found that information from the registration records was passed by the registrars to local Public Health Authorities who did permit him access.

In a few instances, members of some group can be detected from lists not specifically designed to identify them. Himmelfarb (1974) needed a sample of Jews in order to assess the effects of differing levels of religious schooling on adult religious practice. Although Jewish charities keep detailed lists of donors, these lists could not be used for the research envisaged because of their bias towards the more committed, who were likely to have had high levels of religious education. The donor records did, however, yield a further list of distinctively Jewish names, which Himmelfarb then used to sample from local telephone directories. The sample obtained in this way was not representative, but did allow the effect of differing levels of religious schooling to be assessed. Subsequently, Himmelfarb et al. (1983) have shown that Jews with distinctive Jewish surnames differ little in their demographic characteristics from the Jewish population as a whole. (For a further use of distinctive name sampling, see Dench's [1975] survey of Maltese immigrants living in London who were selected by searching electoral registers for distinctive Maltese names.)

Name sampling, of course, is only useful where the group concerned can be unambiguously identified by name. Those who change their names in order to 'pass', out-marrying women who take their husband's name on marriage, and some of the offspring of intermarriage in the previous generation will not be detected. Benson (1981) tried to sample Anglo-African marriages in a racially mixed area of London by using the distinctive names approach in a search of local electoral registers and registrations of intention to marry. These searches, however, yielded few traceable interracial couples. In addition, the couples who were identified by this procedure were somewhat suspicious and disliked the fact that their names had been obtained from official records. Conversely, and perhaps unexpectedly, this kind of irritation was not voiced in Marris's case. The widows he studied accepted without comment that they had been selected on the basis of death registration information. Perhaps widows, who, as Lopata found, are often in fact anxious to talk about their bereavement, might be less concerned about the origins of the sample than is the case for interracial couples, who may fear racial harassment.

Besides the irritation their use may cause to members of vulnerable groups, lists are subject to the usual difficulties involved in using sampling frames: the inclusion on the list of blank or ineligible elements, duplicates and the systematic omission of some segment of the population (Sudman, 1983). Even where these problems exist, lists may still be useful in providing the seed for a snowball sample, or for checking the validity of data collected by some other methods (see, e.g., Tracy and Fox, 1981; Sudman and Bradburn, 1982; and, for a critique of this procedure, Miller and Groves, 1985). In addition, Sudman and Kalton (1986) point out that where a list is incomplete it may still be advisable to use it if the proportion of the population *not* on the list is small and the cost of screening for non-listed individuals is high. Such a decision can only be made, though, on an empirical basis depending on the size of the sample, the accuracy desired and the relative costs involved.

Multi-purposing
An existing survey can sometimes be used as a vehicle for reaching the population of interest. Access to a special population can be achieved either by 'piggybacking' the sampling of the special population on to an existing survey, or by using an 'amalgam' approach in which a survey is employed simultaneously to locate a number of different rare populations (Tourganeau and Smith, 1985). Alan Walker's (1982) study of the problems of handicapped young people in the labour market used a sample of 18-year-olds whose handicap had already been identified on an earlier wave of the longitudinal National Child Development Survey. In a similar way, a longitudinal survey of redundant steelworkers in South Wales provided Leaver (Harris et al., 1987) with a sample of previously financially secure families who were now facing financial hardship, and Bytheway (1986) with a sample of older workers whose labour market future was uncertain because of their age.

As Catherine Hakim points out

> Hitching a ride on an existing multipurpose survey carries enormous advantages in terms of savings in costs . . . and in obtaining access to a wide range of complementary data on other topics. (1985, 14)

The disadvantages of multi-purposing include the problems of confidentiality which may arise if respondents' names are to be made available to another researcher, and the organizational difficulties of running different but interconnected projects in tandem (Tourganeau and Smith, 1985). In addition, the main survey may not actually be an entirely ideal vehicle for investigating the topic of interest on the subsidiary study (Hakim, 1985). Multi-purposing seems most feasible as a means of reaching a special population where some kind of organizational context already exists in the form of a longitudinal, or a recurrent, survey. Such contexts, however, produce their own problems for, as Hakim notes, those who run recurrent surveys are often under tremendous pressure to piggyback special projects.

Screening

Screening or 'sift-sampling' involves the systematic canvass of a particular location in order to identify members of some requisite population. As a method, it is labour-intensive, requires fairly sizeable resources and may only be operable over a relatively limited area. It may also produce only a limited 'strike rate'. In a study of women homeworkers, Hope et al. (1976) canvassed 216 houses in two streets in North London. Even within this limited geographical area fieldwork took two-and-a-half months for a yield of 11 interviews, 10 refusals, and information on a suspected further 11 homeworkers. To take another example, Susan McRae (1986) wanted to generate a sample of households in which the occupational status of the wife was higher than that of the husband, for an intensive interview study of couples in cross-class marriages. She distributed, in all, 2,155 screening questionnaires to women in non-manual occupations employed mainly in health, social services and education in a number of locales. Some 603 questionnaires were returned which yielded 24 couples suitable for interview. In both these cases, the resulting sample was appropriate to the exploratory aims of the study. Nevertheless, the effort required to screen the relevant population was considerable, and where, as in the study by Hope et al., screening forces reliance on an extremely limited geographical area, it is hard to suppress doubts about how far the results obtained can be generalized.

In an effort to reduce the costs and time involved in screening, a number of studies have made use of 'batch testing' strategies. Batch testing appears to have been developed in the United States from the application to area sampling of methods originally suggested by Waksberg (1978) for improving the efficiency of telephone sampling (Tourganeau and Smith, 1985), and independently – under the name of focused enumeration – in the United Kingdom (Brown and Ritchie, 1981). The essence of the method is that, having selected a sample of geographical clusters or segments (often on the basis of a known concentration of members of a rare population), full screening of the cluster only takes place if a member of the rare population is found at an initial randomly selected dwelling unit. For example, in a study of the attitudes of Black Londoners towards the police (D.J. Smith, 1983), a sample of census enumeration districts (typically containing around 150 households) was selected, but with enumeration districts having very low concentrations of Asians or West Indians being excluded. Where Asian and West Indian residents comprised more than 10 per cent of the population of the enumeration district, screening was carried out by enumerating the members of every household. With concentrations under 10 per cent, however, focused enumeration was used. Here, an interviewer called only at every fifth dwelling unit and asked whether any Asian or West Indian residents were to be found in the five dwelling units to the right and left of the selected dwelling unit. If the household chosen contained an Asian or West Indian resident, or if any mention was made at the first household of Asian or West Indian residents in any of the five households to right or left, then all the intervening households were screened.

Methods of this kind do reduce considerably the costs of screening for rare populations. They work best, however, where the population of interest is either geographically concentrated and/or visible. Focused enumeration might, for example, be less successful where one was attempting to sample, say, a religious minority rather than a racial one.

Networking
In network sampling the researcher starts from an initial set of contacts and is then passed on by them to others, who in turn refer others and so on. Because of the way in which the sample is presumed to grow, network sampling is also often described as 'snowball sampling'. Traditionally, snowball sampling found little favour in survey research. More recently, however, in the guise of 'multiplicity sampling', it has been recognized as having considerable potential for the sampling of rare populations (Sudman and Kalton, 1986). In this variant of network sampling, snowballing is used to increase the yield from screening interviews by asking respondents to supply information about someone related to them but not residing in their household. One example of the use of this technique comes from a survey of Vietnam war veterans by Rothbart et al. (1982). In this study a stratified sample of 8,698 households was screened for a yield of 535 eligible veterans. Survey respondents were also asked, however, to supply information on kin who had been veterans of the war in Vietnam, a procedure which

yielded an additional 476 veterans. Rothbart et al. report few difficulties in locating nominated veterans, with most of the work of locating being done by telephone. Cost savings using this method were substantial, although there is some danger of sample bias in cases where kin vary systematically in their ability to nominate potential respondents.

Snowball sampling is ubiquitous in the study of deviant populations because it often represents the only way of gathering a sample. However, the intuitively appealing notion of the 'snowball' can be taken too much at face value. As a result few attempts have been made critically to evaluate snowball sampling as a strategy (Biernacki and Waldorf, 1981). Because of its ubiquity and relative lack of critical scrutiny snowball sampling, therefore, deserves some extended discussion. Despite its name, snowball sampling does not inevitably lead to an inexorably growing mass of contacts. Rather, as a number of researchers have found (Davis, 1982; R.M. Lee, 1981; 1992), what it often produces is a slow and uneven accretion of additional data points. As originally conceived, snowball sampling involved the attempt, as Coleman (1958) puts it, 'to sample explicitly with reference to the social structure'. The starting point for a snowball sample is therefore most properly an initial random sample from which further sample elements are selected for inclusion on the basis of a predefined sociometric relation to those already chosen. Where, as in the search for members of a rare population, the interest is in attributes rather than relations, one may gain some advantage in not having to predefine the sociometric criteria for inclusion in the sample. A pair of contacts in a chain need be linked by no more than knowledge of the existence of one another. Even so, in most cases – although this is rarely made clear – one is still sampling with reference to the social structure, though this time in an *implicit* manner.

This can be put another way. The inclusion of additional sample elements depends on the social ties between members of the study population, as well as on the links which exist between them and the wider population. Other things being equal, movement through informal networks will be easier in a numerically small group with well-developed patterns of social organization. That Goldstein (1984) was able to generate what was an apparently complete list of doctors who performed abortions in the Los Angeles area before legalization was probably due both to the relatively small number of doctors involved and the likely prior existence of an already organized professional referral network. In the case of religiously intermarried couples in Northern Ireland (R.M. Lee, 1981), snowball sampling proved difficult.[4] First of all, couples have little basis for interacting with one another. Second, in urban areas at least, even *knowledge* about intermarried couples may not be well distributed among the population at large in Northern Ireland. Unlike interracial couples, say, the religiously intermarried are not immediately visible, and, in Northern Ireland, they develop strategies for concealing the 'mixed' nature of their relationship from those around them (R.M. Lee, 1981). (On what might be a slightly different situation in rural Northern Ireland, see McFarlane, 1979.) In such situations sampling takes on an 'excursionary' character with progress being made from an initial starting point before contact depletion makes it necessary to return and begin the search for contacts all over again. Where this happens the snowballing metaphor can be seen not to be entirely apt, as the sampling process proceeds in a slow and halting way.

Snowball sampling does have advantages in cases where those being studied are members of a vulnerable or highly stigmatized group. 'Security' features are built into the method because the intermediaries who form the links of the referral chain are known to potential respondents and trusted by them. They are thus able to vouch for the researcher's *bona fides*. However, intermediaries can produce difficulties if they give a misleading account of the project and its aims. This can lead to a diminution in the flow of contacts, or, as Biernacki and Waldorf (1981) point out, to the researcher being inundated by large numbers of ineligible respondents. The eligibility criteria in Biernacki and Waldorf's study were in fact quite stringent, which may have made the problem particularly acute for them, but most researchers who use snowball sampling will need at some stage to build in procedures for verifying the eligibility of respondents. Since direct contact is not made with prospective informants it can become difficult to keep an accurate tally of refusals. Refusals may be reported when in fact the intermediary has not actually contacted a prospective respondent, or an intermediary may try to avoid the embarrassment of reporting a refusal by claiming not to have been able to make a suitable contact (R.M. Lee, 1981).

Bias is an almost inevitable feature of snowball samples because the social relations which underpin the sampling procedure tend towards reciprocity and transitivity (Davies, 1986; Rapoport and Horvath, 1961). In other words, if x and y are two points on the sample network and x is related to y in some way, then so too y will be related to x. In addition, it is also probable that the friends of y will be the friends of x. As a result, networks tend to turn in upon themselves and to be homogeneous in their attributes, rather than providing linkages to others whose social characteristics are different (Granovetter, 1973). This point is not being made to decry the utility of snowball sampling. As pointed out earlier, in many instances using a snowball sample is often the only possibility open to a researcher, and normally in these cases it will simply have to be accepted that the sample eventually obtained is unrepresentative.

That caution is necessary, however, is clear from the study of Catholic–Protestant intermarriage mentioned earlier where it was possible to assess the extent of bias involved by comparing the characteristics of the snowball sample against figures obtained from a special tabulation of the Northern Ireland Census. (For more detail and a discussion of the limitations of the Census data, see R.M. Lee, 1981; 1985a.) By comparison with the Census, the sample gathered showed a sharp bias towards young, recently married couples, mostly without children and with relatively high levels of educational attainment. There are two points to note about this. One is that the Census figures strongly contradict an assumption common in Northern Ireland that religious intermarriage is predominantly a middle-class phenomenon. In the absence of this additional evidence, there would have been a strong temptation to claim in line with this assumption that the use of the snowball procedure had in fact produced an adequate representation of the population under investigation. The second point is that, because snowballing tends to produce samples which are relatively homogeneous, the possibility of making internal comparisons across cases within the sample becomes more difficult than would be the case were the sample to be larger and more diverse.

Biernacki and Waldorf (1981) argue that, in order to maximize sample variability and the theoretical utility of snowball sampling, researchers need to make conscious efforts to pace and monitor the referral chains which they generate. From this point of view, snowball sampling is best seen as proceeding through a number of phases. In the beginning the aim is simply to make sufficient contact in order to get the project started. As time goes on, however, Biernacki and Waldorf suggest that the researcher should begin to exercise more control over referral chains; for example, by using as wide a variety of starting points as possible so as to ensure extensive coverage of the study population. Later, in a process akin to theoretical sampling (Glaser and Strauss, 1967), an attempt may be made to identify specific kinds of respondents whose utility to the researcher lies in their ability to illuminate emerging theoretical formulations. Finally, some referral chains may be developed in preference to others because they are thought to allow the possibility of verifying developing theory. In each of these cases,

Biernacki and Waldorf point out that the temptation to follow up referrals as quickly as possible needs to be tempered by the need to reach theoretical goals, which, in turn, requires the researcher to pace and monitor chains of referrals.

Outcropping
The notion of 'outcropping' as applied to sampling is based on a metaphor taken over by Webb et al. (1966; 1981) from geology to refer to the opportunistic exploitation of data points which are readily available. In other words, one method of sampling a rare or deviant population is to find some site in which its members congregate and to study them there. Where sampling is carried out on a probability basis, this implies the use of what might be called 'spatial outcroppings'. That is, the ability to produce a sample containing sufficient members of the group under consideration depends on the group being geographically segregated in some way. This allows areas of high concentration to be sampled using modifications of cluster sampling or stratified sampling; for example, the use of large sample clusters or disproportionate stratified sampling (Tourganeau and Smith, 1985; Kish, 1965). Qualitative researchers, on the other hand, tend to seek out 'relational outcroppings', that is, specific settings which bring together members of the group being studied. In practice, of course, the distinction between spatial and relational outcroppings is an artificial one, since geographical clustering and relational density normally imply one another. On the other hand, many deviant groups are probably not readily identifiable on a geographical basis, but are still based around extensive interactional contact between members.

Locating oneself 'where the action is' has a long and venerable history in sociology stretching back at least as far as Nels Anderson's (1923) study of Chicago's 'Hobohemia' and possibly further (Gouldner, 1973). There are, however, two broad problems with the use of relational outcroppings for sampling purposes. The first of these relates to the data collection process itself. When a setting has a high turnover of participants, data capture becomes problematic. In other words, while observation in the setting may be relatively straight-forward, it can be difficult to collect background data. Thus, although Humphreys's (1970) observational study of homosexual 'tearooms' has rightly attracted much attention because of the ethical considerations involved, it is clear that the collection of social and demographic data on participants was also problematic. This was not simply because of the sensitive nature of the research, but also because the behaviour being studied had a highly transitory and impersonal character. This, in turn, led to Humphreys having to adopt a convoluted and even more ethically dubious survey strategy involving deception and disguise.

The second problem involved in sampling relational outcroppings is that of sample bias. There is simply no guarantee that a sample selected from among those found in a particular setting is representative of the wider population of interest to the researcher. Indeed, there are usually grounds for assuming that the opposite is in fact the case. In the first place, those who make no use of the setting cannot be studied (Becker, 1970). In some cases this may not be a problem. However, by definition, one is automatically excluding social isolates and solitary participants from the sample. Furthermore, participation by the members of some group in a particular setting often reflects patterns of internal differentiation within that group, as when, say, a deviant subculture is organized into a series of non-overlapping 'scenes' which reflect differing styles of deviant expression (see, e.g., Plummer, 1975).

Although they are attractive because of their accessibility, populations which have been bureaucratically processed in some way are markedly subject to problems of sample bias. For this reason, Polsky (1971) has argued strongly against an over-reliance in the study of criminals on those who have been incarcerated, since those who find their way into prison are likely to be amateurs, or the less successful who are more easily caught. Thus, the prison population is unrepresentative of the wider criminal population although, as Becker (1970) notes, there are some criminal trades, like embezzlement, where the activity is both individual and secretive, and where prison may be the only feasible source for obtaining a sample at all.

A further problem is that, because the sampling of outcroppings often represents the path of least resistance in a research situation, a cumulative bias can come to be built into a field of study. For example, redundancy studies are often highly sensitive from the point of view of managers, who fear worker resistance or the disruption of remaining production (Wood, 1980). As a result, redundant workers have most often been studied in situations where the management has a paternalistic concern for its workforce, or where the plant is large and well-unionized (R.M Lee, 1986a). The consequence of this is, however, that the experiences of workers, such as women (Callender, 1986) or minority group members (Cornfield, 1986), who are likely to be made redundant from small-scale or non-unionized plants have remained relatively unstudied.

Advertising

Where other means fail, it might still be possible to obtain a sample through advertising. Beer (1983) used newspaper advertising as one strategy for obtaining a sample of househusbands. His initial advertisements in the *Village Voice* and the *New York Review of Books* drew little response, but advertising in local papers produced an acceptable return. Beer notes that those who responded and who were eligible for inclusion in the sample tended to be skewed towards the more highly educated, although it is not clear whether this reflects the social characteristics of househusbands, local newspaper readers, or those who answer advertisements.

In fact, it seems likely that there is considerable opportunity when advertising for sampling purposes to use quasi-experiments (Cook and Campbell, 1979) in order to identify the best wording to use, and the best locations for placement. Indeed, one could also presumably draw on research into the use of covering letters sent with mail questionnaires (Dillman, 1978) to obtain clues to the wording of advertisements in order to maximize returns. However, virtually no attention seems to have been paid to any of these issues. The experience of a number of writers suggests that if one is forced to advertise, it probably pays to take the whole enterprise rather seriously. Silver et al. (1983) in a study of the effects of incest on its victims, and Bart (1981), who studied rape victims, gathered their samples by advertising. In each case, as well as advertisements in public places, use was made of press releases, radio and television announcements and personal media appearances. Presumably the importance of these tactics is not only that they give the research wide coverage, but also they allow the study to be presented in a positive and non-threatening light which may encourage respondents to come forward. In both cases, samples of adequate size for the purposes of the study were obtained. Moreover, Bart (1981) found that, except for some overrepresentation of white women, the 94 women who came forward in response to her advertising strategy had broadly similar social characteristics to women reporting rape on victimization surveys. There was also no single particular route by which women came to hear about the study.

If one of the major advantages of advertising is that it is possible to obtain wide coverage, a major disadvantage is a lack of control over who responds, in terms of either representativeness or suitability. Biernacki and Waldorf's comments on network sampling are equally applicable to advertising:

> Revealing too many of the eligibility criteria can result in problems relating to verification, while revealing too few details can produce

management difficulties related to screening and perhaps difficulties in turning away non-eligible but willing study participants. (1981, 149)

The problem of obtaining respondents who might be unsuitable in various ways is graphically illustrated by Henslin's (1972) study of illegal abortion. Henslin had broadcast the fact, by word of mouth, that he would like to be put in contact with an abortionist. Subsequently, he was put in touch with an abortionist who, allegedly, had shot to death a former client and her boyfriend in a dispute over fees. As Henslin put it, 'In spite of the commitments I feel to research, I passed up this "opportunity".'

Servicing
It is sometimes possible to obtain research subjects by offering them a service of some kind. Thus, Fineman (1983) used his participation as a counsellor on a government-sponsored career review programme in order to study white-collar unemployment. Offering a service as a means of gaining a sample may have particular utility when one is studying members of a deviant group. As Becker (1970) points out, those who are deviant in some way often prefer to utilize non-conventional legal, medical or therapeutic services. In this way, Becker notes, Bryan (1965), who studied call-girls, was able to obtain some respondents by offering them psychotherapy. One difficulty with this kind of approach is that it becomes difficult when evaluating the research to judge how far the processes of counselling and data collection may or may not have had an effect on one another.

A further, obvious, limitation of this strategy is that it depends on the ability of the researcher to offer an appropriate service. Sometimes, however, researchers who do not set out to provide a service come to do so because they are approached by people who know of their interest in a particular topic, and who assume that they can offer advice. Eileen Barker (1984) found when carrying out a study of the Unification Church (the Moonies) that she was not infrequently approached by parents alarmed about a child who had joined the Church. Not only was Barker able to give advice to these people, but also her interviews gave her additional and useful data about recruits' home backgrounds, and about the ways in which the Moonies were perceived by those outside the movement. John Lee (1979), a sociologist also widely known as a spokesman for the Gay Liberation Movement in Canada, similarly records that one source of data he has collected on the development of a homosexual identity was men who were in the process of 'coming out', and who approached him for advice.

Professional informants

Becker (1970) has pointed out that, as well as or instead of studying deviant groups directly, the researcher can and should utilize whenever possible a variety of indirect data sources. These may include a variety of archival and running records (Webb et al., 1966; 1981). Thus, agency files, transcripts of legislative hearings, the results of medical and legal research, popular literature and the self-justifying literature deviant groups often produce about themselves may all be mined for the data they contain. In addition, Becker suggests, it is also often possible to gather information from those, such as police, social workers, probation officers and the like, whose work brings them into contact with the group in question. What lies behind Becker's suggestion are two observations. The first is that those whose work brings them into contact with deviants are 'wise' in Goffman's (1963) sense of the term. As a result they have opportunities not afforded to others for routine interaction with and observation of deviants by virtue of the servicing or control functions they are presumed to perform. Second, as a result of this privileged access, they are also assumed to have available to them what Sudnow (1965) refers to as 'prototypical portrayals and knowledge of operative social structures'; a fund of typifications, in other words, concerning the social characteristics and activities of the group of interest.

There are a series of constraints which operate to diminish the willingness or the ability of professionals to provide suitable information. First of all, professionals rarely see a full spectrum of types. Drug users encountered by the police, for instance, are likely to be quite different from those seen by medical practitioners, who in turn might be different from users in contact with paramedics or social workers (Hartnoll et al., 1985a). Second, some professionals may have only fleeting contact with the researcher's target group. For example, priests and ministers in Northern Ireland have relatively little knowledge of or familiarity with religiously inter-married couples (R.M. Lee, 1981), partly because rates of Catholic–Protestant intermarriage are low and such couples are, in fact, rarely seen. In addition, where contact with couples does take place, it is within the relatively transitory and formal context of arranging for the marriage ceremony to take place, and, here, for Roman Catholic clergy at least, bureaucratic pressures exist to define the situation in an extremely routinized way (R.M. Lee, 1981; see also Fulton, 1975). Third, in some cases, professionals may be inhibited from sharing information with those outside the profession. Thus Hartnoll et al. (1985a) note that police drug squad officers are often unwilling to impart information which has a bearing on operational matters. Moreover, where there is mutual suspicion between two professional groups – police and social workers, say – neither group may be prepared to provide information for fear of its being passed on to the other. Fourth, some professionals, for example, lawyers, are constrained within very strict rules of confidentiality, while others may hold professional ideologies which inhibit the kind of generalization of most use to researchers. This was true, for instance, of marriage guidance counsellors approached for background information about religiously intermarried couples in Northern Ireland (R.M. Lee, 1981). Counsellors were able to say little, not only because of their very strict rules concerning client confidentiality, but also because it was taken by them as an article of faith that each individual case was unique, and did not, therefore, provide any suitable basis for wider generalization.

Notes

1. Some portions of this chapter have appeared in a slightly different form in R.M. Lee (1992).

2. Sampling in field research should be seen, strictly speaking, as an ongoing feature of the research process in which the further selection of sample elements is guided by theoretical understandings, reflections and judgements which emerge over the course of the research (Glaser and Strauss, 1967; Denzin, 1970). In practice sampling and access are inextricably intertwined in field research. Access is treated separately here for two reasons. First, where sensitive topics are involved, it is often the initial selection of individuals or settings which is problematic. In this instance, sampling is logically prior since if one cannot even locate cases for study access remains an impossibility. Second, whereas in survey research extensive discussion of sampling was matched only late in the day by a concern for 'access' in the shape of informed consent (E. Singer, 1978), the business of selecting respondents or informants has often been taken more or less for granted in the field research tradition, relatively little discussed against a recurrent preoccupation with problems of access.

3. One difficulty with Gillespie and Leffler's position is that they tend to associate 'scientific conservatism' in favour of rigorous sampling and measurement with political conservatism. It can be argued, however, that this association is a contingent rather than a necessary one. For example, inflated estimates of the extent of the underground economy in Britain, based on largely anecdotal evidence and often promoted by a right-wing press, have been used to justify punitive treatment of welfare recipients (Golding and Middleton, 1982). The substantial methodological problems involved in measuring the underground economy mean that such assertions cannot easily be refuted unless methodological development takes place to produce more reliable estimates (see, e.g., J.J. Thomas, 1990).

4. The methodology of this study is discussed in more detail in R.M. Lee (1992).

5

Asking Sensitive Questions on Surveys

Survey researchers have put a considerable amount of effort and ingenuity into finding ways of asking sensitive questions. To do this, they have used the survey itself as a vehicle for methodological experimentation into its own procedures. This chapter draws on that tradition of methodological experiment to look at a range of topics, including question design, the use of vignette methods and a variety of statistically based 'dejeopardizing' approaches for asking sensitive questions.

Designing questions for sensitive topics

The imagery lying behind methodological writing on the asking of sensitive questions on surveys is implicitly Goffmanesque. It is assumed that respondents wish to manage impressions of themselves in order to maintain their standing in the eyes of the interviewer. For the researcher to cope with this situation, methods have to be found which allow the respondent to provide potentially discreditable information without disrupting the interaction or causing embarrassment or loss of face to the participants. It has long been recognized, for instance, that 'loading' questions in various ways can encourage greater reporting of behaviours which might not otherwise be admitted. Early versions of this technique were pioneered by Alfred Kinsey and his colleagues in their studies of sexual behaviour (Kinsey et al., 1948; 1953; see also Madge, 1963, chap. 10; A.J. Barton, 1958). One strategy is for the questioner to presume that the activity of interest has actually taken place. Questions are therefore asked about its frequency rather than about whether it has occurred at all. Other variants depend on communicating through the wording of the question that the behaviour referred to is common or not especially untoward. Thus, a question about abusive behaviour might be prefaced, for example, with a phrase such as 'Everybody loses their temper now and again . . . .'. Alternatively, a casual approach can be used, employing the phrase 'Do you happen to . . . .' in the question to diminish the apparent importance of the topic. Sudman and Bradburn (1982, 76) point out that, for what they regard as moderately threatening topics at least, this last technique may not actually be very effective. Comparing survey responses to a range of questions about gun ownership, they conclude that using the phrase 'Do you happen to . . .' in a question does not increase levels of reporting – indeed it does rather the opposite. Instead of stressing the ubiquity or supposed innocuousness of a particular behaviour, a further way of loading the question is to use an authoritative source to justify it. The rationale here is that respondents will respond more positively to statements which employ endorsement by a group with high status or particular expertise. An example Sudman and Bradburn give is: 'Many doctors now think that drinking wine reduces heart attacks and improves digestion. Have you drunk any wine in the last year?' (1982, 76).

As Sudman and Bradburn point out, particular techniques for loading questions usually emerge out of survey practice rather than from methodological research. Together with a number of colleagues they have attempted to develop a more systematic framework for asking about sensitive topics on surveys (Sudman and Bradburn, 1974; Bradburn and Sudman, 1979; Sudman and Bradburn, 1982; Bradburn, 1983). Drawing on their own large-scale methodological experiments, as well as a systematic review of a large number of previous studies, they have examined ways of asking about a range of sensitive behaviours. (These extend from gambling through drinking behaviour and drug use to questions about the frequency of a range of sexual behaviours.) As a result of this work, they have made a number of suggestions and recommendations for reducing the under-reporting of behaviours normally regarded as threatening or sensitive.

Other things being equal, Sudman and Bradburn suggest following an number of rules for encouraging frank reporting by respondents. In summary, open questions should be preferred to closed, and long questions to shorter ones. Respondents should be allowed to describe activities in words which are familiar to them. Questions about activities to which respondents find difficulty admitting should be located within appropriate time frames or embedded in various ways within the wider context of the questionnaire. (Needless to say, Sudman and Bradburn advocate a judicious following of these rules rather than a slavish adherence to them.)

Open questions
Closed questions on surveys offer advantages in terms of reliability and ease of processing. Despite this, Sudman and Bradburn (1982) give a number of reasons for using open questions when asking about threatening topics, particularly if one is interested in the

frequency of behaviour. First of all, pre-coded responses must be organized into a logical ordering with the highest and lowest frequencies at each end of the list. Since respondents tend to avoid the extreme response categories on a pre-coded list, those who indulge heavily in an activity may under-report. Alternatively, pre-coded lists may encourage under-reporting because the response categories have to be closed somewhere, and in some cases this may miss respondents with very extreme responses. Coxon (1986; 1988) has also pointed out that pre-coded responses for frequency behaviour often have an implicit logarithmic distribution which encourages under-reporting. Speaking of question forms often used in AIDS research to provide estimates of the number of sexual partners an individual may have had, he notes that:

> Significantly these categories are rarely equal interval, but instead follow an implicit power relation: small intervals at the least frequent working up to large ones at the most frequent end – thus producing as an artefact the evidence of 'promiscuity' so often uncritically quoted in the medical and other press. (Coxon, 1986, 26–7)

Long questions

Sudman and Bradburn argue that there is some benefit to using long rather than short questions, particularly when one is dealing with a topic which is threatening. The rationale, in general terms, for using long questions may not be obvious. Conventional wisdom has it that questions on a survey questionnaire should be kept short (Payne, 1951; Hoinville and Jowell, 1978; Sheatsley, 1983). Sudman and Bradburn (1982, 50–1) accept that short questions are better when asking about attitudes, but argue that their research and that of others suggests that long questions should be preferred when one is asking questions about behaviour. They give three reasons why this should be so. Longer questions can be used to provide the respondent with memory cues. In other words, by giving examples in the question one can stimulate recall. Longer questions also take more time for the interviewer to read out. As a result, the respondent is given more time to think, and the longer one has to think, in general, the more one will recall. Finally, they argue that there is a tendency for the length of a reply to be related to the length of the question which elicited it. In taking longer to answer, respondents may cue themselves into remembering additional information.

To the extent that respondents may themselves suppress recollection of undesirable behaviour, aiding recall may be important when asking sensitive questions. Sudman and Bradburn found (1982, 73) that long questions reduced under-reporting of the *frequency* of behaviour reporting in response to questions on threatening topics. Question length, however, had no impact on reports of whether respondents had ever engaged in the behaviour. It is not clear from their discussion whether length alone encourages the reporting of 'sensitive' topics. In other words, do respondents find it difficult to recall such behaviour, and thus need to be given more time to do so? Or, is it the case that longer questions help to desensitize the topic by stressing, to use one of Sudman and Bradburn's examples, that a particular topic is one about which people are in fact prepared to talk freely. It should also be recognized that continued use of long questions may induce fatigue in the respondent (Tanur, 1983–4, 20).

Using familiar words

In asking questions about behaviour the admission of which was threatening to the respondent, Bradburn and Sudman (1979) experimented with the use of 'familiar words' in questions. A familiar word in this context is one which is supplied by the respondent. The argument is that such words make the respondent feel more relaxed and aid in the understanding of the question. For instance, Bradburn and Sudman asked a series of questions about drinking behaviour. Before beginning the series, the interviewer described intoxication as 'Sometimes people drink a little too much beer, wine or whiskey so that they act different [*sic*] from usual' (1979, 18). The respondent was then asked 'What word do you think we should use to describe people when they get that way, so that we will know what we mean and feel comfortable talking about it?' The word chosen by the respondent was then substituted in the questions that followed. In cases where the respondent could not supply a word, or supplied an inappropriate word (Bradburn and Sudman do not give examples of such words or how interviewers dealt with them), a fallback word was used. The use of familiar words did not enhance levels of reporting on sensitive topics to a statistically significant degree. Used with long, open-ended question forms, familiar words did, however, produce a consistent pattern of improvement in levels of report. Bradburn and Sudman suggest, therefore, that it may often be worth using the familiar words strategy with long, open questions where other factors, such as the overall length of the questionnaire, do not militate against its use.

Embedding the question

As Bradburn and Sudman point out, the overall context of a questionnaire has an effect on the extent to which particular questions are likely to be perceived as sensitive. Questions about drinking behaviour, to take their example, will be less threatening on a survey of consumer habits than on one devoted to alcoholism. More specifically, the questions which surround those asking about sensitive behaviour can also have an effect. There are a number of ways of 'creeping up' on the respondent, as Cisin and Miller (1981) put it. It may be easier to admit to past indiscretions than to current ones. So, respondents may be asked whether they have 'ever, even once', engaged in some activity. If they respond affirmatively, they are then asked whether they have engaged in that activity during some more recent period. Threatening questions on one topic can also be desensitized by embedding them within the questionnaire in a variety of ways. One can, for instance, lead up to a sensitive topic gradually through a series of less threatening questions. Though a rather wasteful strategy, it may be appropriate in some contexts to embed a threatening question on one topic within a series of questions on other, relatively *more* threatening topics, In this case, the more sensitive questions are 'throwaway' items. Their purpose is to reduce the threat of the later question by comparison with the earlier ones.

Vignettes

The use of vignettes is a survey-based technique which has some affinities with experiments, on the one hand, and simulations, on the other. Vignettes, according to Alexander and Becker, are 'short descriptions of a person or a social situation which contain precise references to what are thought to be the most important factors in the decision-making or judgement making processes of respondents' (1978, 94). Respondents can be asked to respond to these descriptions in various ways. The advantage behind their use is that, unlike attitude statements on surveys, vignettes present the respondent with concrete and detailed situations. It becomes possible, therefore, to discuss norms and beliefs in a situated way which accepts the complexities normally surrounding them. Moreover, the various elements which go to make up the vignette can be systematically varied across respondents in a factorial design. This allows one to implement within a survey something like a completely crossed experimental design (Rossi and Anderson, 1982; Alves and Rossi, 1978; Jasso and Rossi, 1977).

One example of a vignette is the following:

> Mr. Miller is a salesman who works for you. He comes into your office one morning to tell you he has been drinking on the job. Miller is white, about 22, has been working for you for three months, and shows an average performance record. (Alexander and Becker, 1978, 94)

Different versions of this vignette can be allocated at random to respondents on a survey. The sex, job, race, age, length of service and performance of the person described can all be systematically altered, and variations in the judgements respondents make about the situation can be measured and analysed. One difficulty is that the number of different versions of the vignette increases rapidly the more the characteristics of the fictional situation are varied. For example, in the vignette above there are six variables. If each of these is dichotomized the number of possible vignettes is 64 (that is, 2^6). It is convenient, therefore, to use computer programs to produce the vignettes. The use of a computer also permits randomization of the combination of characteristics, and allows them to be reduced in number to those of most analytic interest (Alexander and Becker, 1978; Converse and Presser, 1986). There is some evidence that the number of vignettes presented to respondents should be limited to avoid problems of fatigue and boredom (Converse and Presser, 1986; Finch, 1987, 107). A decision also has to be made about whether respondents should be presented with separately drawn samples of vignettes or with a set of standardized vignettes common to all respondents. There are advantages and disadvantages to both approaches; the decision depends on the aims of the study. (For a brief discussion of relevant considerations, see Alves and Rossi, 1978, 544, n.3.)

In Finch's (1987) British study, vignettes are used in a somewhat more qualitative way than is typical of the American studies mentioned so far. For her, vignettes provide an opportunity to employ on a survey a non-directive question form which allows the respondent rather than the researcher to define the meaning of the situation. Finch argues that vignettes as typically used by American researchers have a somewhat static character in which respondents make judgements about a particular set of circumstances at one point in time. In her study the vignettes depart from this static model 'by building into the story certain changes which occur over time and also by focusing on questions on what should happen next' (1987, 106). So, for example, a vignette might have three stages. Respondents are presented with a situation to which they are asked to respond. More information is then given which makes the original choice more complex. Finally, in a third stage, the story is moved on further in time and a slightly different set of choices is offered. According to Finch, the advantage of this strategy is that the hypothetical situation presented comes to have a history, and allows, for example, those in the situation to build up obligations to one another, the nature of which can be explored with respondents. (It seems, however, that it is difficult to continue adding stages to the story 'before respondents begin to lose the thread, forget some of the earlier details, or confuse the dramatis personae with one another' [Finch, 1987, 109].) With Finch's approach, respondents are encouraged to respond to vignettes in an open-ended way, and Finch also combined the vignette survey with a second-stage qualitatively based study.

There are clearly difficulties in generalizing from the judgements respondents make when confronted with a vignette to their actual behaviour when faced with a comparable situation. Indeed, vignettes are probably best seen as devices for studying normative rather than behavioural patterns. This does not mean, however, that the use of the vignette technique is limited to topics which are bland or consensual. Rossi and Anderson (1982) in fact suggest that areas which are controversial as a consequence of changes to the normative consensus surrounding them are very readily studied with vignettes. The specific examples they give include studies of sexual harassment, child abuse and drinking problems (see, more generally, Rossi and Nock, 1982). Finch (1987) also stresses the utility of vignettes as a means of studying sensitive topics. She argues that because the situations presented to respondents are hypothetical there is a distancing effect. As a result, the vignettes are less personally threatening than direct questions would be, and so they may allow sensitive topics to be discussed in a relatively neutral way.

Although computers have been used to develop factorial designs on vignette surveys, they can also provide a means to facilitate the kind of approach favoured by Finch. Holden (1988) has briefly described a methodology based around what he refers to as 'Computer Presented Social Situations' (CPSS). He has developed a computer simulation, DAYSIM, in which parents are presented with a range of child-rearing situations over the course of a simulated day. The simulation elicits from parents information about the frequency, content and quality of their responses to the presented situations. The use of the computer allows the simulation to be personalized to make it more 'realistic', and permits complex branching responses to particular situations. Holden also suggests that because no interviewer is present social desirability effects may be minimized. A further example of this kind of approach in a situation where physical danger makes research difficult is in the study by Ekker et al. (1988). They have described the use of a microcomputer simulation to study the response of families to the volcanic eruption of Mount St Helens. Families played a game on the computer in which they had to manage a small family business. During the course of the game participants received messages of varying degrees of seriousness relating to volcanic activity. Families were asked to make decisions about the possible relocation of the business in response to the messages they received.

The families' deliberations and the decisions they made were recorded and analysed. Decisions in response to the simulated danger compare well with data on evacuation behaviour in response to the actual eruption, and to natural disasters in general. Simulation, therefore, provides, according to Ekker et al., a 'valuable, as well as relatively inexpensive, methodological tool for the study of human behavior under highly threatening circumstances' (1988, 104). They also point to two other advantages of the method they used. First, discussions held by participants yielded a considerable amount of information about family dynamics, some of which might have therapeutic value. Second, the simulation had implications for the development of public policy on disasters. Ekker et al. note that disaster policy is usually based around notions of evacuation. The simulation, as well as other studies, underlines, however, that people are generally reluctant to take protective action in the face of a possible disaster.

CPSS appears to be a novel, useful and important development. For the moment, though, there are technical limits on the diffusion of the technique. To be used more widely, CPSS needs to be adapted for use on portable computers which can be brought to respondents, rather than requiring respondents to be brought to the computer. There is also, presumably, a need to develop authoring languages to make the construction of CPSS programs easier for non-computer specialists. However, there seems no reason why the method could not be extended to cover situations which are socially rather than physically threatening. Methodologically, CPSS is akin to the use of vignettes. With its 'as if' character and the absence of an interviewer, it also has some of the features of the kinds of dejeopardizing techniques described in the next section of this chapter. Presumably, too, it would be possible to enhance the protection given to participants by programming the computer in some way to anonymize results. As in the vignette approach developed by Finch, the method allows data to be collected on 'complex, mutually contingent sequential actions' (McFarlane, 1971, 155). It also benefits from the immediacy and flexibility typical of methods based around role-playing and simulation.

Dejeopardizing techniques

A number of specialized techniques have been developed to help researchers ask questions about sensitive matters. Their purpose is to minimize the respondent's feelings of jeopardy when asked to admit to behaviour which is stigmatizing or incriminating in some way. Specifically addressed here are a number of such 'dejeopardizing techniques': the *randomized response* method, the *nominative technique*, and the use of *microaggregation*.

Randomized response
In its original form, as proposed by Warner (1965), this technique involves presenting the respondent with two statements; for example, 'I am an "A"' (where A is a sensitive attribute) and its converse, 'I am not an "A"'. The respondent is then asked to choose one or other question to be answered using some kind of randomizing device such as a die, and to respond to the question indicated by making a *truthful* 'Yes' or 'No' answer only. The interviewer receives no information about the question answered and records merely a 'Yes' or 'No' response. Some care needs to be given to setting the probability level for the selection of the sensitive question. The nearer the probability is to 1 the more reliable the estimate, but the less protection provided to the respondent. (For some discussion of competing design criteria in developing randomized response questions, see Fox and Tracy, 1986.)

Since the interviewer cannot know which statement was chosen, the respondent is protected from self-incrimination (and, incidentally, the researcher is protected from having to maintain a data file containing incriminating information [see Boruch, 1979].) However, Warner showed that provided the probability of selecting the sensitive statement is known, then an unbiased estimate of the proportion of those possessing the sensitive attribute could be calculated for the sample as a whole from the following formula:

$$\hat{\Pi}_A = \frac{\hat{\lambda}(1 - p)}{2p - 1}$$

where:
$\hat{\Pi}_A$ = the estimate of the proportion having the sensitive attribute,
$\hat{\lambda}$ = the proportion of 'Yes' answers,
and
p = the probability of selecting the sensitive question using the randomizing device (and where $p \neq 0.5$).

Warner's initial design has been enhanced and extended in a variety of ways. Extensions of the method include its use to estimate the proportions in a population belonging to two or more mutually exclusive groups (Abu-Ela et al., 1967) and the development of designs for use with continuous variables (Greenberg et al., 1971; Himmelfarb and Edgell, 1980). Perhaps the most important enhancement of the method has been the introduction of the 'unrelated question' design. Here the sensitive statement is paired, not with its converse, but with an unrelated statement referring to some innocuous attribute such as the month of birth. Where the proportion in the population possessing the non-sensitive attribute is known (or can be estimated using a split sample), an estimate of the proportion in the sample bearing the sensitive attribute can be calculated using the following formula (Greenberg et al., 1969):

$$\hat{\Pi}_A = \frac{\hat{\lambda} - (1 - p)\pi_y}{p}$$

where:

$\hat{\Pi}_A$ = the estimate of the proportion having the sensitive attribute,
$\hat{\lambda}$ = the proportion of 'Yes' answers,
π_y = the proportion possessing the non-sensitive attribute,
and
p = the probability of selecting the sensitive question.

A further variant of randomized response useful in situations where a researcher wants to obtain a numerical response to a question about some sensitive activity is known as the 'additive constants' model. The basic idea behind the additive constants model is a simple one: respondents are asked to add a constant chosen at random to the true value of their response to the sensitive question. As in other variants of randomized response, the interviewer is, in principle, unable to give any meaning to the actual value reported. (Since difficulty in performing even simple mathematical tasks is widespread in the population [Webb and Wybrow, 1982], respondents are usually provided with a calculator to help them perform the necessary addition.) The randomizing device normally used is a pack of cards on which the constants are printed. In the version of the additive constants model developed by Himmelfarb and Edgell (1980), constants can be any number, positive or negative, as long as they appear with a known probability and can be zero a known proportion of the time (i.e. the respondent is instructed to give the true value without, of course, telling the interviewer that this is the case). Duffy and Waterton (1984) have shown that the procedure has greater statistical efficiency if zero is not used as a constant – in other words, if respondents never give the true value of the sensitive characteristics – and if constants are generated in an exponential random manner, with the mean of the exponential distribution chosen, if possible, to be close to the putative mean value of the sensitive attribute.

Difficulties associated with randomized response   As with any other research technique, there are difficulties and drawbacks associated with the application of the randomized response technique. For a long time it was considered that an extremely serious limitation of the technique was its inability to provide anything other than frequency data. The 'noise' introduced into the questioning process by the randomized selection of the question protects the respondent, but it also makes it impossible for individual responses to be linked together. It is not therefore possible to look at patterns of association between variables. One cannot examine, for example, the characteristics which distinguish those possessing a sensitive attribute from those who do not – something, very often, of most · interest to the investigator. More recent work, however, has suggested a number of approaches for dealing with this particular problem (see, for example, Kraemar, 1980; Edgell et al., 1982; Fox and Tracy, 1986).

On a practical level there are a number of additional problems. The procedure which must be adopted in the interview situation when one uses randomized response is more than a little complex. Opportunities, therefore, exist for respondents to become confused or unsure about what they must do. Since the interviewer does not know which question is being answered, there is no possibility of checking whether the respondent has in fact answered the appropriate question, and has not, for instance, chosen simply to answer the innocuous question whatever happens. On the additive constants model, a very high total value may indicate that the respondent has at least engaged in the activity under consideration. In addition, respondents may not be totally convinced that they are not somehow being tricked. They may suspect that the procedure has been set up in some way which permits the interviewer to know which question has been answered. Finally, and more technically, indirect techniques such as randomized response tend to produce larger sampling errors than will a direct question. The effects of this may be offset somewhat, though, by a reduction in non-response bias.

Validation studies of randomized response While there has been considerable interest in the use of randomized response, there have been relatively few validation studies (Umesh and Peterson, 1991). As might be expected, a major difficulty is in finding independent valid estimates of the sensitive behaviour under consideration. A number of studies have shown that RRT (the randomized response technique) reduces the under-reporting of behaviour judged to be 'sensitive' in some way (Goodstadt et al., 1978; Bradburn and Sudman, 1979; Zdep et al., 1979; Boruch and Cecil, 1979). As Tracy and Fox put it:

> randomized response is far less susceptible to systematic response bias than is the more direct question approach. Consequently, the validity of

inferences drawn from the randomized response technique would appear to be far greater than for other methods which are vulnerable to systematic response bias. (1981, 199)

However, as Umesh and Peterson (1991) point out, in a range of studies where validation data were available, randomized response produced estimation errors of anywhere between 5 and 35 per cent. Other studies have also cast doubt on particular variants of the method (Duffy and Waterton, 1984), or on its applicability in particular kinds of situations, such as the study of attitudes rather than behaviour (Wiseman et al., 1976). Even among those who have found in favour of the method (Bradburn and Sudman, 1979; Tracy and Fox, 1981; Zdep and Rhodes, 1976), there is general agreement that the technique does *not* provide a panacea, and that, in particular, if it is to work the method requires careful piloting. Thought must be given to the setting of the various probability levels required by the method and means found to ensure that the respondent both understands the method and trusts it to provide protection against possible jeopardy.

The nominative technique
The nominative technique is a recently developed and promising alternative to the use of the randomized response question as a means of obtaining reliable estimates of behaviour likely to be under-reported in response to direct questioning. The technique had its origins in the 'multiplicity techniques' developed by Monroe Sirken and his associates in order to study the incidence of rare health events. Procedures of this kind depend on the generation of a 'shadow sample' of those possessing some rare attribute or exhibiting some rare behaviour by asking survey respondents to provide information about relatives and friends. Since members of the shadow sample may be reported more than once using this procedure, additional data must be used in order to assign weights which compensate for multiple counting. The multiplicity technique has been used to make estimates of the incidence of diabetes in the United States (Sirken et al., 1975), and to estimate the extent of under-registration of births and deaths. (Another application of multiplicity techniques is in the 'network sampling' of rare or 'special' populations discussed in Chapter 4.)

Sirken's (1974) suggestion that a technique using information supplied about nominated others could be extended to the exploration of sensitive topics has been taken up by a number of writers. Bradburn and Sudman (1979) used a version of the nominative technique to examine levels of drinking behaviour and marijuana use. They found that the method led to increased levels of reporting, even for respondents who felt very uneasy about the question. Sampling variances of the estimates using this method were also reduced. They concluded that the results of their experiment were 'encouraging enough to make further testing of this procedure desirable' (1979, 150). Subsequently, the most detailed and extensive study of the use of the method for obtaining reliable estimates of heroin abuse has been carried out by Patricia Fishburne. Fishburne (1980, 71–2) argues that the advantages of the nominative technique in relation to threatening topics are as follows. First, since information is gathered about a nominated but unidentified other, the anonymity of both respondents and nominees is maintained. This in turn should reduce the level of threat posed by the asking of potentially sensitive questions. In so doing, interviewer and interviewee reluctance to deal with the sensitive topic should be reduced, as should the level of under-reporting of the behaviour in question. Second, the technique produces a larger sample size by allowing individuals to be enumerated at a larger proportion of households. One consequence of this, especially where the attribute in question is relatively common, may be a lower sampling error than could be obtained using direct report. Third, the nominative technique potentially yields a more complete coverage of the population of interest since it may be possible for those frequently missed by household surveys (e.g. those living in various kinds of institutional accommodation) to be enumerated in the shadow sample. A further possible advantage not mentioned by Fishburne is that the researcher is not required to hold information on individuals which is potentially incriminating, and which might be subject to legal seizure.

Against these advantages can be set the following disadvantages (Fishburne, 1980, 72–3). The nominative technique is of little utility in the investigation of essentially private activities like sexual behaviour where the amount of knowledge available to others may be severely circumscribed. Nor is it useful where the population of interest contains a large proportion of social isolates. In addition, because the possibility of multiple counting is inherent in the procedure, the nominative technique cannot be made to work in the absence of reliable data on respondents' relational involvements to be used for weighting purposes. (For further discussion of this point, see R.M. Lee, 1986b.) Furthermore, there is no guarantee that respondents will accept the informant role, nor is it clear how far there may be systematic tendencies to over- or under-report the activities of others.

On the basis of extensive, detailed and careful pre-testing Fishburne developed a set of questionnaire items for inclusion in the

1977 US National Survey on Drug Abuse. Using data from a shadow sample of individuals nominated by survey respondents, these items were used to provide prevalence estimates of heroin abuse in the United States. In the form finally adopted after pretesting, respondents were asked to specify how many of their close friends they knew for certain to have used heroin. Interviewees were then asked to think of one user-friend chosen at random and – without identifying the individual – to supply information on that person's age, sex and pattern of heroin use. In addition, responses to a number of further questions were obtained. These were designed: (a) to help assess the credibility of the respondent's report; (b) to supply the necessary information to allow the weighting procedure to take place; and (c) to gauge the extent to which the respondent found the nominative question series difficult to answer.

The nominative technique yielded good results on the national survey. As expected, the heroin prevalence estimate produced by the nominative technique was a good deal higher than that based on direct report, suggesting that the method had successfully reduced under-reporting of heroin use. Construct validity appears also to have been good; that is, associations between variables such as age and drug use, whose relationship is well-known on the basis of existing studies, were reproduced in the nominative data. Fewer than half of one per cent of interviewees refused to respond when confronted with the nominative series, while a very substantial proportion of those giving information about a nominee gave evidence of having had direct first-hand evidence of the nominee's heroin use. It proved possible, too, readily to obtain the information necessary for weighting purposes. Taken overall the results suggest, according to Fishburne,

> a relatively high level of veracity on the part of the respondents. The patterns between variables were as expected, and there was a logic and consistency about the data which would not have been present if large numbers of respondents had misrepresented their knowledge of user-friends. (1980, 202)

As with randomized response, it should not, however, be assumed that the nominative technique is capable of being automatically transferred to other topics or contexts. In this regard, Fishburne concludes (1980, 220) that the nominative technique could only be used successfully where it could be demonstrated on the basis of pre-testing that the following conditions were met:

1   the behaviour under consideration is of a kind likely to be known to other people;

2 the behaviour under consideration is sufficiently salient to respondents for it to be easily remembered by them;
3 a prior determination has been made concerning the reference group *most knowledgeable* about the behaviour in question;
4 a prior determination has been made concerning the reference group *most willing to report* the behaviour in question.

Microaggregation methods
Microaggregation techniques were originally designed to protect the confidentiality of data held in archives (Feige and Watt, 1970). It is also possible, however, to use microaggregation strategies on respondent rather than archival data. One method suggested by Boruch and Cecil (1979) is for the members of a sample to be aggregated into a set of clusters (or, where appropriate, grouped into naturally occurring aggregates). Members of each cluster are then requested to forward to one of their number anonymous questionnaires. The recipient of the questionnaires then averages the replies and forwards the averages to the researcher. The researcher therefore at no point has access to identifiable data. Clearly there are problems of securing co-operation with this method. A more useful model is that known as the Block Total Response (BTR) method (Smith et al., 1974). In this method, respondents are presented with sets of questions concerning the frequency with which they engage in certain kinds of behaviour. These questions are organized in blocks containing sensitive and innocuous questions. Different blocks are offered to different sub-samples. A coding procedure is used to provide numerical responses to each block but without indicating which questions are being answered. From this it is possible to estimate an average value for the prevalence of the behaviour of interest. (For more on the statistical background to the method, see Boruch and Cecil, 1979, chap. 5; Smith et al., 1974.)

Miller and Cisin (Cisin and Miller, 1981; Miller, 1984; Miller and Cisin, 1984) have field-tested a microaggregation technique known as the item counts/paired lists method which has the considerable advantage of simplicity. Two lists of behaviours are constructed, one of which contains the sensitive topic while the other does not. Each list is administered to a split sample. Respondents are instructed to return the number of activities in which they have participated but not to indicate to the interviewer what those activities are. The mean counts for each list are then subtracted from one another to give an estimate of the prevalence of the sensitive behaviour.

There are a number of disadvantages to these techniques (Boruch and Cecil, 1979; Fox and Tracy, 1986). The arithmetic involved may be a problem for some respondents, although in practice calculators could be supplied. As with the additive constants version of randomized response, high scores when the blocks are summed may jeopardize some respondents. One also needs a sample big enough to accommodate the number of sub-samples needed. Finally, the attributes entered into the blocks must be statistically independent from one another. This is a requirement which is likely to be difficult to attain since in many cases the necessary statistical information will be unavailable.

Validating self-reports

Midanik (1982) notes that most researchers choose not to validate their results by comparing them with data from other sources. The procedures involved are tedious and expensive, and in many cases where the interest is in sensitive issues, the necessary data are simply not available. Many kinds of behaviour are not, of course, amenable to validation even in these terms, and this is probably particularly true of 'sensitive' behaviour. There are a number of different sources of criteria which can be used to assess the validity of self-report data. These include: (a) other information obtained from within the interview itself; (b) data from other surveys; (c) collateral reports, for example, from family members, partners and so on; (d) the use of official reports; (e) episodic data such as sales records; (f) observational data and chronological records such as diaries; (g) chemical, electronic and mechanical tests (Bateson, 1984; Midanik, 1982; Sudman and Bradburn, 1982; Webb et al., 1966; 1981).

One way, used by Kinsey, of assessing validity from within the interview itself is to ask about the same topic several times over (Kinsey et al., 1948; 1953). Not surprisingly, as Sudman and Bradburn point out, this carries with it the risk of irritating respondents. Where questions with a high level of threat are used on a questionnaire, a more useful tactic, according to Sudman and Bradburn, is to discover at the end of the interview how respondents perceived the threat posed by particular questions. In the Sudman and Bradburn experiments several indicators of threat were used (Bradburn and Sudman, 1979; Sudman and Bradburn, 1982). Levels of non-response to particular items on the questionnaire were recorded. At the end of the interview interviewees were invited to indicate questions which were 'too personal' or, more indirectly, those topics which they thought 'most people' would feel uneasy discussing. Interviewers were also asked to rate the difficulty posed by particular topics.

Only the more indirect approach, where respondents were asked to assess how far most people would feel uneasy answering questions to a particular topic, proved to be a good indicator of threat. Neither levels of item non-response nor direct questions about which topics were too personal proved to discriminate between topics. Except for questions on income and on sexual behaviour, the proportion of 'no answer' responses to ostensibly threatening questions, such as those on gambling, drinking behaviour and drug use, rarely rose above 1 per cent. It seems that respondents prefer not to admit to behaviours which might be deemed to be sensitive, rather than refusing to answer questions about them (cf. P. Young, 1986). In a similar way, there was little variation, except again in relation to questions on income and sexual behaviour, in the topics respondents reported as being 'too personal'. Bradburn and Sudman (1979, 66–7) interpret these findings to mean that direct questions about threat are themselves threatening. In their view, indirect questions about the levels of uneasiness felt by most people in relation to question topics more clearly reflect perceptions of societal norms governing the disclosure of particular topics to strangers, and thus, it can be presumed, of the sensitivity of the topic. Bradburn and Sudman found that respondents who thought most people would be very uneasy answering questions on a particular topic were less likely to say that they had ever engaged in that activity. Levels of uneasiness, however, appear to affect whether a behaviour is admitted to, but once it is admitted has no effect on frequency reports. Bradburn and Sudman suggest that simple adjustment methods might be used to improve survey estimates. Specifically, they suggest that those who record the highest levels of uneasiness about questions relating to particular activities are at least as likely to engage in those activities as those who are moderately uneasy.

For many surveys, particularly those dealing with deviant activities, the results of other surveys often provide the only source of validation data. Having developed a new survey-based technique for studying heroin abuse, for example, Patricia Fishburne (1980) could only validate her survey results based on the nominative technique against existing self-report studies. Comparing the results of one survey with those of another has the merit of being convenient. As a means of validating self-report data, however, comparisons with other surveys can be rather hazardous. Some survey organizations, particularly government agencies like the

Office of Population Censuses and Surveys in Britain, consistently produce high-quality surveys. Overall, though, surveys vary considerably in their quality. As a result, there is often no reason to suppose that the data from one survey are any more valid than those of the other (Bateson, 1984, chap. 3). Martin (1983), for example, points to a number of instances of substantial, and in some cases inexplicable, divergences between the results obtained from supposedly comparable surveys. As she notes, even quite minor changes in survey instruments, sampling definitions, interviewer training, and coding and classification procedures can all produce non-comparability even in ostensibly similar surveys.

Survey non-comparability may also be a feature of repeat surveys where the same questionnaire is administered to the same sample at two different time periods. Sudman and Bradburn warn that 'high reliability on several waves of a panel study is no indication of validity. High threat behavior may be reliably over- or under-reported' (1982, 83). On the other hand, Livesley and Waterton (1985) note that somewhat higher responses to questions on a number of sensitive topics were obtained on the second wave of the panel element of the British Social Attitudes Survey. They suggest a conditioning effect may operate on panel studies. As a result of their first interview experience, respondents realize that their responses will not be received by interviewers in a judgemental fashion. Therefore they feel more relaxed on the second wave of interviewing about disclosing sensitive information.

Sudman and Bradburn argue that in some instances 'proxy' respondents may give 'better' reports on other's behaviour than would be obtained by direct report (a strategy on which the nominative technique described earlier is founded). Reviewing the literature on drinking behaviour, Midanik (1982) notes that most studies show relatively high levels of agreement between respondents and family members. She points out, however, that if a family member, say, offers a higher report than the respondent, it is typically assumed that this is because the respondent has under-reported. The collateral report, in other words, is assumed to be more valid than the respondent report. If the collateral report is lower, however, the discrepancy is usually explained away in some manner.

The use of official records as a source of validation data is only, of course, possible for activities of the kind for which records are kept (Bateson, 1984). Even if data exist at an individual level suitable for validation purposes, it may not be possible to gain access to them because of concerns over data protection. (The direct matching of interview reports against written records is not possible for methods such as the randomized response techniques which produce anonymized reports. It is possible, though, to estimate *levels* of agreement.) Sudman and Bradburn recommend that, even where individual level data are not available, it is wise to compare self-reports against aggregated data. Even here there are difficulties, though, for, as Bateson (1984) points out, data can be aggregated in different ways. As a result, although marginal frequencies may appear similar, there is no guarantee that bivariate and multivariate relationships remain unaffected.

It is also the case that one may have to deal with a considerable lag between the origination of the written record and the survey self-report. The written data themselves may be in error, while the matching procedures may be open to question. A study by Miller and Groves (1985), in which survey data were matched with written records using a variety of manual and computer procedures, found wide variations in the number of matches found. Again, there is no reason to suppose that levels of agreement between survey data and official records will necessarily be high. Bateson argues that, since written records often depend on the respondent, invalidities found in the self-report data may also be found in the written record. In some cases the written records may be more reliable than the respondent's account. Cannell and Kahn (1968) note, for example, that patients often lack detailed knowledge of the surgical procedures performed on them. In these cases, one would expect hospital records to be more reliable. In a similar vein, Midanik (1982) remarks that alcoholics may not recall events surrounding their hospitalization as a result of having been too drunk or too confused at the time it occurred.

Besides official records other kinds of written records can be used for validation purposes. These can include what Webb et al. (1966; 1981) call 'running records'; that is, those that are routinely produced and archived such as actuarial records, and 'episodic records' of a more discontinuous kind such as sales records. Of this last type, consumption figures derived from sales data have been fairly commonly used in studies of drinking behaviour. Midanik (1982), however, points to some of the difficulties inherent in their use. Principally, purchasing and consumption are not the same. Sales data will not include alcohol which was home-made, or purchased from a duty free shop and therefore untaxed. Problems also arise due to alcohol used in cooking, bottle breakage, and stockpiling. There may also be some difficulty in making meaningful comparisons between estimates based on widely different units of measurement. Drug abuse studies (Hartnoll et al., 1985a) have also made use of episodic records relating , for example, to the seizure of drugs, deaths due to drug overdoses, and the notification of diseases such as viral hepatitis often associated with drug addiction. These, however, provide very imperfect measures of the number of drug users or the volume of drugs in circulation.

Diaries and other chronologically based methods of recording activity patterns, such as time-budgets, provide a potential source of validation data. Provided they are not too burdensome (Conrath et al., 1983) and are filled in regularly and in a timely fashion, diaries avoid some of the difficulties associated with recall on interview methods. Since the data source for both diaries and interviews is the same person, there is no guarantee that under-reporting on one measure will not be repeated on the other (Midanik, 1982). However, Conrath et al. (1983) have argued on the basis of a comparison of diary and traditional interview techniques for recording organizational communication patterns that diaries are inherently more reliable.

An important class of what Webb et al. (1966; 1981) refer to as 'unobtrusive' or 'nonreactive' measures are those based on the erosion of the physical environment or accretion to it. Precisely because these are nonreactive, such measures lend themselves to validation studies. Rabow and Neuman (1984) attempted to use an accretion measure based on the contents of garbage cans for validation purposes. They were interested in looking at the effect of a liquor store opening in a residential locality. They therefore compared survey data with alcohol consumption as measured by counting empty bottles appearing in garbage cans. Interestingly, by comparison with the direct measure of consumption derived from the garbage can study, the sample survey seriously underestimated consumption. Rabow and Neuman attribute this underestimate to a high refusal rate and the exclusion of teenage drinkers. In the end, however, they were forced to abandon the garbage can study. They had a high refusal rate when they asked people if they would permit their garbage to be sifted, and were eventually threatened with a lawsuit if they persisted with the study.

Besides erosion and accretion measures trace methods may include the use of chemical, mechanical and electronic procedures which may be more or less reactive. For example, a range of chemical tests is available for measuring levels of alcohol in blood, and it is also possible to use devices such as the breathalyser. In a study of adolescent smoking behaviour Akers et al. (1983) used a variety of measures. These included direct report, the use of a randomized response model, and a biochemical approach which measured levels of salivary thiocyanate (a metabolized residue left in the body after smoking). The use of a biochemical procedure established what Akers et al. refer to as a 'bogus pipeline' condition. The bogus pipeline works on the principle that people will tell the truth if they think their real answers will be found out anyway. Since respondents knew that their smoking behaviour could be detected from the biochemical tests, it was reasoned that they would be less likely to conceal their smoking behaviour when asked about it directly. There was substantial agreement between direct reports and the results obtained using randomized response, suggesting that the self-reports obtained were generally valid. The bogus pipeline, however, does not seem to have produced appreciably more valid responses.

Clark and Tifft (1966) asked undergraduates on a survey to admit to a range of deviant behaviours. Respondents were then asked at a later date anonymously to modify the responses to their questionnaires to bring them up to 100 per cent accuracy. In fact, initial responses to the questionnaires had already been surreptitiously recorded to see whether any changes were made. Respondents were also asked to take a voluntary polygraph test. Despite the use of the polygraph test, inspection of the questionnaires suggested that the initial self-reports were in fact reasonably valid. The use of mechanical, chemical or electronic devices for the measurement of social behaviour can give rise to instrumentation problems (Webb et al., 1981). The bogus pipeline strategies used in both these studies raise ethical issues since they involved deception. One feature of the studies by both Akers et al. and Clark and Tifft is that it seems as though where technology is available researchers find it hard not to use it, even if it leads them in ethically dubious directions.

Conclusion

The asking of sensitive questions in the survey interview labours under the joint constraints of ensuring reliability and not compromising the respondent. This has a number of consequences. First, methods for asking sensitive questions have been restricted, by and large, to the measurement of prevalence and incidence. This is something, it can be argued, that the survey does relatively well. Second, the asking of sensitive questions requires that careful attention be paid to the methods employed. Many of the traditional critiques of the survey interview (see, e.g., Cicourel, 1964) are simply less applicable to well-designed surveys (Marsh, 1982; Schuman, 1982). Third, it has been possible to tailor particular solutions to particular problems. This is crucially so where the researcher wants to obtain potentially incriminating information, and where dejeopardizing techniques provide a high degree of protection to researcher and respondent alike. Even so the results have not been completely impressive. In terms of eliminating under-reporting, the techniques described above are palliatives rather than remedies. Even where appropriate question wording strategies and other methods for improving reporting on sensitive topics are used, comparisons with other records tend to show levels of under-reporting. Furthermore, reliance on the 'more is better' syndrome, as Midanik (1982) calls it, is a serious weakness. Increased levels of reporting using a particular method are taken unproblematically to mean that the various factors which encourage under-reporting have been successfully diminished. The difficulty with this approach is obvious. There is no understanding of the underlying processes which have produced the apparent improvement in reporting levels (see also Bateson, 1984).

A final, and important, difficulty with dejeopardizing techniques is that, although they provide protection for the individual, they do not preclude the possibility of collective jeopardy. For example, the uncovering of high levels of some undesirable activity may lead to an increase in social control. This is particularly likely to be the case if the techniques are used on a local rather than a national scale, or with a specific rather than a general population. The paradox is that in such situations increases in social control have of necessity to have a generalized rather than a specific target. As a result, the 'innocent' may fall under suspicion as well as the 'guilty'.

6

Asking Sensitive Questions: Interviewing

Techniques for drawing from people what they would prefer to keep hidden are hardly new. If one leaves aside torture, some of them at least became codified in the fifteenth and sixteenth centuries. At that time a new doctrine of sin began to emerge in the Western Church. This stressed less strongly than previously social obligations to one's neighbours, and dwelt instead on individual, personal, and especially sexual, lapses (Bossy, 1985). In order to deal with this new situation, priests had to be taught, by means of written manuals, to probe the minds of penitents in order to bring forth admissions of sinfulness. Not a few of the techniques which appear in those manuals (Tentler, 1977) are still used today by sociologists for asking 'sensitive' questions in research. For example, as Tentler shows, confessors were admonished by sixteenth-century commentators 'not to show amazement; exhibit a contorted face; show revulsion (no matter what enormities are confessed) rebuke the penitent; or exclaim "Oh, what vile sins!"' (1977, 94); sentiments endorsed again centuries later in Kinsey et al.'s (1948; 1953) pioneering studies of sexual behaviour. Even that favourite device of social scientists for obtaining self-reports of deviant behaviour, collecting data under conditions of anonymity, has its parallel in the invention of the confessional box by Archbishop Borromeo in 1565. Indeed this parallel is even more striking when one realizes, to anticipate a point made later, that one reason for this technological innovation was to help overcome the unease of the questioner rather than of the informant (Bossy, 1975).[1]

A common insight lies behind pre-Reformation penitential practice and modern methods of social research. Telling another about those aspects of one's self which are in some way intimate or personally discrediting – confessing in other words – is a difficult business. It becomes less so where privacy and anonymity are guaranteed and when disclosure takes place in a non-censorious atmosphere. Researchers have developed the implications of this in sharply divergent ways. Survey researchers have generally assumed that optimum levels of report can be produced by manipulating in various ways the conditions which promote disclosure. By contrast, researchers in the qualitative tradition see the disclosure of sensitive information as implying much more than the management of civility between strangers. According to Madge:

> As the techniques of questioning were refined it came to be taken almost for granted that some form of psychoanalytic penetration into the near unconscious was the proper method of handling difficult affect-laden topics. Among such topics it would be assumed that those dealing with sexual behaviour would rank high, and that exceptional psychological tact would be needed to obtain correct answers on such questions. (1963, 534)

In this context, privacy, confidentiality and a non-condemnatory attitude are important because they provide a framework of trust. Within this framework, researchers can lead those studied to confront, in a fundamental way, issues which are deep, personally threatening and potentially painful.

This chapter begins by looking at attempts by survey researchers to isolate the effect interviewers have on the propensity of respondents to disclose sensitive information. This is followed by a detailed discussion of depth interviewing as a method for exploring sensitive topics. A final section considers the use of diary methods, a research technique which has sometimes been proposed as an alternative to the interview in research on sensitive topics.

Survey interviewing

Sykes and Hoinville (1985) point out that it is possible to advance two contradictory hypotheses concerning how the physical presence of an interviewer might affect reporting on sensitive topics. On the one hand, it can be argued plausibly that when an interviewer is not present respondents are less likely to feel threatened by questions about sensitive topics. On the other hand, it can also be argued that the presence of an interviewer encourages respondents to feel relaxed and therefore more forthcoming. There are three main methods of administering questions on surveys: face-to-face using an interviewer, telephone interviewing where the interviewer is heard but not seen and the use of self-completion questionnaires where the interviewer is absent or is present but passive. There is little evidence that *in general terms* any one method should be preferred over the others. Bradburn and Sudman (1979) found that varying the mode of administration of a questionnaire in itself had no consistent effect on the results obtained. Similar patterns emerge from much of the recent work which has focused on telephone interviewing versus other methods (Dillman, 1978; Cannell, 1985; Groves and Kahn, 1979; Sykes and Hoinville, 1985). Sykes and Hoinville (1985) found few differences in the distribution of responses to a range of sensitive questions whether the interview was carried out face-to-face or by telephone. In subsequent work Sykes and Collins (1988) have pointed to a consistent tendency for telephone interviews to yield a pattern of greater disclosure. However, the differences between modes remain small.

In the Bradburn and Sudman (1979) experiment, where survey responses were compared against official records, under-reporting of 'socially undesirable' behaviour occurred whichever method of questioning was used. However, face-to-face interviewing tended to depress reports of socially undesirable behaviour more than did telephone interviews. Self-administered questionnaires fared relatively poorly. There was a small but consistent tendency for respondents using self-completed questionnaires to report lower levels of socially undesirable behaviour than was true of the other methods. Moreover, response rates were lower for this mode of administration than for the other methods. Randomized response, the most anonymous condition, produced the lowest levels of under-report. Even so, for a question relating to drunk driving there was still a level of under-report of around one-third. In other words, as Bradburn puts it, 'Contrary to common belief favouring face-to-face interviews, there is no clearly superior method that yields better results for all types of question' (1983, 294). A further possible conclusion from these studies is that there is a need, as yet unmet, for a more sophisticated understanding of the conditions under which one method of eliciting sensitive data is more useful than another (Bradburn, 1983).

Interviewer effects
There are many ways in which interviewers can affect the validity of the responses they receive. (For reviews, see Collins, 1980; Bradburn, 1983.) In relation to sensitive topics, interview effects of two kinds have been thought to be important. First of all, it has long been suspected that the social characteristics of the interviewers themselves might have a biasing effect on results. A second source of bias has been sought in the expectations interviewers have about the interview itself.[2]

In what would now be called a 'meta-analysis' (Glass et al., 1981), Sudman and Bradburn (1974) undertook a systematic review of a very large number of studies which have looked at response effects. They conclude that in many instances interviewer effects do not exist or are small compared with other kinds of effect (although there may be differences depending on whether the questions asked refer to attitude or behaviour). Bradburn comments:

the belief in pervasive and substantial interviewer effects is a consequence of the intuitive appeal of the idea and the ready availability of data on these variables rather than on empirical demonstrations of the comparative size of response effects arising from different sources. (1983, 311)

If interviewer effects are neither pervasive nor substantial across a wide range of studies, there is still reason to believe that they may occur under specific conditions, and particularly where the topic of concern is a sensitive one. Johnson and Delamater's (1976) study of the sexual behaviour of young people in Madison, Wisconsin, found only limited interviewer effects. Overall, interviewer characteristics, such as gender, sexual experience, their rapport with subjects and their technical competence, had only a modest relationship to variations in respondent reports, with few obvious patterns in the results. However, females in general were more comfortable when interviewed by a female interviewer. In the case of males, there appeared to be some relationship between the interviewer's assessment of rapport and greater levels of report for a variety of sexual behaviours.

In a study by J. Allen Williams (1964) both Black and White interviewers were used. Differences in socio-economic status between interviewer and interviewee were taken to be a measure of social distance, and Williams used three independent judges to rate questions for the level of threat they were likely to pose to respondents. The race of the interviewer appeared to have an effect on responses only in cases where there was appreciable social distance between interviewer and respondent, and where the threat potential of questions was high.

The city of Detroit saw fierce urban riots in 1968. During the year Schuman and Converse (1971) surveyed the attitudes of a representative sample of Black Detroit residents in a study which used both Black and White interviewers. They found that the race of the interviewer did not affect responses to *all* areas of their questionnaire. For example, there was little evidence that the race of the interviewer had an influence on responses to questions relating to racial discrimination, poor living conditions or personal background. They did find, though, that the race of the interviewer had a quite large effect on responses to what they term a 'militancy scale', based on questions concerning the acceptability of militant protest and hostility towards Whites. Black respondents were less likely to express hostile attitudes towards Whites to White interviewers than when the interviewers were Black. An obvious solution to situations of this kind is to match the social characteristics of interviewers with those of respondents. However, the information to permit matching may not be available from the sampling frame. Furthermore, as

Martin (1983, 712) points out, an unanticipated consequence of this strategy is that apparent trends which emerge when one looks at survey data over time are likely to be artefacts of changes in interviewer composition.

Interviewer expectations
If interviewer effects due to the social characteristics of the interviewer are less marked than has sometimes been thought, there remains the question of how far interviewer expectations about the difficulty of particular kinds of questions may affect responses (Bradburn and Sudman, 1979, 52–3). Johnson and Delamater (1976) found relatively high response rates on their study of young people's sexual behaviour. From this they argue that sexual behaviour may be a less sensitive topic than is often assumed. Problems of obtaining reliable information on surveys dealing with sensitive topics may have more to do, they suggest, with interviewers feeling uncomfortable about asking questions than with the interviewees being embarrassed (see also Collins, 1980, 80). In a similar way Bradburn and Sudman (1979) argue that there is likely to be a relationship between interviewers' expectations of the difficulty of a survey and the actual difficulties they experience. Interviewers employed on the question-wording experiments carried out by Bradburn and Sudman completed a questionnaire about their expectations of the survey before going into the field. The effect of interviewer expectations on responses was not very large, but Bradburn and Sudman's initial hypothesis was supported. Those who did *not* expect difficulties obtained higher levels of report on sensitive questions – of the order of 5 to 30 per cent depending on the question – than those who expected difficulty. When other confounding variables were taken into account, interviewer effects contributed only between 2 and 7 per cent of the total variance. Nevertheless, Bradburn (1983) suggests that if one is going to mount a survey on a sensitive topic, it is important to discover something of the expectations interviewers have of dealing with threatening questions. It might be worthwhile, therefore, not to use interviewers who expect to have difficulty, or to give them additional training.

Depth interviewing

Many researchers have epistemological and ethical objections to the use of survey research. Even at a purely technical level, many topics – especially of a sensitive kind – remain ill-suited to study by means of the survey. In these circumstances, a preference has commonly been voiced for the use of unstructured or 'depth' interviewing. The depth interview should not be seen, however, as it sometimes is, as merely derivative from the survey interview. It has an equal, if not prior, historical claim to consideration (Roethlisberger and Dickson, 1939; Merton and Kendal, 1946; Madge, 1963; Converse, 1987; Malsteed, 1987). Despite this, as Bryman comments, it is rather surprising 'that the widespread acceptance of interviewing in qualitative research has not been given greater critical attention' (1988, 114; see also Briggs, 1987). A number of writers (Spradley, 1979; McCracken, 1988) have given general guidance on the conduct of the depth interview. There has, however, been little specific advice about question strategies which might be used in the case of sensitive topics. Yet, there is no reason to suppose that qualitative interviewers will feel any less uncomfortable or concerned about broaching sensitive topics than do survey interviewers, or that interviewees will not find the interview difficult.

In a recent review, Brannen (1988) has discussed a range of issues which arise when qualitative interviewing is used to research topics which are highly personal, threatening or confidential. Such interviews, according to Brannen, are distinguished by a number of features which make them problematic. The interview is typically a stressful experience for both the interviewee and the interviewer. Moreover, in written reports respondents are easily identified by themselves and others close to them because the data are unique and personal. Identification carries with it the risk of sanctions or stigma from various sources. As a result, the researcher has responsibilities to the respondent such that 'Protection is required both with respect to the confidences disclosed and the emotions which may be aroused and expressed' (1988, 553). Brannen suggests that there are four sets of contingencies which surround the exploration of sensitive topics by means of qualitative interviewing. These are: (a) approaching the topic; (b) dealing with the contradictions, complexities and emotions inherent in the interview situation; (c) the operation of power and control in the interview situation; and (d) the conditions under which the interviewing takes place.

Approaching the topic
Where the topic of the research is a sensitive one, presenting it to respondents may not be easy. As a matter of strategy, the researcher must decide whether or not the topic of the interview should be described in detail at the outset. If so, there is the further problem of just how the research is to be described. Defining the

boundaries of the research topic too tightly may inhibit respondents from defining it in their own way. In addition, as Cunningham-Burley (1985) points out, defining the interview in one way may preclude the raising of other topics. Having obtained respondents' trust, it may be difficult to inquire into aspects of their lives not apparently related to the topic at hand.

Brannen (1988) points out that where the interview is addressed towards behaviour which is problematic or stigmatized respondents may be alarmed by the broaching of the topic. With some topics they can have difficulty in making sense of what might be unfamiliar or distasteful to them. Interviewees may not have the vocabulary which allows them to discuss the problem, or they may deny it, or project it on to someone else. In some cases, even, as Van Maanen points out, dramatic and stressful events may be recounted in an 'existential fog' in which 'informants are as unsure and equivocal as to what happened, what is happening, or what will happen as the fieldworker' (1982, 140–1).

Brannen suggests that the topic of the research should be allowed to emerge gradually over the course of the interview. This, however, raises the issue of informed consent. Indeed, it can be argued that depth interviewing poses more acute problems of informed consent than do survey interviewing or participant observation. While the survey interview runs the risk of depersonalizing respondents, its relatively brief span and its very superficiality may pose little direct harm to those who participate in it. This may even be true where sensitive topics are broached if steps of the kind described earlier are taken to 'dejeopardize' respondents. In participant observation, the fieldworker spends considerable time in the field. The obtaining of consent in this context can be seen as the outcome of a developmental process (Wax and Cassell, 1979b). Disclosure of sensitive or confidential information is usually only possible in these situations once trust has been established between the fieldworker and the people being studied. Where this has been done consent becomes implicit. By contrast with both these situations, the person from whom a depth interview is sought must agree at the behest of a relative stranger to give a not inconsiderable amount of time and effort to the interview. They may be asked to reveal a great deal about themselves, perhaps at some emotional cost. Moreover, there is no guarantee that informants will realize before an interview begins what they might reveal, in what ways, or at what risk. Nor may it be easy for the researcher to convey all of this in an informed manner before beginning the interview. (For some discussion of these issues, see Kay, 1989.)

Contradiction, complexity and emotion

Depth interviews are seen to have advantages over survey interviews. As a number of writers have pointed out (Coleman, 1958; Galtung, 1967; Graham, 1983), surveys, in treating the individual as the basic unit of analysis, abstract from social positions and social relations. The survey assumes that social phenomena have an external, stable and verbalizable form. It is therefore an inappropriate instrument for investigating aspects of experience which are internal, fluid or expressed in non-verbal ways (Graham, 1983). The measurement procedures typically used by survey researchers force experience – often by fiat – into pre-determined and frequently inappropriate categories (Cicourel, 1964). In contrast, it is argued that interviewing in depth produces more valid information. Such interviews provide a means of getting beyond surface appearances and permit greater sensitivity to the meaning contexts surrounding informant utterances. This is particularly so when sensitive topics are studied. Brannen argues that sensitive topics are difficult to investigate with single questions or pre-coded categories. She comments:

> Respondents' accounts of sensitive topics, such as marital difficulties, are frequently full of ambiguities and contradictions and are shrouded in emotionality. These form an integral part of the data set and therefore need to be confronted and taken account of in their interpretation. (1988, 553)

In a similar vein Laslett and Rapoport (1975) have advocated an approach they refer to as 'collaborative interviewing and interactive research'. As will be seen, some researchers prefer collaborative research relationships for ethical and political reasons. Laslett and Rapoport, by contrast, argue that achieving a sense of collaboration in the interview enhances the quality of research by increasing internal validity. Such an approach, which they see as being particularly appropriate for studying the private and intimate aspects of family life, depends on 'being responsive to, rather than seeking to avoid, respondent reactions to the interview situation' (1975, 968). To do this Laslett and Rapoport aim for systematic exploration of the topic to hand, but avoid interviewing in a standardized way, which they see as a route to superficiality. Interviews in collaborative research are lengthy, demanding and require negotiation. The research strategy advocated by Laslett and Rapoport is, therefore, explicitly longitudinal. Repeated interviews are carried out with several members of the same family. Specially trained interviewers are used, with interviews being carried out by more than one person, whose work is monitored. The interview itself is organized around an interview guide which may be used by both interviewer and interviewee. As presented by Laslett and Rapoport, the collaborative research method is apparently not suitable for one-person research. It is highly labour-intensive, and its organization involves a division of labour which incorporates, it would seem, differentials of power and status between different team members. Lone researchers may have to develop slightly different strategies, as did Cannon (1989; 1992) in her study of women suffering from breast cancer. Interviewees at each interview were encouraged to discuss the previous interview and their feelings about it, as a way of involving them actively in the production of the data.

Laslett and Rapoport (1975) are insistent that the research strategy takes into account the psychodynamics of the interview situation, and the effects they have both on interviewers and interviewees and on the quality of the data. A major aspect of the kind of interviewing they advocate is the attempt to make inter-viewers aware of their feelings during the interview, and of the ways in which these feelings may affect the interviewing process. In particular, Laslett and Rapoport make use of the concepts, derived from psychoanalytic theory, of *transference* and *countertransference*. In its original psychoanalytic context transference refers to feelings derived from earlier experiences which are projected on to the analyst. Countertransference refers to similar feelings on the part of the clinician. With respect to interviewing, Laslett and Rapoport use the terms in a slightly looser but analogous way to refer to situations where, for example, the interviewee develops an identifi-cation with the interviewer or vice versa. As a result, respondents may produce what it is assumed the interviewer wants to hear, or interviewers may accord particular features of the respondent's experience undue prominence.

Although transference may arise out of past experiences or relationships, Laslett and Rapoport also suggest that an additional source for transference effects is to be found in social characteristics of interviewer and interviewee such as social class. Whatever their origins, however, these psychodynamic manifestations are regarded as data, not as a problem or a nuisance. In consequence, inter-viewers in their study were helped to detect and manage these processes, in order to minimize invalidity in the data collected. Nevertheless, Laslett and Rapoport's discussion at this point is somewhat unsatisfactory. They do not indicate how, in the absence of psychoanalytic principles, one can identify transference in this wider sense.

Interviewing about sensitive topics can produce substantial levels of distress in the respondent which have to be managed during the course of the interview. Brannen argues that faced with such distress interviewers may want to help but should strongly question their motives for doing so. Such feelings on the part of the interviewer, she suggests, 'often have more to do with helping the helper than those who are in need' (1988, 559). All that may be possible in these situations is for the interviewer to undertake the difficult task of enduring and sharing the pain of the respondent.

It follows that if the interview can be distressing to the respondent, it can also be stressful for the interviewer. In the kind of approach taken by Laslett and Rapoport, interviewers are closely supervised. There is extensive discussion of transcripts and close attention is paid to the feelings of the interviewers, especially in relation to those topics which are threatening and/or worrying to the interviewer. One major part of this process is detailed writing up. This kind of context, however, is presumably unusual. As Brannen notes, the stress induced by interviewing respondents in depth about sensitive topics, and ways of dealing with that stress, have largely been ignored:

> Researchers who are entrusted with the confidences of their respondents ought to be protected by some of the safeguards that customarily are associated with the role of the confidant. Confiding is normally a reciprocal process. Even professional confidants – counsellors and psychotherapists – have their own confessors. (1988, 562)

Taking this last comparison further, Brannen points out that other professionals are able, by virtue of their superordinate position, to develop structured ways of dealing with stress. They practise on their own territory, work within set time limits, and can usually call on therapeutic support. By contrast, those who collect interview data are in a less favoured position. While they stand in a relation of superordination in relation to the respondent, researchers in many instances may be 'hired hands' (Roth, 1966) whose position in the research organization for which they work is frequently a subordinate one. As a result, Brannen argues, researchers must often try to cope with the stresses and strains of interviewing as best they can. This they do usually by turning for support to others in the same predicament (see also Smart, 1984, 256–7), something not always possible for the lone researcher.

Brannen noticed that her respondents would frequently anticipate the emotional demands which the interview was likely to make on them. They would try to ensure that support from friends would be available after the interview had taken place, or else they used alcohol as a crutch during and after the interview. In fact Brannen suggests, although she does not fully develop the point, that the emotional risks attached to the interview may have actually made them attractive to respondents. Whether they have anticipated it or not, the depth interview can often be a cathartic experience for interviewees (see, e.g., R.M. Lee, 1981). Faraday and Plummer collected life-histories from a number of sexual deviants by means of detailed and repeated interviews. They record that one of their informants wrote to them as the interviews proceeded, saying:

> I feel I am overburdening you as an outlet for my personal troubles, but it has been a case of opening a valve and being reluctant to close it until some of the pressure was spent. (1979, 789)

They point out, however, that being an outlet in this kind of way brings with it a range of difficulties. Because respondents feel grateful for the opportunity to express their feelings, they often respond by overwhelming the researcher with gifts of various kinds. Over time this may lead to a growing closeness which creates a blurred line between the role of friend and that of research participant. Because of this blurring it becomes difficult not to worry that the friendship aspect of the relationship is being exploited for research purposes. A further difficulty, particularly with those who are 'deviant' in some way, is that the articulation of hitherto private feelings may encourage a growing sense of a particular identity. Faraday and Plummer note examples in their study of people developing the self-confidence to 'come-out' in various ways as the interviews proceeded. Such decisions, of course, have wider ramifications for which, conceivably, the researcher may have a responsibility.

Power in the interview

In recent years, an important area of discussion within the literature on interviewing has revolved around the role of power in the relationship between interviewer and respondent. One difficulty with this literature is that it is by and large divorced from theoretical debates about the nature of power and the means by which it is exercised (see, e.g., Lukes, 1974; Giddens, 1976; Benton, 1981). The notion of power is used in a rather loose and common-sense way. This is true, for example, of Elliot Mishler's (1986) work. Mishler discusses the power dynamics in interviewing solely in terms of the status distance between interviewer and interviewee. This not only conveniently neglects situations where interviewer and interviewee are of equal status, or, as in élite interviews, where the interviewer has a lower status. It also continually begs the question of how disparities of status actually manifest themselves in power terms within the interview.

Despite difficulties of this kind, the existence of power relations in the interview, once recognized, becomes difficult to overlook.

This is particularly so given the work of feminist writers like Oakley (1981), Graham (1983) and Finch (1984). These writers have argued that within the 'traditional' survey interview interviewers have power because of an asymmetrical distribution of rights and obligations. In particular, there is a disparity of disclosure rights. The interviewer may obtain revelations from the respondent but need not reveal anything in return. Despite admonitions in the literature to establish 'rapport' with the respondent, the disparity of rights between interviewer and interviewee gives that rapport a spurious and ultimately instrumental character. As Oakley puts it:

> 'Rapport', a commonly used but ill-defined term, does not mean in this context what the dictionary says it does ('a sympathetic relationship', *O.E.D.*) but the acceptance by the interviewee of the interviewer's research goals and the interviewee's active search to help the interviewer in providing the relevant information. The person who is interviewed has a passive role in adapting to the definition of the situation offered by the person doing the interviewing. The person doing the interviewing must actively and continually construct the 'respondent' (a telling name) as passive. (1981, 35)

Looked at from this point of view, the standardized interview, with its closed questions and rigid pre-specification of topics, does not enhance disclosure but precludes it. In the case of women, feminist writers argue, the survey interview objectifies female experience and mutes women's self-expression. As a consequence, survey research tends to operate in an oppressive way which mirrors and promotes wider patterns of social disadvantage. For reasons of this kind, writers like Oakley and Finch eschew survey methods in favour of qualitative research strategies. They stress as a matter of ethical commitment a style of interviewing based on reciprocity and a process of mutual self-revelation. In addition, both Oakley and Finch argue that women researchers and female interviewees share the same subordinated structural position in a male-dominated society. This provides them with a shared identification with one another as women. One outcome of this identification is that it promotes a genuine rapport in the interview, which leads to greater self-disclosure and, thus, to the collection of 'better' data. It follows from this that a lack of shared identification constitutes an impediment to the relationship established between a male interviewer and a female respondent.

The critique of the traditional survey interview put forward by writers like Oakley and Finch has been influential. Their work has not, however, escaped criticism from within the feminist tradition, notably by Wise (1987; see also Smart, 1984; Warren, 1987). Wise argues that the kind of ethical critique produced by Oakley and

Finch is 'both more complacent and more sophisticated than previous accounts'. Oakley, in particular, in her view, uses the shared structural position of women as a 'magical device for the instant dissolution of inequalities' (1987, 66). In other words, even where gender differences are absent, Wise argues that imbalances of power can still exist between researcher and researched. This is so because power has a variety of social structural bases, for example, in class relations, which may still operate even in the presence of a shared gender identity. As a result, along with a number of other writers (Brannen, 1988; McKee and O'Brien, 1983), Wise argues that success in interviewing depends more on a complex interrelation between the relative structural positions of interviewer and interviewee and the interviewer's skill and personal style, than it does on a simple identity of gender.

Implicit in Wise's critique of other feminist writers on the interview is a wider distrust of the interview as a therapeutic event. Drawing an analogy with the relations between social workers and clients, she argues that even ostensibly equal or mutually satisfying research relationships may nevertheless conceal more subtle forms of domination. A further point related to this is that, as a number of micro-sociological studies of power and exchange suggest, reciprocity and self-revelation can be deployed strategically in social relationships. They may be used, for example, as ingratiation tactics, or as a means of increasing the social indebtedness of the other (Kollock and Blumstein, 1987; Leifer, 1988; see also Blau, 1964b; Richard M. Emerson, 1962; Cook and Emerson, 1978). In other words, as Finch (1984, 81) acknowledges, strategies used to ensure a non-hierarchical relation between interviewer and respondent can come to be regarded simply as a set of techniques divorced from the ethical foundations upon which they are based.

Wise (1987, 66) also asks 'what does Oakley do with the women that she does not like, or who don't like her, or those who's (*sic*) perceptions of their lives differ from hers?' This is an interesting question because it brings into focus again the issues of transference and countertransference raised by Laslett and Rapoport (1975). Oakley mentions Laslett and Rapoport's discussion of transference effects briefly in a footnote. However, she does not discuss whether such effects, at least in their more 'social' form, were present in her own interviews. This, therefore, leaves unanswered the question of whether, in deepening disclosure, a non-hierarchical, mutually self-revelatory interviewing style might also distort, in a variety of subtle ways, what is disclosed. Interesting in this regard is the literature on psychotherapeutic interviews. There, the emphasis seems to have shifted away from justifying the role of self-disclosure in the interview. Instead, research has been directed to the conditions under which self-disclosure by the interviewer will enhance the therapeutic encounter, or be harmful to clients (Anderson and Mandell, 1989).

Brannen speaks of power in two senses. One, related to that just discussed, is the ability to *control* the interaction itself by dictating the form taken by the interview, and its content. Where the format of the interview is not rigidly specified by prior standardization, it is possible to see the exercise of power in the interview as a two-way process: it can be exerted by both interviewer and respondent. According to Brannen and others (Wise, 1987; McKee and O'Brien, 1983), the locus of control in the interview emerges from the interrelation between the topic, the particular method of interviewing used and the respective statuses of the participants. Thus, in one of the cases Brannen describes status equivalence between interviewer and interviewee resulted in an interactive conversational interview. In another example which she discusses, the topic was an extremely personal one and the role of the interviewer was deliberately non-interventive. Here, interviewees became so engrossed in their own stories that they become relatively impervious to interviewer interventions. In other words, in this situation respondents exercised control although not in an entirely conscious way. Even when this does not happen, respondents may still retain power. As Brenner (1978) points out, interviewers have few sanctions which they can deploy should a respondent decide not to accept their definition of the situation (see also Cunningham-Burley, 1985). The relative powerlessness of the interviewer is reinforced by the etiquette of the interview itself. This generally forbids even the self-disclosing interviewer from being openly judgemental about the respondent. There may thus be situations where the interviewer has simply to endure the interview with gritted teeth. Even when respondents put forward views of an offensive kind which, in other circumstances, would normally bring forth a swift and sharp rebuke, the interviewer may choose to remain silent (Smart, 1984; McKee and O'Brien, 1983).

A further sense of power referred to by both Brannen and Finch is the ability to have power *over* the informant by virtue of possessing potentially damaging information which may have been revealed in the interview. This vulnerability can be personal as when individuals reveal personal details about themselves in the interview which may spark reaction or intervention from those near at hand. In situations of this kind, others, unsympathetic or hostile to the research, may overhear what has been disclosed and subsequently intervene to the respondent's detriment. Brannen (1988,

560) gives a number of examples of situations in which she feared a negative reaction from husbands to information disclosed by their wives during interviews concerning marital difficulties. (She also notes that wives sometimes concealed the topic of the research from their husband, presumably for fear of their reaction.)

Respondents may also be vulnerable in a collective way (Finch, 1984; Brannen, 1988) since they have little control over the ways in which the data are interpreted. Finch records, for example, her worry that data she had collected from women on the basis of trust could, given a particular interpretation, be used against their interests. The dilemma here is not simply, as Finch argues, an ethical one, but ultimately involves a political choice of the 'whose side are we on?' kind (Becker, 1967). However, as both Finch and Brannen point out, the difficulties here may be particularly acute for the interviewers who are 'hired hands' (Roth, 1966). In these situations control over the data typically passes from their hands to those of powerful others who may have less concern for the interests of the respondents.

Interviewing conditions

Perhaps because of its roots in the survey tradition, the literature on interviewing tends to assume that those interviewed will be unrelated to one another. Particular difficulties arise when research on 'sensitive' matters is carried out with members of the same family. Drawing on Simmel's analysis of triadic relations, Carol Warren (1987) suggests there is a range of patterns with may emerge in the relationship between husband, wife and interviewer. Each partner may seek to obtain confidential information about the other from the interviewer. The partners may collude in various ways, often to withhold information from the interviewer. Alternatively attempts may be made by each partner to draw the interviewer into a collusive relationship in order to keep information away from the other partner. Finally, the interviewer may become a *tertius gaudens* (Simmel, in Wolff, 1950): the third party who benefits from the conflict of two others. In this case, presumably, conflict between the partners leads, deliberately or inadvertently, to increased disclosure. This is not to say, of course, that interviewers will necessarily feel happy with this situation. Indeed, the interviewer may have to engage in conversational 'repair work' where arguments and disagreements break out between respondents (Cunningham-Burley, 1985).

Brannen (1988), on the other hand, distinguishes three kinds of situation in which interviews are to be carried out with marital partners. The most difficult situation from the interviewer's point of view, according to Brannen, is where each partner must be interviewed alone in his or her own home. The one-to-one interview can produce over-intensity and embarrassment, and it is very easy for the interviewer to become drawn into the interviewee's problems. A very much more favourable situation, Brannen suggests, is where two interviewers are used to interview the partners separately but simultaneously. Using a strategy of this kind leads to a feeling of equity in the interview situation. Each partner has a researcher who is neutral in the sense of being uninvolved in the marriage, but who is also partisan in the sense of 'belonging' to that partner. It was precisely for reasons of this kind that Laslett and Rapoport (1975, 971) used more than one interviewer per family, and adopted a strict rule that no member of a family could give permission for any other family member to be interviewed. Between the one-to-one interview and the use of interviewers for each respondent is a further situation where two interviewers are used with each interviewee. In these situations, while one interviewer carries out the interview, the other interviewer remains passive in an observer role. This particular configuration, while yielding additional information about non-verbal interaction, helps to ease the intensity of the interview. It also serves to give the 'active' interviewer support. Brannen, however, does not indicate what effect the second interviewer might have on the respondent's willingness to self-disclose. (A further reason for using two interviewers when dealing with some kinds of sensitive topics is suggested by Braithwaite [1985]. Faced with possible libel suits arising from his research on corporate crime in the pharmaceutical industry, Braithwaite decided in a subsequent study to work with a second interviewer who could serve as a potential corroborative witness in any possible libel action.)

For Brannen, one important aspect of interviews dealing with sensitive topics is that they should have a one-off character. In other words there should be no fear on the part of the respondent that the paths of interviewer and interviewee will ever cross again. In Brannen's view this is essential to ensure trust. The disadvantage of this rather transitory relationship from the respondent's point of view is that the researcher can not be used subsequently as a source of help or support. However, Brannen, referring to her research on marital difficulties, goes on:

> In response to a question about what they considered to be the 'ideal situation' for disclosure . . . a significant number mentioned the characteristics of the research situation (for example, anonymity or its one-off nature) or the research situation itself. Even the majority who were already in receipt of counselling rarely mentioned professional help as an

ideal. Thus our tenuous links with respondents were both potentially exploitative but also served to increase respondents' trust in us. (1988, 559)

In one sense this is not surprising. It can be argued that the relationship between disclosure and intimacy is a curvilinear one. The stranger, according to Simmel, 'often receives the most surprising openness – confidences which sometimes have the character of a confessional and which would be carefully withheld from a more closely related person' (Wolff, 1950, 404). In other words, the recipients of intimate details about one's life are most likely to be either those standing in a very intimate relation to oneself, or those who are socially remote (for a review of research on social distance and self-disclosure, see Day, 1985, chap. 7).

Brannen's emphasis on the importance of the 'one-off' interview stands in some contrast to the advocacy of repeated interviewing by Laslett and Rapoport (1975) and by Oakley (1981). Oakley argues that the single interview encourages what she describes as an 'ethic of detachment' (1981, 44), which makes difficult the development of a deep, lasting and genuinely collaborative research relationship. Pointing out that multiple interviewing has been little discussed in the methodological literature, Laslett and Rapoport (1975) stress the importance of what they call the 'inter-interview dynamic'. In particular, they argue that the period between the first and second interview is of crucial importance. The initial interview typically raises anxieties on the part of the interviewee, and generates resentments directed towards the interviewer. Provided these anxieties and resentments can be handled by the interviewer, Laslett and Rapoport suggest that a different kind of data will be collected in the second interview. They argue that, characteristically, what is brought forward in the first interview is a more publicly acceptable, 'surface' account. Typically, however, a fuller, deeper and more complete account is more likely to emerge at the subsequent interview.

It is difficult to resolve the competing claims of one-shot versus repeated interviewing. Repeated interviews have undoubted advantages in terms of the quality of both the data and the relationship which can be established with respondents. They may not necessarily be needed, however, in a number of circumstances. If carefully handled, some kinds of topics, say of an incriminating rather than an intimate kind, may be brought to the surface fairly readily. In a similar way, where the interviewer is introduced to the interviewee by an intermediary, a sufficiently high level of trust may be present for a single interview to suffice. Finally, the respondent preference for single interviews uncovered by Brannen probably should not be taken lightly. This is so not simply because of the benefits of anonymity, but also because the single interview is less demanding on the respondents themselves. It may therefore avoid the paradoxical situation in which the interviewer, to be collaborative and non-hierarchical and to avoid exercising power, has to make substantial demands on respondents.

Whatever interview strategy is used, termination of individual interviews and of the interview series is important. As Laslett and Rapoport put it, 'Both methodological and ethical considerations require that terminal sessions be well managed' (1975, 974). Specifically, and in line with their commitment to a collaborative interviewing style, Laslett and Rapoport argue that concluding interviews should give something back to the respondents. They therefore gave their interviewees feedback about their analysis of the family, and, it would seem, provided them with counselling about the potential longer term consequences of the interviews within the family itself. They also took the opportunity to correct errors or uncover remaining disagreements about how particular events were to be interpreted. At this stage Laslett and Rapoport also made agreements with their respondents about the conditions under which research accounts were to be published. For example, interpretations which were disputed by the respondent could be omitted or the respondent provided with the opportunity to present a dissenting account. Sometimes, of course, termination may be difficult for the researcher. Particularly when a study has been long and relations have been built up with respondents, the researcher may experience guilt, alienation and melancholia when those relations come to an end (Roadberg, 1980). In some circumstances such feelings can become even more intense and distressing. Over the course of her study, Cannon (1989; 1992) had become close to a number of the cancer sufferers she interviewed. A difficult problem for her as the research progressed was, therefore, how to come to terms with their deaths. Once again, it may be that the lone researcher is particularly vulnerable in this regard. As some AIDS researchers have discovered (Zich and Temoshok, 1986), the ability to mobilize support for researchers from team members can be indispensable when research participants die.

Diary methods

Diaries provide an appropriate data collection method where one wants to measure activities over time, the frequency or salience of which makes recall difficult. Plummer (1983, 17–20) distinguishes three forms of diary: (a) logs, the most clear example of which is the time budget; (b) the 'requested diary', where informants are given diaries and asked to keep records of their day-to-day lives; and (c) the diary–diary interview. Time budgets are detailed diaries in which a random sample of respondents keep a record of their daily activities. As they provide a means of 'tracking' people's activities, time budgets provide a way of finding out about activities which a respondent might not disclose in interview. Time budgets therefore have been used in studies of the 'hidden' economy to give an indication of the extent to which people officially defined as unemployed undertake paid work 'on the side' (Trew and Kilpatrick, 1984). Time budgets potentially yield a great deal of detailed, potentially generalizable data. However, the method can be burdensome to the respondent. A further major drawback of this method is that, without other information, all one knows about are activities, but not the contexts in which they take place. To stay with the hidden economy example, the recording of an activity as paid work will not of itself reveal, say, that tax payments are being evaded. Nor is there any guarantee that potentially incriminating activities will be recorded in the first place. As Harding and Jenkins (1989) point out, if time budgets are to be used in these kinds of studies they need normally to be harnessed to other data collection strategies.

Coxon and his colleagues have made use of diary methods in a study of changes in the sexual behaviour of gay and bisexual men under the impact of AIDS/HIV. Coxon (1988) argues that reports of sexual behaviour based on pre-coded questionnaires and clinical data are unreliable. This is because accurate recall is difficult, reported frequencies are often an artefact of the pre-coding procedures, and it is not clear what meanings terms such as 'sexual partner' have to respondents. For these reasons, according to Coxon, diary methods should be more reliable than retrospective accounts provided they are kept on a regular day-to-day basis.

The diaries used in Coxon's study are different from literary, biographical or life-history diaries in that they are systematic and based on externally defined categories. In this they resemble expenditure diaries. The activities to be recorded were coded in terms of three elements: contexts, acts and accompaniments. For each diary session, letter codes were assigned having the following form: a root code referring to a specific kind of sexual behaviour, a prefix referring to its modality (what Coxon [1988] describes as the 'binary, directional relational specification of the act'), and a suffix designating the outcome of the session.

Coxon notes that in using such methods there is a trade-off between the complexity of the coding scheme and the willingness of respondents to use it. The codes used were mnemonics comprising the initial letter of natural language terms referring to a variety of sexual activities. The subject codes were included in the diary, although respondents did not necessarily use them. The codes, which are machine-readable, are capable of being read and manipulated by a database management program. Coxon concludes that the strategy used is sufficiently structured to allow direct comparison between records. At the same time, it is sufficiently life-like to be used easily by respondents, and produces easily retrievable data.

Zimmerman and Weider (1982) describe what they call the diary–diary interview method. They developed this method in a study of the counterculture as part of an ethnographic research strategy they refer to as 'tracking'. They argue that within a given setting participants may be engaged in a wide range of roles which may contain within them a number of diverse aspects. Moreover, participants' activities are also temporally, spatially and interactionally diverse. Ethnographers face the problem of keeping track of the diversity of roles and activities in ways which avoid reactivity, the ethical problems which arise from covert research, and their inability to be everywhere at once. The rationale behind the diary–diary interview method is to use the informant as an observer of the social scene in which he or she participates. By this means the researcher is allowed a vicarious entrée into the temporal, spatial and interactional facets of subcultural behaviour in natural settings. Informants were requested to complete a detailed diary over a relatively short span of time (seven days). The diary was then made the basis for a lengthy unstructured interview with the diarist. The diaries had a 'Who?', 'What', 'When', 'Where', 'How', format. In other words, in their diaries informants reported on daily activities, the relationship they had to other people who were involved, described the location, timing and duration of their activities, and the logistics involved in carrying out the activities. Detailed questions were then prepared on the basis of the diaries and used as the basis for depth interviews with informants. Zimmerman and Weider argue that, using the diary–diary interview method, they were able to detect stable and recurrent patterns of culturally sanctioned social organization in the countercultural world they were studying which would have been difficult to uncover by other means.

From these examples, it would seem that diaries have a role in the study of sensitive topics. Their application in such circumstances remains constrained, however, by the problems normally associated with their use (see, e.g., Moser and Kalton, 1971, 340–1). Those who agree to keep diaries or logs may differ in their social characteristics from those who do not. There may be reactivity effects. People, through keeping a diary, may become aware of their behaviour, and in consequence change it. Finally since diary-keeping can be onerous, there may be problems of sample attrition.

Conclusion

Cannell recounts that one early source of interest in interviewer effects derived from a study of the destitute carried out during the Great Depression (Cannell, 1985; Cannell and Kahn, 1968). The researcher, Stuart Rice, noticed that while one of his interviewers consistently attributed destitution to economic factors, another emphasized the adverse effects of alcoholism. Rice, on talking to the interviewers, found the first to be a socialist, and the second an advocate of Prohibition. Cannell comments, 'This suggested that the causes of bias are in some way located in the interviewer, and the whole concept of interviewer bias ran widely through the field' (1985, 4). Improved interview training and procedures have muted that worry somewhat for the modern survey researcher. It seems, however, that interviewer effects are not independent of survey topic. Interviewer characteristics as well as the concerns interviewers have about the questions they have to ask apparently affect the validity of survey responses. As Graham, a critic of the survey interview, has pointed out: 'Surveys, precisely because they conform to the rules of the public domain, have played an important part in raising the consciousness of those within the scientific and political world' (1983, 146). This has been particularly so in the study of sensitive topics, because questions relating to the incidence of 'sensitive' behaviour, and its distribution, are not unimportant. Even so, it is clear that standardized interviewing allows experiences to be expressed in only narrow and truncated ways, and within a social context that some have found ethically dubious. At best, this is unsatisfactory and points to the need for alternative methods of asking questions about sensitive topics. It should be clear, however, that alternatives like the depth interview are not themselves without difficulty.

Notes

1. This, of course, was not the only function of the confessional. It helped to reinforce the social distance between priest and penitent and to minimize physical contact between priests and female parishioners (Bossy, 1975; Hepworth and Turner, 1982).

2. Research on interviewer effects is bedevilled by methodological problems. As Martin (1983) points out, the demographic character of field forces has changed over

the years, and the training of interviewers has improved (Bradburn, 1983). This means that research in this area may be more than usually historically specific. Differential turnover rates for different kinds of interviewer produce systematic differences in experience levels which confound comparisons based on interviewer characteristics. In addition, statistical comparisons are also frequently hazardous because interviewing assignments are usually clustered. This means that comparisons between interviewers are not, strictly speaking, based on independent trials (Collins, 1980).

7

The Access Process in Research on Sensitive Topics

Field research, based on qualitative methods such as participant observation or depth interviewing, has often seemed like the method of choice in studying sensitive topics. Thus, while applied social research in the United States has traditionally had a quantitative character, federally funded community-based research on AIDS has relied heavily on ethnographic methods (Kotarba, 1990). As Kotarba points out, qualitative researchers were able to gain access to at-risk populations, such as prostitutes, who were difficult to locate because of their social invisibility and deviant social status. The use of ethnographic methods in contemporary AIDS research parallels in many ways the prominence of qualitative research during the 1960s and 1970s in studies of urban social problems like drug addiction, juvenile crime and poverty. Although few of the issues involved were entirely new – a number, for example, had been aired by William H. Whyte (1955) in *Street Corner Society* – much of the methodological writing associated with this earlier work dealt recurrently with the conditions under which trustful relations could be established with deviant or disadvantaged subjects.

This chapter looks at a particular aspect of that process, the methods researchers use to enter settings in order to carry out socially sensitive research. Despite an extensive literature which has grown up around the topic, there are a number of difficulties if one tries to look in more detail at the processes involved in gaining access. One is the suspicion voiced by some writers (Fielding, 1982; Polsky, 1971) that much of the discussion on the problems of gaining access in fact hides a reluctance to go out and face those problems by actually entering the field. A further problem is that there is usually little incentive for a researcher to dwell on the reasons why a request to grant access was refused. The pressure to move on and seek entry to another site is usually too great. Nor are researchers necessarily wise while in the field to look too closely at why access has been granted. In so doing they might raise further and unwelcome questions in the minds of gatekeepers about whether the decision to permit the researcher entry was correct in the first place.

Writing about access is also subject to a peculiar limitation. The difficulties of gaining access are extensively discussed in the literature on field research. One justification for field research is that it provides researchers with a method for seeing social situations 'in the round' by trying to understand how all of the participants in a setting are acting and thinking. The paradox is that much of the social science writing on field research in general and on the problems associated with access in particular is based, as it inevitably must be, on the researcher's own account. It is usually the one part of a study which is only ever written from one side. What is usually lost thereby are the understandings those who are being researched have of being studied (Warren, 1984; Bittner, 1973; see also Shipman, 1980, for one account by a sociologically informed gatekeeper). (Survey researchers face a similar problem when they try to use survey methods for the study of non-respondents on surveys [Goyder, 1987].)

Even where researchers have been able to say something about why they were granted access, the reasons given have usually been rather varied, and often expressed in vague and general terms. The managers who allowed Wood (1980) access to their firms did not expect that his research would be of any direct benefit to them. Rather they couched their acceptance of him in terms of a general sense that the research 'would do some good', and that it would help him with his education. Some of those studied by Winckler (1987) were flattered by the prospect of being studied, some co-operated in order to pay off obligations to the sponsors of the research. Others thought that the study would provide intellectual stimulation, or else they were sympathetic to research, or to the project itself.

A further problem has to do with the way in which reflexive accounts of field experience are used as aids to the socialization of novice ethnographers. (For example, Rosalie Wax's [1971] book on fieldwork is explicitly subtitled *Warnings and Advice*.) While in many ways laudable, much of this writing tends to be underpinned by a view which sees entry to the field as a rite of passage. Accounts of field experience serve in this literature both an initiatory and a moral purpose. Neophytes are allowed to enter vicariously into back-regions so that they may be allowed to learn some of the more disreputable secrets of the trade. They are also encouraged to understand that research involves asceticism, anomie and atrocity. In other words, the message is that fieldworkers are the kinds of people who can put up with constant and dedicated hard work, loneliness, powerlessness and confusion, and, quite possibly, some suffering at the hands of those being studied. (For an alternative view, drawing on the experiential learning paradigm, see R.M. Lee, 1987; 1988.)

Clearly fieldwork *is* difficult and stressful. As Sanders (1980) has suggested, one cannot hope to 'learn the ropes' of being a field researcher without suffering from 'rope burns'. Field research by its very nature, he argues, requires people to carry out tasks which run against the grain of earlier socialization and social experience. Thus, it is difficult to avoid the fear of being a stranger, the fear of rejection when seeking personal details about people's lives, and the fear of violating the normative standards of those being studied. It is hardly surprising, then, to learn that fieldworkers on occasion exhibit physiological symptoms associated with stress such as diarrhoea, nosebleeds and vomiting (see, e.g., Walford, 1987; J.M. Johnson, 1975; Punch, 1979). The drawback is that, in stressing the difficulties of field research, what results is largely a set of 'heroic tales' in which the reluctance of those being studied is overcome as a result of the researcher's diligence, cleverness or artifice. (See J. Hunt, 1984, for a particularly clear example of this genre.) By contrast, as Form (1971; 1973) has pointed out, there has been very little attempt *systematically* to examine the social dynamics of access processes. Neither has much attention been paid to patterns of access and non-access across studies, or to the potential consequences of differential accessibility to some settings rather than others. (Although the use of simulation as a tool for understanding the access process has been advocated on occasion, developments in this direction still remain limited [R.M. Lee, 1987; 1988; see also Form, 1973].)

Access careers

John Johnson (1975) argues that gaining access is unpredictable because the thing one needs to ensure success is a detailed theoretical understanding of the social organization of the setting one is attempting to enter. In other words, that which is most likely to secure access can only be gained once the researcher is actually inside the setting and has carried out the study! Along with a number of other writers (Warren, 1984; 1988; J. Hunt, 1984; Adler and Adler, 1987) he has stressed rather strongly the view that gaining access is situationally specific. Johnson notes, for example, that, judging from published accounts, researchers seeking access face what he describes as 'seemingly unlimited contingencies . . . ranging from being gleefully accepted to being thrown out on one's ear' (1975, 50).[1] Johnson (1975) argues from this that access should not be thought of as an initial phase of entry to the research setting around which a bargain can be struck. Instead, it is best seen as involving an ongoing, if often implicit, process, in which the researcher's right to be present is continually renegotiated. Looked at in this way the access career can be thought of as both continuous and precarious. Some individuals in the setting ('freeze-outs' in Johnson's terminology) may never come to accept the researcher's presence, and even where the researcher has been accepted, the legitimacy of his or her presence can still be questioned or revoked.

While there are good reasons to stress the continuous and precarious nature of the access career, there are some disadvantages to doing so. First, the paradox Johnson points to – that the knowledge one needs in order to gain access to a setting can only be gained once entry to the setting has been achieved – is less striking than it first appears. Johnson does stress as a way of overcoming the problem the importance of a 'pre-research' phase in which detailed information about the setting is gathered prior to the attempt at entry. However, in saying that the contingencies which face researchers are 'seemingly endless' he also seems to be implying that the uniqueness of each individual attempt at access means that little can be said about entry situations in general. However, it is a truism to say that the *specificity* of new situations cannot be experienced in advance. This does not mean that they cannot be apprehended in their *generality*. Taken to its logical conclusion, Johnson's position would mean that it would never be possible to learn from one's own experience, or from the experiences of others.[2]

Second, writers like Johnson, Hunt and the Adlers move the researcher to the centre of the stage. In so doing, they replace an earlier conception of the researcher as 'detached' from the setting with one in which the researcher affects the setting as much as the setting affects the researcher. Alongside this, they promote an open and 'confessional' style of reporting on field experience which discusses topics – such as the role of sexual relations in field research – which were previously relegated to 'corridor talk' (Warren, 1988). A penalty involved in doing this is that the power relations embedded in the setting slip from view. It is recognized that the resources researchers bring with them in terms of power and status are usually meagre and unlikely to match those of the gatekeeper. There is little sense, however, of how gatekeepers actually exercise power. Form (1971), who has made a similar point, has noted that it is precisely the imbalance of power between gatekeeper and researcher which leads directly to bargaining in the access situation.

Third, few people would argue that access, in the sense of

maintaining a presence in the setting, does *not* involve an ongoing process of negotiation. There is no reason, however, why, in some kinds of settings at least, this process should not be more explicit at certain points, and certainly at the beginning of the research, than during its progress (Hammersley and Atkinson, 1983, 76). In other words, it may be important to maintain the distinction, which Johnson and others dissolve, between 'physical access' and 'social access' (Cassell, 1988).

The gaining of access in situations where research is potentially threatening inevitably revolves around what Form (1973) has called the 'politics of distrust'. Whether a person trusts or not depends on whether he or she is willing to embark on a risky course of action confident in the expectation that others will act in ways which do not threaten the trusting person's interests, activities or self-presentations. In interpersonal relationships, trust is facilitated because those within the relationship have much information about each other arising from self-disclosure and from observations of past actions. Moreover, because a breach of trust in these situations has a high emotional cost to all involved, it is likely to be avoided. There are many social situations, however, and seeking entry to a new social setting for the purposes of research is one of them, in which individuals must trust one another, despite potential conflicts of interest. In these situations, those involved may have little information about how the other is likely to act (Moe, 1984; see also Luhmann, 1979), and there may be few emotional costs to disrupting the relationship. In other words, while social access crucially depends on establishing *interpersonal* trust, gatekeepers who control *physical* access will often seek ways of ensuring *impersonal* trust.

Shapiro (1987) suggests there are a number of strategies which can be used to reduce the risk involved in trusting a stranger in situations where the outcome of the relationship is uncertain. First, risk can be *avoided*. It is not unusual, for example, for a researcher to meet with a point-blank refusal to grant entry. Although, as in Josephson's (1970) study in Harlem, it is possible for *community* resistance to a research project to be mobilized, direct denial of access is presumably most common where attempts are being made to study an organization. Gatekeepers in these situations have both the power and the authority to prevent entry. This can be clearly seen, for example, in a study of major redundancies at a large manufacturing plant (reported in Harris et al., 1987) where the management curtly refused co-operation with a group of researchers, saying simply that 'These workers are no longer our employees.'

Second, risk can be *spread*. In economic relations this is often done through the use of insurance arrangements (Shapiro, 1987). Such arrangements have no *precise* analogue in social relations. However, in uncertain situations informal social ties may be used to spread risk, as when kin can be relied upon to mitigate the effects of economic hardship (M. Anderson, 1971), or when employers avoid potential 'troublemakers' by taking on workers who have been vouched for by an existing employee (Jenkins et al., 1983; R.M. Lee, 1985b). In research settings, the use of sponsors or intermediaries can serve as a form of social insurance which spreads the risk of being studied for those in the setting.

Third, risk can be controlled. This can be done in one of two ways. Either the relationship can be *proceduralized* or it can be *personalized*. That is, the parties can either formally agree to be governed in their dealings by a set of explicit procedures, or they can convert their impersonal relationship into an interpersonal one. The rest of this chapter considers: (a) the ways in which gatekeepers control physical access through proceduralization; (b) the role of sponsors and intermediaries; (c) the process of establishing social access, and (d) the indirect consequences which flow from the complete denial of access to research settings.

Conditional access

Gatekeepers often allow researchers into a setting but use formal agreements and procedures in order to control their activities. Data collection, for example, can be limited by placing *restrictions* on the kind of material which can be made available to the researcher. It is not uncommon in organizations for certain kinds of documentary information to be placed 'off-limits'. Robert Burgess (1984) records that the otherwise co-operative head-teacher of the school he researched would not allow him to look at staff files. More widely, governmental organizations in particular may formally restrict the disclosure of potentially embarrassing information. Documents may be classified in ways which permit them only a limited circulation and which proscribe their disclosure to those outside the organization. In Britain, this might include the possible use of the Official Secrets Act to prohibit the publication of information gained inside a government establishment (Cohen and Taylor, 1977). In other, ostensibly more open, societies it is still possible for the researcher's data collection efforts to be frustrated. At the West Point Military Academy during Spencer's (1973) time there, documentary materials were classified in a variety of ways in order to limit their availability to outsiders. In some cases, documents were specifically designated as pertaining to the internal administration of the Academy to avoid their being treated as public documents, and, therefore, open to inspection. Alternatively, papers could be labelled 'For Official Use Only', a classification designed to restrict circulation on a 'need to know' basis, but which was used routinely whenever documents contained information which was sensitive or potentially embarrassing to the military.

A further way of constraining access is by subjecting the researcher to some kind of surveillance. Often in organizations this takes the form of chaperonage. In one of the redundancy situations Wood (1980) studied, he was required to report to the personnel manager each time he entered or left the premises. Whenever he was present, the personnel manager made regular visits to see what he was doing. Researchers who visit the West Point Military Academy, according to Spencer (1973), are escorted throughout their visit, while Carter (1987) and a group of colleagues on a field trip to Rajneeshpuram, a religious settlement set up in Oregon by the followers of the Bhagwan Shree Rajneesh, had their activities closely monitored. They had to permit themselves and their cars to be searched, were required to wear green armbands to designate their visitor status throughout their time in the settlement, and found their opportunities to speak to devotees severely limited.

Gatekeepers often seek to impose explicit conditions on research in ways which affect both the processes by which a particular study is carried out and its published products. A number of clear examples of this tendency are provided by Platt (1976). Even in a relatively small number of projects (55 in all), she uncovered frequent attempts by gatekeepers to frustrate or circumscribe the conduct of the research. From the researcher's point of view, gaining access under these conditions often takes on the character of a bargaining situation, particularly where the topic of study is sensitive in some way. Access, in other words, has to be 'bought' at the cost of restrictive conditions being imposed on the researcher's activities. Broadly speaking, in these situations three major kinds of condition are imposed by gatekeepers on researchers. These are: (a) restrictions on the methodology used by the researcher; (b) the completion of a piece of research *for* the gatekeeper in return for access; and (c) the right of the gatekeeper to examine, modify or censor published material arising from the study.

Sometimes gatekeepers have preconceptions about the way in which research should be carried out. Walford, seeking research access to a number of independent schools in Britain, describes his initial encounter with the principal of the one of the schools he eventually studied in the following way:

I had intended, in true ethnographic style, to develop my research strategy once inside the school. The headmaster, however, had a rather different idea of how research should be conducted, where questions are tightly framed, questionnaires or interview schedules developed, and representative samples drawn from populations. It quickly became obvious that the role of 'open ethnographic researcher' was one which he would not entertain. This was the first occasion when it became clear to me that possible research roles were structured by the definitions of others. (1987, 50)

Platt (1976) gives an instance of a gatekeeper who found the use of sociometric techniques objectionable on the grounds that the methodology required his staff to make judgements about one another. The 'structuring of possible research roles' by gatekeepers, however, seems – as Walford's experience implies – most often to be inflicted upon qualitative researchers. (Quantitative researchers are perhaps more vulnerable to the argument that the paraphernalia of survey research is a potential source of administrative disruption.) The distrust of qualitative methods may partly reflect simple ignorance, given the greater public visibility of survey research, although, as Patton (1980, 18) remarks, it is frequently the product of methodological prejudice. Writers sympathetic to qualitative research (e.g. Finch, 1986), who have looked at the commissioning of research by policy-makers, have noted that, technically and logistically, survey research provides more opportunity to scrutinize and control the activities of the researcher than does qualitative research. The point might be extended to suggest that gatekeepers are also likely to prefer research methods which give them scope for scrutiny and control, something more easily done where – as with survey research – much of what will be carried out inside the setting can be pre-specified and where there is instrumentation in the form of questionnaires and so on which can be inspected.

In some cases, the gatekeeper will offer to provide access to the setting but only if the researcher agrees to study some aspect of it on the gatekeeper's behalf, or to produce a report of the findings for the gatekeeper's use. Bargains of this kind may represent either a demand for reciprocity or an attempt at co-option. Thus, some minority communities, in which the recurrent attention of researchers has become experienced as a form of exploitation, have become increasingly unwilling to allow access without some assurance that the product of the research will be of direct benefit to them in some way (Blauner and Wellman, 1982). Possibly less common but more insidious from the researcher's point of view are the kinds of attempts described by Argyris (1952) in which pressure is put on the researcher to act as a detective or an informer on behalf of management. Few researchers, one would assume, would allow themselves willingly to be co-opted to a gatekeeper's control purposes. Offers of access based on a reciprocal trading of in-house research in return for access are, on the other hand, presumably more difficult to refuse. Considered in exchange terms there are three reasons for this. First of all, researchers are usually in a weak position when seeking access because they can deploy few bargaining resources beyond their academic respectability and the appeals they are able to make to the rhetoric of science (J.M. Johnson, 1975, 64–5). Second, being in a weak bargaining position in itself produces pressures towards reciprocity. To draw a not entirely fanciful analogy with courtship (Waller, 1938), the partner who gives most in a relationship is the partner who, faced with the other's disinterest, has most to lose. Thirdly, from the researcher's point of view the bargain potentially being struck is apparently a 'good' one since the ability to do the research is produced at a small marginal cost to the researcher, that of the additional labour required to produce the report.

Judging from published accounts, situations in which researchers have made bargains of the kind just described often appear to have unhappy outcomes, especially when the research has been carried out in a formal organization. Although there are clearly exceptions (e.g. Form, 1971), it seems not uncommon for the final report when it appears to be greeted with hostility and indignation (see, e.g., Platt, 1976). Sometimes, negative reaction of this kind can be valuable. Jenkins (1987) looked in his research at patterns of discrimination against Black workers in recruitment for employment. Faced with hostile reactions to consultancy reports he had produced for employers as a *quid pro quo* for gaining access, he notes that the negative responses he received were nevertheless useful. First of all, he became convinced as a result of the arguments put to him that some of his interpretations were erroneous. Second, he came to regard the reactions he received as a useful ethnographic resource in that they brought to the surface underlying attitudes and expectations about race.

Jenkins points to one way of salvaging what is often presumably a difficult and unpleasant situation. The literature on evaluation research also provides some discussion of the issues surrounding the reception of research findings. It might be anticipated that an evaluator who, after all, enters a setting by invitation and on the basis of valued expertise would have few problems in presenting findings. However, as Rossi and Freeman point out, evaluators, on producing a report, frequently find themselves being confronted by 'a torrent of criticisms of and negative reactions to the findings' (1982, 311). Rossi and Freeman argue that responses of this kind arise for two reasons. First, decision-makers prefer research which has a short-term instrumental utility. Second, evaluation often takes place within an essentially political context in which the 'stakes' power-holders have in particular policies may be threatened by outside appraisal. Rossi and Freeman's solution to this problem is to advise evaluation researchers to take conscious steps to ensure that their findings are received sympathetically and are robust enough to survive possible attack. In particular, they argue that the evaluator should try from the beginning of the research to build a consensus among all concerned about its conduct, purpose and possible consequences. They also suggest that researchers should strive to develop research designs which are 'tight', in the sense of being relatively immune to methodological challenge.

Unfortunately, these are conditions which are rarely likely to be met outside the evaluation context. In these cases, once access has been granted there is often – deliberately – little contact between the researcher and the gatekeeper. Little basis therefore exists for the development of mutual trust. Far from producing consensus, such situations often instead produce shared misunderstandings. Indeed, it is probable that the research bargain itself will be perceived in different ways. For the researcher, the access provided by that bargain is likely to be seen as its most important outcome, while the report itself is more likely to be of consequence from the gatekeeper's point of view. Even where this is not the case, those who have been studied often assume, as Becker (1964) points out, that the researcher 'will abide by the ethics of the group, not realizing the scope and force of the scientist's impersonal ethic and, particularly, of the scientific obligation to report findings fully and frankly'. Fullness and frankness may well be seen as the final indiscretion of a never very welcome guest. However, few researchers outside the evaluation context are likely to feel happy about shaping their research design to minimize possible hostile reactions from a gatekeeper. Furthermore, although conflict between researcher and gatekeeper may jeopardize subsequent research access, hostile reaction to a report is less problematic in overall career terms for a researcher who is not routinely involved in evaluation than for someone who is.

As Platt (1976) suggests, the most common way in which gatekeepers try to control the research process is by attempting to secure the right to inspect, modify or suppress the published products of research. In this regard it is interesting to look at an attempt to simulate the access process (R.M. Lee, 1987). In this simulation, groups of students were asked to deal with a request for access to a fictitious college in order to study 'deviance and the student lifestyle'. The simulation was designed primarily for teaching purposes and the request for access was, to that end, deliberately couched in terms likely to make the granting of access seem problematic. As a result its wider applicability to other access situations is obviously limited. Nevertheless, one striking feature of the simulation is how often the students who participated sought the right to examine, approve and, in some cases, suppress altogether any written work arising from the 'research'.

Becker (1964) notes that one possible solution to problems of restricted access might be to 'drive the hardest bargain' with those who control entry to a setting, compromising on publication only 'in order to gain access to a theoretically important class of institutions that would otherwise be closed'. Unfortunately, Becker does not develop this argument to show more clearly the kinds of compromise he might or might not be prepared to make. Instead he goes on in his subsequent discussion to consider the entirely separate problem of those in research situations whose lack of familiarity with the research process might encourage them to make research bargains which are disadvantageous to them. On the other hand, some researchers (e.g. Galliher, 1973) argue that restrictions on the sociologist's capacity to report are most likely to serve the interests of the powerful. From this point of view, attempts to reach an accommodation with gatekeepers should be avoided altogether. Instead, 'conflict methodologies' should be adopted which do not require the co-operation of powerful subjects: the use of covert research, the analysis of publicly available data, the seeking out of dissatisfied or former employees as informants and so on.

This last approach has been criticized by Sullivan and Cornfield (1982). Primarily interested in the problems of access which arise in the study of large-scale corporations, they argue that conflict methodologies defeat their own purpose. Covert studies of organizations, they point out, often only provide opportunities for entry to low-level positions. In a similar way other related kinds of strategy restrict the researcher only to data which are potentially deficient. Publicly available material, for example, may be seriously incomplete or 'stage-managed'. Obtaining information from informants who are peripheral, dissatisfied or retired is often to rely on those not in positions closely to observe, or with an interest in exaggeration or distortion. As a result, Sullivan and Cornfield argue, conflict methodologists are normally prevented from being able to study at first hand the actual processes of élite decision-making which are in fact their primary concern.

Sullivan and Cornfield suggest an alternative strategy. First of all, they argue that it is important to negotiate directly with top management in order to legitimate the research and to distinguish the role of the researcher from other roles such as that of the journalist. They argue that managements are concerned in case potentially discreditable information flows outwards to competitors and regulatory agencies and downwards to unions and employees. It is possible to alleviate fears about the outward flow of information without altogether restricting access by making an explicit bargain with management officials. Under the terms of this bargain, management may inspect the manuscript of the final report prior to publication and suggest changes which may be made to it. However, under the agreement this right of inspection and modification *can only be exercised in relation to the preservation of anonymity*.

Sullivan and Cornfield make a strong case for utilizing explicit agreements of this kind in a way which helps to overcome the power imbalance between individual researchers and large-scale organizations. There are, however, a number of problems with their approach. Sullivan and Cornfield are in fact suggesting that an inducement to co-operate (Rainwater and Pittman, 1967) should be made available to organizations which researchers have long extended to individuals – the promise of anonymity. However, one point the conflict methodologists are making is that bureaucracies are publicly accountable in a way that individuals are not. Researchers, therefore, may have a greater obligation to expose public wrongdoing than they would cases of individual deviation. In addition, Sullivan and Cornfield are rather coy about the details of negotiating such agreements. It is not clear, for example, whether rights of inspection and modification over pre-published material in order to ensure anonymity should be offered right away or only as the kind of last-ditch compromise of which Becker speaks. Neither is it clear how far, in practice, there are grey areas in which gatekeepers might attempt to 'stretch' the definition of anonymity in order to distort or minimize substantive findings. Additionally, while the strategy Sullivan and Cornfield advocate deals effectively with the problem of *outward-flowing* information, it deals less well with fears about the *downward* flow of information. Managements, in fact, may be particularly sensitive to the gaining of information by workers and unions, who of course are in a uniquely favourable position to pierce the disguise of anonymity. Finally, there are, of course, some situations where guarantees of anonymity are difficult to give. Where a local economy is dominated by a particular employer, for example, it can be virtually impossible to disguise the company under discussion, especially in cases like plant closure or workforce reductions which are highly visible and have major local consequences.

Sponsors

'Doc', perhaps the most celebrated and exemplary sponsor in sociology, told William Foote Whyte:

> Well, any nights you want to see anything, I'll take you around. I can take you to the joints – gambling joints – I can take you around to the street corners. Just remember that you're my friend. That's all they need to know. I know these places and if I tell them that you're my friend, nobody will bother you. You just tell me what you want to see, and we'll arrange it. (1955, 291)

Embodied in these words are the three major roles which a sponsor can perform: as a bridge, as a guide, or as a patron. (These are, of course, analytic distinctions; an individual sponsor will normally combine them in various ways.) The 'bridge' provides the researcher with a link into a new social world. For the researcher who studies sensitive topics, bridges are often necessary even to make contact with deviant worlds. The Adlers, for example, eventually discovered that one of their neighbours was a drug smuggler, who subsequently provided them with an entrée into the world of illegal drug importers and distributors (P.A. Adler, 1985). The 'guide' is someone who, as it were, maps a way for the researcher through unfamiliar social and cultural terrain. Such an individual points out to the researcher what is going on, and explains features of the setting which might be puzzling. The guide can also provide warnings against possible *faux pas*, as Doc did by alerting Whyte whenever his questions strayed into sensitive areas to do, for example, with racketeering. The 'patron' is someone who, simply by associating with the researcher, helps to secure the trust of those in the setting. Doc's phrase 'Just remember you're my friend. That's all they need to know.' captures rather nicely the nub of the relationship between researcher and patron.

A sponsor, who acts in a bridging or a guiding role, serves indirectly to facilitate acceptance of the researcher. Introducing a stranger to a new social world – especially if it is a deviant one – is in itself to provide a guarantee of the stranger's trustworthiness. ('Tally' acted in this way for Elliot Liebow [1967].) In a similar way, a researcher who is able to avoid, with the help of a sponsor, over-inquisitive or naive questions, or inappropriate actions, aids acceptance by allaying suspicion. Having someone act as a patron serves more directly to secure acceptance for the researcher. This is so, because, first of all, in exerting influence on behalf of someone else, the reputation of the intermediary is potentially put at risk. Second, the patron can potentially act as a channel for informal social control should the person sponsored act in an inappropriate way. Similar considerations are likely to apply to the relationship between researcher and sponsor.

Acquiring a sponsor is often treated in the fieldwork literature as a matter of good fortune. In fact, the availability and usefulness of sponsors are frequently structural matters which depend on factors such as the size, density and character of social networks (see Boissevain, 1974; see also Granovetter, 1974, on 'luck' as an outcome of structured social relations). According to Form (1973), access to an organization is likely to be easier when there are dense linkages between it and other organizations. Access is facilitated in these situations because a greater number of potential sponsors exist. Conversely, although marginal individuals are often useful informants (Dean et al., 1969), it is unlikely, for example, that a social isolate would make a good patron.

Sponsorship appears to be closely tied to prestige. Doc was, of course, the leader of the 'Nortons', the gang Whyte studied. Sponsorship may be more problematic in organizations, since as Form argues, 'Sponsorship, like prestige, is not necessarily transferable; it can be contested at any time by any faction in an organization' (1971, 7). It was noticeable in a study of redundant steelworkers (reported in Harris et al., 1987) that some of the people initially contacted, such as trade union officials, would assert their ability to facilitate access by speaking to some powerful or strategically placed individual. Often, however, what had been promised would not materialize. In the specific cultural context within which the research took place, men, especially, tended to maintain their social identity by deploying their social networks in an instrumental manner. It may be that by exaggerating the character of their relationship with a powerful other or that person's ability to deliver what was required, some of the men involved were trying to assert claims to power and status which had been undermined by the impact of the redundancies.

Of course, apparently willing sponsors may not always be what they seem. At least one researcher has been approached by a potential sponsor who was apparently a hoaxer (Bruce, 1987). In another instance, in Northern Ireland, an initially helpful but subsequently elusive intermediary may in fact have been checking out the researcher on behalf of a paramilitary group (R.M. Lee, 1981). Peritore (1990), describing his experiences of carrying out research on left-wing parties in Brazil, also notes that apparently innocuous informants can turn out to be members of the security services.

From physical to social access

Physical access is a precondition of social access. With the former secured, however, the latter can remain problematic. For example, where settings are organized formally, there often exists a 'hierarchy of consent' (Dingwall, 1980) in which it is assumed that superiors have the right to permit their subordinates to be studied. Often, however, this consent, once given, produces little more than the token co-operation of subordinates, particularly if they would prefer to keep certain aspects of their work lives from their superiors. Berk and Adams (1970) have argued – perhaps over-pessimistically – that it can also be difficult to establish and maintain rapport with members of deviant groups (see also W.G. West, 1980; Power, 1989). Past experiences often make group members cynical; they will often assume the worst about an outsider until their fears have been proved unfounded. Because of the social distance which often exists between researcher and researched, the researcher is also likely to be culturally incompetent and to make mistakes. Such errors lead to negative evaluations by those in the setting which produces in its turn a lack of trust. In addition, some of those studied may be 'question-wise' from their dealings with state bureaucracies and social control agencies, adept at looking behind questions and 'prudently trying to psych out and con their questioner' (Beck, 1970, 19). Since they do not trust outsiders, people in the setting may erect 'fronts' (Goffman, 1956; D. Douglas, 1972; J.D. Douglas, 1976) designed to impede the researcher's progress through concealment, obfuscation or deception.

Fronts
Fronts conceal by ensuring that the researcher has only a limited opportunity to observe what is going on. Deviance is often possible because, to paraphrase Goffman (1961), licence has a geography. That is, deviant activities are obscured from view by what Best and Luckenbill (1980) refer to as the 'command of place'. By means of physical separation and the use of shielding mechanisms (Rock, 1973) participants free themselves from surveillance by social control agencies. In so doing they also protect themselves from the unwitting and the curious, and present barriers to the researcher.[3] Obfuscation is common in settings where physical access has been

granted but where social access has not yet been attained. While apparently assenting to the researcher's presence those in the setting engage in activities designed to keep the outsider at bay. Daniels (1967), for example, found that the army officers she was studying feigned interest in her research but perennially missed or were late for appointments and frequently found reasons for cutting interviews short. Argyris (1952), too, gives several instances of researchers in industrial organizations being met with surface 'co-operation' which was in fact designed to hinder their progress. In one case, the researchers found themselves being deluged with irrelevant information. In another, requests for data were continu-ally referred back to 'head office' for clearance. Those in the setting may also try to deceive the researcher. In some cases the deception can become quite elaborate. Dorothy Douglas (1972), who studied a commercial ambulance service, discovered, for example, that the ambulance crews she was observing went to considerable lengths – including the setting up of a fake despatch office – to present her with an innocuous view of their work.

Some writers, discussed in detail elsewhere, argue that fronts are pervasive and durable. Researchers need, therefore, to adopt an aggressive 'frontbusting' style or use covert penetration in order to 'crack' the front. By and large, however, field researchers have avoided such methods. Instead, as John Johnson points out, in order to establish trustful relations fieldworkers usually adopt a 'progressive entry' strategy. Progressive entry involves the researcher making 'gradually increased requests for more open access' (1975, 64), while at the same time 'defocussing' the study. This is done by presenting the research topic in a general rather than a specific way. In so doing, one allows those within the setting to define the research according to their own concerns rather than those of the researcher (see also Schatzman and Strauss, 1973). For example, according to Berk and Adams (1970), when dealing with deviant groups it is important to minimize any suggestion that the research is concerned with social problems. Instead researchers should stress that they are curious about the lives of the researched, and express a desire to uncover 'their side of the story'.

It should be clear that a strategy of progressive entry will not work if, at any given stage in the process, the researcher disrupts the operation of the setting. Typically, therefore, fieldworkers engage in what Van Maanen (1982) calls 'character display', that is, strategies of self-presentation aimed at finding ways of 'fitting in' to the setting. To do this, as John Johnson (1975) points out, researchers normally minimize the social distance between them-selves and those they study, normalize potentially deviant aspects of identity or biography, and generally 'play it safe' whenever a difficult situation arises.

Progressive entry aims to minimize the potential threat posed by the researcher and to maintain a sustained presence in the setting. In field research, continued presence in the setting is important because it helps to undermine the maintenance of fronts. Considerable effort is usually needed to sustain fronts over an extended period. After a time, those in the setting may forget the researcher's presence or find the effort of maintaining the front too onerous. In some cases, such as occupations where protracted spells of inactivity are common, the front may eventually dissolve because the researcher's company and questions provide a welcome relief from boredom (Brewer, 1990a). Spending considerable amounts of time in the setting – especially at inconvenient hours – also aids acceptance because it can be taken as an indication of the researcher's seriousness and commitment. In addition, with disadvantaged groups, the researcher avoids taking on a 'social work aura' by working outside the 9 to 5 routine (Berk and Adams, 1970, 106; Polsky, 1971). There may of course be some individuals in the setting who refuse to accept the researcher's good intentions. Provided presence can be maintained, however, there are likely to be at least some potential informants more ready to reveal what is going on than others (Dean et al., 1969). Although their accounts may be self-serving in various ways, those who are marginal, frustrated or malcontented may welcome the researcher's presence as an opportunity to 'tell all' or set the record straight. Others may be too secure, too naive, or have too little stake in what is going on to feel inhibited about revealing potentially discreditable information.

In and of themselves, neither time spent in the setting nor the different stakes research participants have in the front will ensure that concealment, obfuscation or deception will disappear, especially if the topic of the research is a sensitive one. Researchers have sometimes been duped for considerable periods (Garfinkel, 1967; Punch, 1989). Furthermore, as Dorothy Douglas notes, even when the initial façade breaks down, a 'retrenchment of the front' (1972, 103) may take place. In other words, the initial front is replaced by a subsequent, though usually less credible, one. There can also be dangers in becoming identified with marginal or disaffected individuals (see, e.g., Blau, 1964a, 34). As a result, continued presence in the setting partly depends on the 'transformation of the researcher's cultural identity from that of untrustworthy to that of trustworthy category of person through the demonstration of membership and participation in the construction of intersubjective meaning' (J. Hunt, 1984, 286). This is particularly so where the researcher has an identity which those in the setting initially devalue. The male police officers studied by Jennifer Hunt (1984), for example, regarded women who operated, like the researcher, within the 'dirty' spatial domain of the street as threatening and untrustworthy. To be accepted, Hunt had to construct an identity which combined aspects of toughness and trustworthiness. She therefore developed prowess at activities the police valued, such as unarmed combat and the use of firearms, and inculcated an identification with rank-and-file policemen rather than their officers. (For an interesting reinterpretation by Hunt of her role in this setting, see J. Hunt, 1989.)

Not all researchers would go quite to the lengths that Hunt apparently did to become accepted. However, Brewer's (1990a) study of routine policing in Northern Ireland shows that the demeanour of the fieldworker in trying circumstances can be important both to the transformation of the researcher's identity and for the identification of underlying taboos. The police in Brewer's study initially welcomed his female research officer. They found her attractive and treated her presence as providing light relief from the demands of their job. Eventually, however, they became suspicious of her. While they were mainly Protestant, she was a Roman Catholic. Relatively innocuous in many other circumstances, this was of considerable significance in the context of the violent social conflict in Northern Ireland. One night, as news of the killing of a fellow officer came in, a policeman launched a fierce verbal assault on the research officer's trustworthiness. Brewer notes that her handling of this outburst aided the research officer's acceptance. It allowed the police officers to define her as a 'decent' Catholic; one who did not support or condone political violence. Brewer adds, however, that the incident had an additional benefit. It brought to the surface issues about the purpose of the study and the potential uses of the data which gave an indication of what those in the setting regarded as sensitive.

Appreciative understanding
Field researchers have tended to study groups for whom they have some liking or sympathy. Indeed, in the Chicago tradition the study of deviant groups by researchers who had been members was something of a commonplace (e.g. Becker, 1963). As a result Chicago school sociologists were particularly wary of 'over-rapport' or 'going native' (Adler and Adler, 1987). Rather less attention has been given to the problems of studying 'unloved' groups (Fielding, 1990), in particular those whose politics or powerful position make

them uncongenial to researchers who have left-wing or liberal sympathies. Studying such groups is often emotionally difficult. Cassell (1988) argues that having fewer resources of power than those one studies makes interaction less emotionally and socially rewarding. She also notes that researchers who adopt the perspectives of powerless groups are less open to professional sanction than those who adopt the perspectives of the powerful.

Field researchers who have studied unloved groups have frequently commented on the moral ambiguities involved. According to Fielding, the 'mechanical demands of participation in certain settings automatically produces deceit' (1982, 89). In other words, one must often apparently assent to what is going on in the setting in order simply to remain in it. As Cassell (1988) points out, such compromises inevitably smack of hypocrisy. However, in Cassell's view, a stance which is openly hostile to those studied potentially blocks the possibility of empathy. While the researcher is not required to love or even totally approve of those studied, it is necessary to like them enough to remain open to their view of the world. Cassell in fact argues that one cannot actually avoid temporarily adopting the perspective of those studied. What is important is that one eventually gains distance on the experiences and that one presents and analyses in published work the processes of identification and disidentification which took place. The process of achieving distance for Cassell is one which takes place after the researcher has eventually left the field. This may be more difficult for some researchers than for others. Although Cassell studied a powerful group – senior surgeons – it was not one she found morally or ideologically repugnant. In these situations it may be necessary to use a variety of devices to avoid becoming engulfed by the demands of the setting and make analytic distance possible. These might include the use of a personal journal devoted solely to emotional reactions to the research, periods of remission from the field and the use of colleagues for support and debriefing (Klatch, 1988; see also Pollner and Emerson, 1983).

Exchange

Early accounts of the trust-building process stressed in particular the importance of reciprocity and exchange (J.M. Johnson, 1975). Those studied were seen to have little incentive to answer questions put to them by inquisitive strangers. Researchers, therefore, were enjoined to 'repay . . . social debts and build up generalized obligations' (W.R. Scott, 1965, 279) which could be drawn on in order to secure co-operation. Many things might form the 'currency' for these exchanges (R.H. Wax, 1952; Gusfield, 1955). At a very basic level, simple 'friendliness' and an openness to questions and enquiries put by those within the setting could be used as an aid to securing co-operation. Alternatively, minor services and favours of a more directly instrumental kind could be performed, such as running errands or providing transportation. Patricia Adler notes, for example, that, in order to cultivate the trust of the drug dealers and smugglers she studied, she and her husband offered respondents 'everything that friendship could entail' (1985, 16). Stopping short of dealing or smuggling drugs themselves, they provided support, advice, loans, the use of their car and phone and so on.

There is some disagreement about the practical and ethical wisdom of providing goods and services to those in the setting. Reciprocity and exchange, particularly where members of deviant or disadvantaged groups are involved, can simply reflect a desire by the researcher not to be parasitical (Power, 1989). Many of the criminals Irwin (1972) studied stumbled from one personal crisis to another. He therefore often found himself acceding to requests for loans, transportation, accommodation and help with 'going straight'. Irwin clearly regarded such requests as legitimate and comments that where those in the setting seek favours the researcher needs to have good reason to turn down their entreaties. On the other hand, Yancey and Rainwater (1970) have argued that gifts or loans from affluent researchers to poor respondents can reinforce paternalist roles. Berk and Adams (1970) also explicitly caution against lending money or providing transportation, except in obvious emergencies, because of the possibility of being 'suckered'. Being too open with services, they suggest, may lead to the researcher being both exploited and denigrated. Neither the researcher nor the researched in their view should find themselves in situations which undermine their identities and self-presentations in the eyes of others. Interestingly, the Adlers had feelings both of guilt and of resentment as a result of the services they provided (Adler and Adler, 1992). On the one hand, they felt insincere when they feigned friendship in order to gain information, or built research materials from people who had become friends. On the other hand, they also sometimes felt that they were exploited by those they studied. While they at all times were expected to be trusting, some of their informants felt no need to reciprocate and took advantage of them in various ways.

Complicity
A number of writers (Polsky, 1971; Irwin, 1972) have noted that in studying deviant groups researchers must expect to gain 'guilty knowledge' about deviance and may face requests to engage in

deviant actions. While researchers commonly reach tacit agreements with those they study not to undermine, challenge or disclose deviant activities which may take place (Klockars, 1979), Polsky (1971) in particular has stressed that it is important to draw a line about what one is prepared to witness or to participate in, and to make clear to those one studies where precisely that line is. According to Irwin (1972), this may not be as difficult as it might seem. The criminals he studied recognized fear of arrest as a legitimate reason for non-participation. However, the Adlers possessed and used small quantities of drugs during their study of upper-level drug dealers and smugglers, arguing that had they done otherwise they would have been regarded with extreme suspicion (P.A. Adler, 1985).

Not all researchers would accept this rationale, or even that a line can or should be drawn. Yablonsky (1965), for instance, has argued that the researcher has an obligation as a citizen to report illegal activities to the authorities. He also suggests that adopting a neutral stand towards the law-breaking activities of those being studied is to reinforce their criminal behaviour. Klockars argues, however, that guilty knowledge is the morally dubious means by which a morally good end – social scientific knowledge – is inevitably attained. It is impossible, in his view, to do research on deviant behaviour without, as he puts it, getting one's hands dirty. Indeed, for Klockars the compromises which surround 'the dirty hands problem' are 'at the ethical core of fieldwork with deviant subjects'. Not to recognize that compromises have to be made is to seek 'to understand how angels behave in paradise' (1979, 265). On the other hand, not to feel moral qualms about guilty knowledge is to develop a romanticized identification with deviant research subjects, and to accept their techniques for neutralizing responsibility.

In some cases, the attainment of guilty knowledge is deliberately engineered by those within the setting as a test of the fieldworker. Tests of various kinds are common in field research; in some cases practical jokes, teasing or the use of somewhat derogatory nicknames may be used simply to gauge the limits of the researcher's perseverance or good humour (see, e.g., D. Douglas, 1972; Brewer, 1990a). Especially in the study of sensitive topics, however, fieldworkers are also subjected to 'trust tests'. They are deliberately provided with discreditable or sensitive information, or are placed in a compromising or difficult situation to see what they do (see, e.g., D. Douglas, 1972, 108; Van Maanen, 1982; R.G. Burgess, 1984, 43). Coping well or ensuring that the information provided does not find its way to outsiders or superiors, is often taken to be a sign by those in the setting that the researcher can be trusted.

Attempts by the researcher to 'fit in', to minimize social distance and to neutralize unsavoury aspects of the situation reflect what John Johnson (1975) calls the 'accommodative morality' of field-work. As Pollner and Emerson (1983, 235) point out, the more one becomes a part of the setting, the more one risks being drawn out of the role of observer and into that of participant. Particularly in the study of deviance, however, the line between accommodation and surrender is a fine one. As a result researchers, have often been enjoined to couple together, in Robert Power's words, both 'an honest, empathetic and non-judgmental approach', and 'a level-headed, sensitive and rational appraisal of potentially compromising situations' (1989, 49). In other words, insofar as the researcher adopts an accommodative morality to the world of the deviant, it is a *tempered accommodation*. One enters a deviant world but tries to avoid being compromised and exploited by those within it.

The consequences of denied access

Platt (1976, 44) remarks that some of the researchers she inter-viewed harked back to a golden age when sociological research was still relatively uncommon and there were few problems about access. More recently, minority communities, at least, have increas-ingly come to feel threatened by the attention of outside researchers (Blauner and Wellman, 1982). In addition, a well-documented decline in survey research response rates which can be linked to growing concerns about privacy (Goyder, 1987) may also suggest an increasing and general disinclination to co-operate in research.

A researcher denied access to one setting can, of course, move on to another. Punch's (1979) inability to gain access to police forces in Britain, for example, led him eventually to study the Dutch police instead. There is, however, a hidden cost to such a strategy. Blau (1964a) notes that researchers will typically expect to find some level of non-response on a sample survey, and that those who do not respond will be different in some way from those who do. Neverthe-less there are well-developed procedures for dealing with the selection bias produced. In cases where one is studying not indi-viduals but organizations, associations or collectivities the problems of dealing with selection bias are much more serious. As Blau puts it, speaking about his research for the study eventually published as *The Dynamics of Bureaucracy* (1955):

> Suppose someone wants to study bureaucratic rigidities and fear of innovation. The very fact that the management gives him permission to conduct his investigation in its organization indicates that it is not resistant to trying something new. It may well be no accident that all old-

fashioned bureaucracies that I approached refused permission for the study and that both organizations that opened the way were relatively young ones founded during the New Deal. Perhaps self-selection makes it inevitable that the organizations we study are those in which bureaucratic rigidities are least pronounced. (1964, 28)

The problem is that if researchers follow the path of least resistance and study only those settings which are easiest to access, the consistent tendency of sociologists to study only the powerless, the near at hand or the relatively innocuous will be reinforced. Moreover, because research which fails or which is never attempted is not usually reported, it becomes difficult to assess just how far the total universe of studies is weighted in a particular way.

Notes

1. One difficulty with Johnson's writing is that he continually uses the term 'contingencies' when he clearly means outcomes.
2. One can make the additional point here that the access process itself often provides important clues to the nature of social relations within the setting. The organizational culture of the firms Wood (1980) studied was characterized by an institutional disregard for subordinates. This, he argues, facilitated his gaining access. Industrial relations in one of the firms he studied were characterized by an 'indulgency pattern' (Gouldner, 1954) in which supervision of the workforce was minimal. Another firm, which also permitted him entry, was organized in a paternalistic way. In both cases, managers assumed that their workers would have no objection to being studied. In the first, 'indulgent', firm, Wood was allowed the access, and was left alone to carry on the research as he pleased. In the firm organized in a paternalistic way, managers presumed to know what their workers were thinking. In this case, they granted Wood access with the expectation that he needed to do little more than to talk to a few workers in order to get a 'feel' for what was going on.
3. Even where public settings are physically accessible, those who use them can still find ways of making them interactionally impenetrable (Cavan, 1966). Gans (1962) notes, for example, that he made strenuous efforts to establish relations with a group of men who regularly frequented a bar in the neighbourhood he was studying. He was never able to do so, however, because they simply excluded him from their company. There are, though, cases in which the simple fact of being present in a setting can be enough to provide the researcher with a legitimate identity. Thus, Warren (1977) was somewhat surprised to find that access to recreational settings for male homosexuals was relatively easy. It was assumed apparently that anyone present in the setting was also homosexual. What still remained difficult for her was to gain entry to more private and intimate settings.

8

Covert, Adversarial and Collaborative Research

The importance attached to trust in the fieldwork literature flows from assumptions about both the nature of field research itself and the preconditions necessary for its successful completion. Field researchers assume that social and cultural worlds must be explored in a naturalistic manner (Rock, 1979). As Matza (1969, 24–5) points out, naturalistic research, especially in the study of deviance, requires first-hand contact with those studied, and a commitment to an 'appreciative' understanding of how those studied define their situation. However, neither contact nor appreciative understanding is necessarily won easily. The successful management of fieldwork 'depends not only on what the researcher says and does, but also upon the willingness of the observed to sustain the presence of such a marginal member in their midst' (Pollner and Emerson, 1983, 236). In this situation, trust is seen as a condition for continued participation, entry into closed spheres of interaction and the dissolution of deceptive self-presentations.

It is possible to challenge this view of trust in two ways. First, as Henslin (1972) points out, researchers may assume they have built up sufficient trust to ensure they are not being deceived. However, it is never possible to be sure that this is so. There are instances, for example, where deviance has been uncovered which had apparently been missed by other researchers (see, e.g., Ditton, 1977, 10). Writers like Henslin have therefore argued that to avoid being duped researchers studying sensitive topics should operate in a covert manner by posing as a member of the setting they wish to study. Second, it has also been argued that traditional conceptions of field relations are based on a consensual view of the world. According to Jack Douglas, this reflects what he calls the 'small-town, Protestant public morality of openness, friendliness and do-gooderism' typical of research in the Chicago tradition (1976, 47). However, both researcher and researched are embedded within relationships of power and socio-economic inequality. From this it can be argued that the researcher should define those studied as political adversaries or allies, and adopt a conflict-based or collaborative fieldwork style accordingly.

Those who advocate deceptive or power-conscious methods typically see the researcher as an unwelcome outsider. To this they couple the view that much of what is worth knowing about social life is surrounded by conflict and/or hidden from view. To conduct research of any relevance, therefore, is inevitably to deal with sensitive topics requiring special, and not always conventionally well-regarded, means.

Covert research

Research is covert when research participants are not aware that they are being studied.[1] A primary justification for covert research is that it avoids problems of reactivity. Because they do not know they are being studied, research participants are not threatened by the research and do not change their behaviour even though to outside eyes it might be regarded as deviant. Covert research is also said to offer an 'inside view' of those being studied. The overt researcher only ever 'speaks about' the insiders' view of the world rather than 'speaking from' that point of view (Henslin, 1972, 46–7). In the case of sensitive topics, however, 'speaking from' may be important because the threat posed by overt research to those in the setting often precludes the easy attainment of inside knowledge.

Despite its apparent advantages, questions have been raised both about the ethical standing of covert data collection, and about its efficacy. Covert studies violate important ethical principles (Bulmer, 1982a). In particular, they negate the principle of informed consent since research participants in covert studies cannot refuse their involvement. Covert studies may involve deception, and frequently cannot be carried out without invading the privacy of those being studied. It is also possible to argue that research using covert methods has longer term undesirable consequences. Such studies may encourage cynicism among social scientists in relation to the rights of research participants, while the wider public may come to distrust researchers (Erikson, 1968).

Social scientists have taken three broad positions in relation to the ethics of covert research. These can be described as absolutist, pragmatic and sceptical. Ethical absolutists hold that the difficulties outlined above fatally compromise covert methods of research. Such methods, therefore, cannot be used ethically. Reynolds (1982) points out that the absolutist position is based on a particular conception of professional conduct. This enjoins researchers to use 'techniques that are models of good behaviour' and actively implies that researchers should try to serve as 'moral exemplars' in their profession.

The pragmatic position recognizes the difficulties associated with the use of covert methods. It accepts the need to protect the rights of research participants and the obligation not to harm them, but sets these considerations against the need to obtain scientific knowledge. Covert research may therefore be regarded – reluctantly – as an acceptable method where the study is not a trivial one and there is no other way for the necessary data to be obtained. In this conception the researcher effectively adopts a utilitarian position, evaluating the costs to the participants of a particular study against the benefits which may accrue from it. Logically, of course, the calculus should also include the costs of *not* pursuing a particular topic (Rosenthal and Rosnow, 1984).

The sceptical position accepts that, far from being used reluctantly, there is in fact positive justification for covert study. In this view refraining from research which it is not conducted openly favours the powerful at the expense of the powerless. Requiring the co-operation of research participants means that, as Galliher (1973) puts it, 'the only secret information obtainable is from individuals and groups who are too ignorant and/or powerless to demand the necessary limitations upon the researchers'. As a result, sociology comes to know a great deal about the lower levels of society, but not about élite groups. In the process sociologists accept as credible the self-presentations of the powerful.

Sensitive topics have a pivotal relevance for the debate about covert methods. Reynolds (1982) points out that choices about the kinds of research methods to be used depend in part on the state of knowledge in a particular field. For example, structured methods such as survey research can be used where knowledge about an aspect of social life is already widely available or can be obtained in an open manner. Where little accurate or relevant information is available on the topic in question, field research involving access to a closed setting might be a more appropriate method. Areas of social life which are 'sensitive' fall more often into this second category than they do into the first. As Reynolds further notes, the absolutist position potentially restricts research to topics which would be regarded as inoffensive. Such a restriction would make it impossible to do at least two kinds of 'sensitive' research. First, research could not be done in which the presence of a researcher is not simply reactive, but potentially catastrophic in the sense of dissolving completely the activity of interest. This was in part the justification used by the late Laud Humphreys for his covert study of impersonal homosexual activities in public restrooms. As he comments, to go into a 'tearoom' as an undisguised observer 'would instantly eliminate all action except the flushing of toilets and the exiting of all present' (1970, 25). The second area which would be threatened are studies which look explicitly at the disjunction between public rectitude and private misdeed. Thus, Fielding (1981) in his partly covert study of an extreme right-wing political party was interested in the disjunction between its public face and the privately displayed attitudes of its members towards political violence.

If the absolutist position would disallow covert research on ethical grounds, research on sensitive topics also poses problems for the pragmatic and sceptical positions. Covert research has often been justified on the grounds that the benefits which flow from greater scientific knowledge outweigh the potential harm to research subjects. Difficulties arise, however, because there is no consensus about the benefits of research (MacIntyre, 1982). Apparently disinterested assertions about risks and benefits may in fact be self-serving. The researcher has greater power than those studied to define what might count as a risk or a benefit and the temptation to find spurious benefits may be particularly strong where a research topic is sensitive or in some way difficult to study. Unfortunately, there are in fact very few empirical studies of ethical decision-making in the social sciences (Stanley et al., 1987). As a result it is difficult to know with any certainty how often or in what circumstances researchers have chosen *not* to pursue a covert study.

Those who are sceptical of ethical proscriptions on covert research point to the sensitive character of research on the powerful. Powerful groups not only often have the means to deny access, they are also more likely to do so if they feel the researcher is set to expose their misdeeds (Cassell, 1988). This argument has been somewhat undermined by the experience of Galliher, a prominent proponent of the sceptical position. Although he is distrustful of ethical codes and quite prepared to use covert methods, Galliher (1980) notes that he has never had to use deception in his research. Indeed, he was surprised to find that he was often told discrediting information by élite informants. Galliher speculates that his informants were so convinced of the rightness of their views, that they did not find his investigation threatening.

Bulmer contends that the proponents of covert research have exaggerated its usefulness, and questions in a general way the extent to which covert research yields better data. He points (1982b), for example, to researchers such as Caudill (1958) who did similar studies using both covert and overt means, but who concluded that overt research provided better coverage and better data. In the pseudopatient study described by Rosenhan (1973), other patients penetrated the deception, even though clinic staff did not. Killian (1981) has argued, for example, on the basis of his own experience as a psychiatric patient, that pseudopatients over-identify with the patient point of view, and so do not get a rounded view. The slights and oppressions of the institution are impressed upon them, he suggests, precisely *because they are not patients*. Real patients, according to Killian, perceive apparently uncaring procedures in a different light, detecting in them potential therapeutic benefits.

Bulmer argues (1982a; 1982b) that it may be difficult actually to carry off a covert role since operating in a covert manner can create practical difficulties for the researcher. For example, in 'pseudo-patient studies', where a healthy researcher feigns illness in order to study the treatment process, the researcher may risk involuntary treatment or incarceration (Bulmer, 1982b). The consequences of revelation can also be serious. Feelings of outrage and betrayal on the part of those studied typically follow the disclosure that a covert study has taken place.

In the study of sensitive topics the practical difficulties involved may vitiate the apparent advantages of covert research. Self-consciousness about the need to maintain 'cover' may interfere with the data collection process (Weppner, 1976). The covert researcher may be unable to ask probing questions in the way that an overt researcher might. In fact, even quite simple questions might be difficult to ask if they concern matters an insider would be expected to know about (Henslin, 1972). It can be difficult to assess how far those in the setting are taken in by the deception. Researchers may unwittingly give off cues which alert those being studied to the possibility that they are being fooled. Ditton (1977), for example, learned after his covert study of 'fiddling' in a bakery was completed that some people had avoided him because they felt that in some way he did not fit into the setting. Particularly in organizations, it may be difficult for a covert researcher to move around without inviting suspicion. This can be particularly so where one is a low-status participant who may be denied access to higher echelons. In some settings it may be difficult to abstain from deviant activities or to avoid pressure to align oneself with one or other faction in a contentious situation. Thorne (1983) records that, although she wanted to observe several different groups, she was forced to take sides among the factions represented within the movement she studied. Thorne's work also provides a reminder that in some settings concern about possible secret identities is endemic. The draft resistance movement studied by Thorne was fearful of infiltration. Such fear induced constant nervous tension among participants which gave rise to the ritual of 'Fed-guessing' in which attempts were made to identify potential infiltrators. Thorne was strongly suspected of being a Federal agent, apparently because her research activities precluded her from becoming a complete participant.

Investigative social research

In his book *Investigative Social Research* Jack Douglas (1976) is critical of what he refers to as the 'classical co-operative paradigm' of field research which originated among the Chicago school sociologists. Douglas acknowledges that the Chicagoans clearly recognized the conflictual character of social life but argues that their approach to research was based on an assumption of community in which society was viewed as homogeneous and non-conflictual. In contrast to the co-operative paradigm Douglas adopts what he calls 'a clearly defined paradigm for people of practical affairs. This is the investigative paradigm' (1976, 55). Douglas sums up the fundamental principle of the investigative paradigm with the phrase, 'Conflict is the reality of life, suspicion is the guiding principle.' In other words, conflicts over interests, values, emotions and activities are endemic in social life. People have reason to hide from others what they are doing, and, as a result, there are good grounds for suspecting whatever it is they say. Another way of putting this is to say that, for Douglas, even ostensibly innocuous topics are more than likely to be sensitive once the surface façade has been penetrated. Douglas does suggest that co-operative and investigative paradigms can be used in tandem (1976, 56–7) but that investigative strategies remain essential as 'a necessary response to the pervasive secrecy, the lies and hypocrisy in society' (Bok, 1984, 246).

Investigative research combines a rugged, combative style of field work with a specific organizational form, that of team research. Although few of the tactics Douglas advocates are entirely unknown in research, it is their welding together into a paradigmatic method underpinned by an organizational structure and an epistemological warrant which constitutes his primary innovation. Couched in suitably aggressive language, the major tactics used in investigative research include, according to Douglas (1976, chap. 8), the infiltrating of the setting to be studied using covert methods if need be, and the 'setting up' and 'opening up' of informants. Researchers may then 'wrench the truth' (1976, 176) from those in the setting using what Douglas describes as 'adversary and discombobulating tactics' to confuse, disorient and wrong-foot them. Douglas acknowledges that, because such tactics are often counter-productive, they are usually weapons of last-resort. However, even in their absence, 'drawing out and phased assertion' tactics can be used in which the researcher asserts a potentially discrediting interpretation of an informant's behaviour in order, hopefully, to produce a confessional response.

Douglas stresses that a team approach is central to the use of investigative methods. Team research provides multiple perspectives on the research problem, multiple vantage points from which to attempt access and to assess the validity of accounts, as well as a range of research roles and skills. Much of what Douglas says about the advantages and disadvantages of teams is unexceptional (see Yancey and Rainwater, 1970, for a further discussion of team research in a difficult setting). He does, however, point to the difficulties of using teams in conflict situations. The team as a whole may be misled if one member or portion of the team is co-opted by one faction in a conflict. There is also a possibility of mistrust developing within the group – a somewhat ironic occupational hazard, presumably, since distrust forms the *raison d'être* of the investigative approach.

The investigative paradigm has met with an adversarial response from other social scientists. An obvious objection to investigative research is that its 'frontbusting' style, while effective, may be counter-productive in the longer term. Researchers who use such methods may meet increased resistance and those who come after them may be denied access in the future. A further difficulty is that the inherent scepticism which lies behind the investigative paradigm may harden into cynicism and a contempt for those studied. Citing Douglas as an example, Van Maanen has commented that:

> In the hands of some sociologists confessions read like debriefings after a ˙ battle in the combat zone with accounts of how informants were bullied, how tactics of coercive persuasion were employed, and how the weaknesses, disunity, and confusion of the natives were exploited. (1988, 98)

Punch (1986, 42) has argued in a similar way that the investigative position might produce a kind of reverse pride in breaking codes of ethics. The difficulty, of course, is that if one is to allow some groups in society to be exempted from ethical strictures because they are thought to have something to hide, then the scene is set for potentially endless debates about which groups can be exempted and which cannot.

Douglas makes much of the Chicago sociologists' failure to study the powerful or to cover systematically in their research a wide area of society. In his view the Chicago sociologists left little more than a series of discrete studies produced by individuals, each of whom studied a separate group. One can question, of course, Douglas's characterization of Chicago school sociology. Much of the recent critical reappraisal of Chicago sociology suggests that its research practice has been mythologized (Harvey, 1987; Bulmer, 1984; Platt, 1983; 1985). But even if Douglas is correct, the investigative paradigm does not seem to be superior in this regard. We seem to be left with a series of discrete studies of (more or less discreditable) settings, but this time produced by teams rather than individuals. The difficulty here seems to be that investigative research is underpinned by a certain ambiguity. One basis for the approach lies in Douglas's assumptions about the inherently conflictual nature of personal experience itself (see also Adler and Adler, 1987, 21–4). On the other hand, the investigative stance might also be underpinned by a structural critique of society. Such a critique would seek to dismantle the fronts and evasions by which powerful institutions hide their activities. While Douglas clearly does not exclude this last approach, the sites of his research, which include naturist beaches and massage parlours, suggest a concern that is more rhetorical than it is radical. There seems no basis, apart from opportunistic access, for choosing these particular settings rather than some others, or for asserting that a series of such studies will aggregate in some way to produce an overall picture of society.

Douglas (1978) has argued that professional ethics are primarily a device for professional aggrandizement. In the preface to *Investigative Social Research* he is openly scornful of ethical debate:

> one might expect that I would deal at length with the tortured moral arguments posed by the revelations in this book. I considered doing so, but the thought made me chuckle. In the end my mirth became uncontrollable and drowned out the considerations. (1976, xiv)

To the extent that he does discuss the ethics of investigative research, Douglas seems to adopt two positions. One is that, since deception is pervasive in social relations, researchers should not be denied ways of acting open to everyone else. The second is that the benefits which accrue from investigative research outweigh the damage caused. Bok (1984) has challenged Douglas's ethical insensitivity. First, she questions whether one can use the pervasiveness of deception as a basis for investigative social research. It may simply be erroneous to assert that people lie. Second, knowing that someone lies no more justifies lying than knowing that someone is a thief justifies stealing from that person. Third, Bok questions justifications for investigative social research in terms of the benefits produced by increasing knowledge. As she rather acidly comments, such defences 'may become more tempting the less justification their work seems to command on its own' (1984, 247). Furthermore, she argues that social scientists do not have the legitimacy to engage in investigative research. There are bodies – the media, law enforcement agencies, for example – which are better placed to do investigative work, are seen to have a legitimate role, and which, moreover, tend to do a better job than social scientists.

Douglas has undoubtedly added to the methodological repertoire. Used sparingly, many of the strategies he describes can usefully be deployed in difficult situations. It seems unwise, therefore, to dismiss the investigative approach out of hand. Yet nagging worries remain about the ethical implications of the investigative style and one is left with the feeling that the whole is rather less than the sum of the parts.

Radical research

Some writers have argued that research is powerfully shaped by the structured inequalities in society. As a consequence, the attention of researchers has been directed and channelled away from the powerful, whose interests are threatened by open scrutiny, and towards the powerless, who must bear the burden of social inquiry. These writers argue that researchers should cease to collude in this situation and should adapt their methods to reflect their political stance towards those being studied. On the one hand, conflict methodologies should be adopted to study the powerful. On the other, researchers should work in a collaborative way *with* the powerless in order to serve their interests.

Conflict methodology
As Robert Emerson notes, investigative social research and conflict methodology 'rest on similar adversarial premises, highlighting the inherent conflict between dominant institutions' control of information and researchers' needs to obtain data' (1981, 367–8). T.R. Young, who apparently coined the term (Christie, 1976), defines conflict methodology as 'comprising those techniques by which information is obtained from and introduced into systems under conditions of hostile contrast' (1971, 279). The term 'hostile contrast' apparently refers to situations in which powerful groups and organizations deliberately withhold or distort information which would serve the wider public interest. In what can probably be regarded as the manifesto for conflict methodology, Lehmann and Young (1974) argue that, by the 1960s, American sociology had reached paradigm crisis. Existing structural functionalist theory,

with its emphasis on consensus and system integration, could not easily accommodate evidence concerning the growing power of corporations, political malfeasance, the conflict over Civil Rights and the war in Vietnam. For Lehmann and Young, an alternative conflict paradigm, which recognized the ubiquity of social conflict and change, was emerging to overthrow functionalism. Theoretical change, however, also required methodological reorientation. Research based on survey research, opinion polling and attitude measurement provided a technocratic élite and the military indus-trial complex with instruments of surveillance and control. The conflict paradigm would only be complete, according to Lehmann and Young, when 'new technologies of research are invented and used by which to breach the barriers to quality information erected by a secretive administration, a conspiring oil industry, an ambitious war department, or a slick commercial organization' (1974, 21).

According to Lehmann and Young, the adversary principle which underpins the Anglo-Saxon legal system provides a basic model for the practice of conflict methodology. This principle assumes that the contending parties to a dispute are partisans whose accounts must be subjected to hostile scrutiny. Like other writers (e.g. Marx, 1984), Lehmann and Young (1974) point out that the courts provide a source of data for social scientists. Thus, researchers can become litigants, using lawsuits, injunctions and freedom of information legislation to secure data about the operation of large bureaucratic agencies and corporations. Lehmann and Young go beyond this, however, by extending the legal analogy to the possible organiz-ational role of the sociologist. Sociologists, in their view, can work alongside radical lawyers to provide various forms of advocacy. These might include 'class-based advocacy' to defend the rights of powerless groups, 'selective advocacy', challenging official decisions and practices, and 'organization advocacy' of the kind seen, for example, in civil rights organizations. Related to this, Lehmann and Young also argue that sociologists need to be involved in the development of radical strategies for community organization and mobilization. What they seem to envisage here is that the sociologist would provide information to community organizations in order to overcome imbalances in the provision of information, which tend to work in favour of powerful organizations.

Lehmann and Young point to two further sources of data which might be used by conflict methodologists. Again, like Marx (1984) and Moltoch and Lester (1974; 1975), they advocate close attention to incidents like environmental disasters or political scandals. In such events the hidden face of corporate and bureaucratic power and irresponsibility is revealed. Lehmann and Young also suggest that conflict methodologists use the kind of ethnomethodological 'demonstrations' proposed by Garfinkel (1967). These 'poke, probe, provoke and puncture normal situations of interaction to uncover the rules and rituals participants take for granted' (Lehmann and Young, 1974, 23).

There is some dispute about the character of conflict methodology. Some writers, like Christie (1976), regard conflict methodology as one element in a wider, political, epistemological and methodological critique of positivistic social research. Others (e.g. Lundman and McFarlane, 1976) see it as a more or less eclectic set of techniques distinguished by a revelatory goal, and an unwillingness to extend the principle of informed consent to powerful actors. Thus, Lundman and McFarlane question the extent to which conflict methodology can be tied to a particular theoretical position. While Lehmann and Young see it as an aspect of conflict theory, others sympathetic to conflict methodology have roots in diverse theoretical traditions including symbolic inter-actionism (Lundman and McFarlane, 1976, 509–10). Part of the confusion here may arise simply because conflict methodology was one strand in a developing anti-positivist critique which at the time was still relatively inchoate. This is perhaps most clearly seen in the conflict methodologists' championing of ethnomethodology. Drawing a parallel with certain kinds of political theatre, Gouldner (1970, 394) notes that ethnomethodological 'demonstrations' had an appeal to campus activists because of the challenge they posed to the 'way things are'. However, the ethnomethodological tradition soon left behind such 'theatre'. Particularly as represented by conversation analysis, ethnomethodology proved radical only in its principled indifference to politics.

Lundman and McFarlane (1976) have presented a series of objections to conflict methodology. First of all, in work of this kind a tension exists between research and advocacy. Indeed, it can be questioned how far the adversary principle in law provides an appropriate analogy for research.[2] The adversary principle assumes that the outcome is not prejudged, but is determined solely on the basis of the evidence. However, in many respects, conflict method-ologists prejudge the issue of whether powerful organizations have a malign influence on society. As Cassell has commented, 'Outrage as a research stance can be as blinding as unquestioning admiration' (1988, 102). Second, the necessity for 'appreciation' poses problems for conflict methodology. That is, it is often difficult to understand the attitudes and motivations of a particular group from the outside. As pointed out earlier, even with 'unloved' groups (Fielding, 1990), whose position is radically at odds with the researcher's own value premises, it may still be necessary to take on the difficult task of entering their world via a minimally non-adversarial stance (Cassell, 1988). Third, as will be seen shortly, Lehmann and Young's call for involvement in community activism echoes that made by a number of other writers of the period. Such activism may, however, undermine conflict methodologies where collaborative relations with the powerless take precedence over adversarial relations with the powerful. In addition, as Hessler et al. (1980) note, the longer term aims of the conflict methodologist may well diverge from those of the researched. Research participants, as a result, are capable of being treated in an instrumental way. A fourth difficulty pointed to by Lundman and McFarlane in their assessment of conflict methodology is that research in this tradition does not cumulate; systematic accumulation of knowledge about society takes second place to radical political action.

Lundman and McFarlane further suggest that conflict methodologists have a simplistic conception of power. Focusing primarily on the malfeasance of large-scale bureaucracies may ignore power that is located elsewhere or is exercised in not entirely obvious ways. Murray Wax (1980) notes that the targets of adversarial research are sometimes caricatured in ways which lead researchers to assume the need for an adversarial style when it may not be necessary. Wax also argues that superordinaton and subordination are relative. Those regarded as superordinates in a particular situation may in their turn be subordinated. Ignoring this fact may mean exposing lower level power relations, but not those at a higher level (see also Gouldner, 1973). Finally, Lundman and McFarlane note that debates about conflict methodology have gone on in academic journals. As a result, the products of conflict methodology have not found their way to wider publics. Redressing the information balance in favour of the powerless, they suggest, may require novel methods for disseminating the products of research based on the conflict model.

While the proposal to adopt a conflict methodology was of its time, how far it seized that time (to use a contemporaneous cliché) is open to question. The longer term impact of the conflict methodologists can be examined using citation counts for Young's initial article (1971) and Lehmann and Young's (1974) article taken from the *Social Science Citation Index*. Young's article received a total of 20 citations between 1971 and 1989. Lehmann and Young received the same number of citations between 1976 and 1989. Although this level of citation is respectable (Oromaner, 1977), citations to both articles had declined to zero within a decade. To assess how far the call to establish a new paradigm actually affected research practice, articles citing the Lehmann and Young article were examined. Conflict methodology does not seem, however, to have reshaped empirical research. One article which could not be traced and two ephemeral sources (one a letter, the other a book review) were excluded. Of the 17 articles remaining only two even made reference to empirical material. Discussion of conflict methodology, in other words, remained at a programmatic level. Looked at with the benefit of hindsight the proposal to establish a conflict methodology did not lead to a new paradigm.[3]

Although one can challenge the premises and the impact of conflict methodology, the question remains: how effective are the methods themselves? Starting from a rather different theoretical standpoint, Gary Marx (1984) has reviewed a number of techniques which help researchers circumvent the control of information by powerful others. For Marx, the ability to uncover hidden information in modern societies depends on a variety of complex organizational, technological and legislative processes. Social scientists, he suggests, need to adapt such processes to their own purposes.

According to Marx, hidden information is yielded up in four broad ways: through deception, coercion, volition or the operation of uncontrollable contingencies.[4] Deception includes not only covert research of the kind already discussed, but also what might be called 'research scams'. The parallel Marx draws here is with investigative journalism and police undercover operations where investigators take on assumed roles, for example, as bribe-takers, in order to uncover deviance or malpractice. Similar techniques have sometimes been used in social research to uncover discriminatory practices (see, e.g., Selltiz, 1955). Marx suggests that a variety of factors makes the use of deception problematic for social scientists. Some of these, including the obvious ethical difficulties, are well-known and have already been rehearsed. He also, however, contrasts covert research as it has traditionally been practised in the social sciences with the 'sting' operations conducted by law enforcement agencies. The former have typically been small-scale, of short duration and have used single investigators. The latter, on the other hand, often carry on over a lengthy period of time and may require extensive funding and personnel. Marx implies that resources of this kind have advantages in terms of the breadth and depth of the information they produce. In a one-person study, cross-observer data are not available for the purposes of validation. Where substantial resources are at hand, more complex deceptions can be mounted. This may in its turn increase the danger of entrapment, but if successful it typically yields massive levels of disclosure.

Coercion refers to what Marx (1984) terms 'institutionalized discovery practices', where individuals and organizations are compelled to provide information under the threat of legal sanction. Like Lehmann and Young, Marx suggests that researchers use such occasions by gathering data from investigative and legislative hearings and from court records. He also advises researchers to make more use of the information professional groups are often required to file on a routine basis; for example, registers of members' interests in legislative bodies. It is difficult to judge how representative the material produced through such discovery practices might be, and steps may have been taken to ensure that certain kinds of information did not enter the written record. The researcher inevitably in these situations is reliant on what information is made available and therefore takes a passive role. In order to use this kind of data effectively, the researcher must know what to look for. According to Marx, there are few ethical problems in using information provided by institutional discovery. The cost of obtaining data in this way is relatively low. In the United States, researchers based in 'an educational or noncommercial scientific institution whose purpose is scholarly or scientific research' are only charged standard fees for the duplication of documents produced under the Freedom of Information Act (Walter and Adler, 1991). However, although some social scientists have used the Freedom of Information Act (see, e.g., Pendakur, 1985, and Coleman and Seligman, 1988), relative to historians, they have been few in number (Relyea, 1989, 65).[5] (Indeed, it seems that most use of the Act is made by businesses seeking information on competitors [Birkinshaw, 1988; Relyea, 1989].)

In part what Marx has in mind when he refers to 'volition' are standard social research methods for eliciting potentially embarrassing or discrediting information: anonymous self-report methods and field research based on overt methods. He also suggests, however, that 'whistleblowing' can provide a source of data. Whistleblowers draw attention to dangers or abuses which exist within the organization for which they work. Marx also mentions what he refers to as 'give aways'. Here someone who discloses information does not recognize its import when used on its own or in conjunction with other information. Marx suggests that whistleblowing is becoming increasingly common. At least in the United States, this has been encouraged by technical developments like confidential hotlines and through legal changes which, in areas like the misuse of toxic substances, encourage and protect whistleblowers. The sources of whistleblowing behaviour sometimes lie, according to Marx, in the disjunction between personal idealism and the realities of organization life, but they may also emerge from personal spite or vindictiveness. These are factors which need to be taken into account when assessing the quality of the data drawn from whistle-blowing incidents. An obvious difficulty with whistleblowing as a data source is that it is the whistleblower who determines what information is made available.

Uncontrollable contingencies are accidents or mistakes which reveal underlying social patterns. Marx distinguishes two categories: traces and mishaps. Traces are residues and remnants of the kind described by Webb et al. (1966; 1981), but which point in this case to the hidden or the deviant. Mishaps are inadvertent happenings which bring to light undisclosed deviance. Thus, technological accidents, like oil spills, and political scandals, such as Watergate, provide strategic research sites which allow researchers to reveal those activities of organizations and élites normally hidden from public view. Echoing a point made by the conflict methodologists, Marx notes that mishaps shatter the façade of normality and provide an ironic counterpoint to official ideologies by revealing the under-life (Goffman, 1961) of institutions and personal lifestyles.

Marx points out that uncontrolled contingencies, 'Strictly speaking, . . . offer an opportunity rather than a strategy, for data collection' (1984, 86). In other words, uncontrolled contingencies are probably more useful for discovering the existence of data than for systematically exploiting it. Since much of the material associated with uncontrolled contingencies appears in the public domain, there are few ethical issues raised by its use. It is also, relatively speaking, a low-cost method. However, relying on accidents and scandals as a source of data suggests that the role of the social scientist is an essentially reactive one. Research agendas thus become shaped by events rather than by a systematic logic, and research studies do not cumulate (Lundman and McFarlane, 1976).

Collaborative research
There is a sense in which until comparatively recently the cultural and socio-economic margins of Western societies provided researchers with a series of more or less 'exotic' locales, much as earlier the imperial empires or their remnants served anthropologists (Hughes, 1976). While this was undoubtedly convenient for the researcher, it eventually began to have a cost. Marginal groups came to feel increasingly threatened by the attentions of researchers. As a result, by the late 1970s in the United States, and rather later in Britain, resentment began to close deprived or minority communities to outside researchers. The concerns and complaints of minority communities concerning research are

remarkably consistent across a range of groups and research situations. Researchers are often seen as predators (Maynard, 1974) or as sojourners (Trimble, 1977). Research, in other words, serves as a vehicle for status, income or professional advancement which is denied to those studied. Blauner and Wellman (1982) note, for example, that it is not unknown for residents in some ghetto areas of the United States to complain wryly that they have put dozens of students through graduate school. Alternatively, researchers come, take what they can get out of a community and they, or the results of their research, are never seen again. In this situation, it is easy for minority communities to feel that there is nothing in the research situation for them. As Joan Moore, speaking about research on Mexican-Americans, puts it, 'As with many other groups, the disinterested pursuit of science is not a particularly meaningful goal to most Mexican-Americans. Some of our predecessors made it even less meaningful' (1967, 232).

Such concerns have produced calls for a collaborative or partici-patory research style (Blauner and Wellman, 1982; Vargus, 1971; Kelman, 1972; Ben-Tovim et al., 1986). (Such calls have also been a feature of feminist writing on methodology, although here the focus has primarily been on the interview situation [see, e.g., Oakley, 1981; Finch, 1984].) Hessler and his colleagues, for example, describe the development a 'research commune' as a way of empowering people in the community which they studied (Hessler and New, 1972; Hessler et al., 1980). In a similar way, Schensul (1980), describing his work on a number of community mental health projects, has advocated the use of 'Community Review Boards', which seem to serve a similar function. Researchers work closely with community activists and attempt to 'facilitate indigen-ous social action programs by supplying data and results which could make significant contributions to the effectiveness of [resi-dents'] efforts' (Schensul, 1980, 313). The community itself helps to structure the research and develop research questions, and community residents themselves can be trained in research skills. This gives the community a continuing capacity to carry out its own research and can provide jobs not otherwise available (Blauner and Wellman, 1982).

On a practical level there are presumably some situations in which it will be difficult to adopt a collaborative research style. The approach seems to depend on the existence of a clear and function-ing community structure. In some cases, however, this may simply not exist (Beck, 1970). More widely, the collaborative approach is open to attack from opposing ends of the spectrum. Commenting on Hessler and New's attempts to establish a research commune,

Gladwin (1972) argues, for example, that what they have done is not radical enough. Offering social science expertise in return for access and involvement does not address wider issues of exploitation. Indeed, it directs attention away from 'the real issues of differential power and access, and how to redress the balance' (1972, 453). James Walsh (1972) argues, on the other hand, that accepting the local community's definition of what should be researched tends to produce atheoretical research in which crucial variables are inevitably overlooked. Goudy and Richards (1973) have also been sceptical of collaborative research. While they agree that researchers may have exploited those they study by ignoring their *social* needs, they argue that sociologists have also been insensitive to the *political* needs of those in disadvantaged communities. As a result they have 'overresponded' to indigenous definitions of research problems. One source of this overresponse, according to Goudy and Richards, has been the assumption of consensus at the local level. However, this may in fact hide a plurality of competing interest groups. Such groups frequently present their interests and objectives as co-extensive with those of the community as a whole. To the extent that some groups may be better able to do this than others they may hi-jack the research for their own purposes by defining the goals of research, intervening in the data-gathering process or controlling the publication or dissemination of research findings. Goudy and Richards contend that where this happens it is the researcher rather than the local community who is exploited.

Jones (1980) has taken a similar position based on his experiences of working with a community action organization in an inner-city area. In the course of his research he charted a growing polarization between the board of directors who controlled the organization and its membership. Although he had initially gained access in part because board members found his political views acceptable, the board attempted to suppress his report. Jones notes that researchers have sometimes drawn too sharp a contrast between disadvantaged groups and the wider society. As a result they have failed to recognize the existence of local internal hierarchies and conflicts. Jones argues that in research *with* disadvantaged groups the issue is 'not one of taking the side of the underdog, but of taking sides without reflection' (1980, 103). Without an attempt to demystify the local, as well as the wider, political context, one may have difficulty in identifying the underdog. Even then, to be on the side of the local population does not necessitate complete agreement with them. Indeed political commitment may require the taking of potentially unpopular positions which transcend local political rivalries.

Many of the issues raised by urban anthropologists in the 1970s re-emerged in the 1980s with the onset of the AIDS crisis. An inevitably fatal disease with a long period of latency, and transmitted through 'sensitive and secretive' activities including sexual behaviour and intravenous drug use, AIDS has 'explosive epidemic characteristics' (Bowser and Sieber, 1992). The nature of the disease demanded a timely and effective response from social, psychological, biological and clinical researchers. AIDS research, however, inevitably raised complex ethical, political, operational and technical issues. Researchers had to seek participation for their studies from members of marginalized, stigmatized and vulnerable groups, though one of these groups, the gay community, was politically aware and relatively well-organized. In a field where, at first, very little was known and research activity was intense, research could impose considerable, sometimes duplicative, burdens on those who were already desperately ill (Zich and Temoshok, 1986). At the same time, the controversy which erupted around clinical trials of the drug AZT suggested that existing procedures for ensuring the conduct of ethically sound research were inadequate (Melton et al., 1988).

In coping with the dilemmas posed by research on AIDS, researchers have turned to community consultation. The purpose of such consultation, according to Melton et al., is 'to enlist potential participants as partners in solving the difficult dilemmas posed in sensitive research' (1988, 576). Such consultation increases procedural justice by giving potential research participants a degree of control over their involvement in the research. In so doing it is likely also to enhance perceptions of distributive justice. In other words, after consultation, the potential risks and benefits of the research are more likely to be seen as having been fairly apportioned. Consulting the community also provides a means by which community members can voice their worries and concerns, and communicates to them that the researcher has regard for them as persons (Melton et al., 1988; Bowser and Sieber, 1992).

AIDS researchers have used a variety of strategies for establishing collaborative research relations with the communities they study. These range from the adaptation of focus group methodology for collaborative ends (Bowser and Sieber, 1992; M. Singer, 1992) to the establishment of community-based ethical review boards (V. Merton, 1990). Focus groups provide a relatively effective, low-cost and rapid method for developing insights into community concerns (M. Singer, 1992; on focus group methodology more generally, see Krueger, 1988). They also can be used in a manner which treats research participants as 'consultants' rather than as 'respondents' (Bowser and Sieber, 1992). As a result, Bowser and

Sieber argue, the method is 'especially useful in engaging difficult to access, potentially mistrustful and alienated subjects'.

Vanessa Merton (1990) has pointed to the efficacy of a community-based model for evaluating clinical trials of new drugs and therapies for the treatment of AIDS. A detailed account of the ethical issues surrounding such trials is beyond the scope of the present discussion. As Melton et al. point out, however, trials of this kind illustrate some of the potential problems involved in community consultation. Some of these problems are of a kind previously discussed, and relate to the availability, representativeness and mandate of local groups. Particularly with deviant or marginal groups, it may be difficult to identify a relevant constituency for consultation, or groups that do exist in the potential research setting may be unrepresentative or factionalized. In these situations, *ad hoc* or surrogate groups of various kinds may have to be established (Melton et al., 1988).

Community consultation provides a means by which potential research participants can be involved in making judgements for themselves about the potential risks and benefits involved in a proposed research project. Making such decisions in groups, however, has hidden dangers. Processes common to group deliberations of any kind may help to diminish rather than enhance protection for research participants. As Melton et al. (1988) point out, social-psychological research on the so-called 'risky shift' phenomenon suggests that often groups are more ready to countenance risks than are individuals (for a brief review of 'risky shift', see M. Douglas, 1985, 66–7). Community consultation may therefore lead to an underestimation of the risks potentially faced by research participants.

To make a further, similar, point, group members asked to reach a decision often experience pressure towards consensus and unanimity. Such pressures can be particularly strong, Melton et al. (1988) argue, in situations like the AIDS epidemic where group members are under stress and are anxious to find a rapid solution to the problems which affect them. As a result, researchers' proposals for research can be subject to insufficient critical scrutiny. Where situations of this kind occur researchers might have to adopt devices such as bringing in group leaders, experts or advocates from outside the local community, or they may need to institutionalize a devil's advocate role in some way. They also suggest that community consultation should be separated in time from attempts to obtain individual informed consent, to prevent group pressure from pre-empting individual decisions to participate.

Community consultation may reveal a conflict of interests

between the needs of potential research participants and those of the wider community. For example, rights to privacy and confidentiality, especially in relation to sensitive issues like sexual behaviour, may need to be weighed against a wider public interest in the reporting and surveillance of infectious disease (Melton and Gray, 1988). Melton et al. (1988) argue that researchers ultimately have responsibility for resolving such issues, even at the cost, sometimes, of abandoning the proposed research. A final difficulty with community consultation is that, paradoxically, it can encourage a degree of ethical insensitivity on the part of the researcher. By seeming to shift the locus of responsibility for ethical decision-making on to the community, the consultation process may encourage researchers to disregard their responsibilities as individuals.

A further, different, style of collaborative research has been suggested by Fielding (1990). According to Fielding, researchers operating in sensitive contexts should consider adopting an 'intercalary role'. The term 'intercalary role' was first used by Barnes (1963). What Barnes had in mind was a situation in which the fieldworker takes on an agreed neutral role between two contending parties, perhaps acting as an honest broker between them. For Fielding, the intercalary role is rather more a reflexive device in which researcher and researched simultaneously inquire into the group's culture and educate one another with respect to it. The field researcher, in taking an intercalary role, is neither the passive recipient of informant accounts nor the sceptical investigator typical of investigative research. Instead, Fielding suggests, fieldworker and study participants co-produce fieldwork. Adopting such a role, Fielding was able to encourage police officers to explore the implicit and contradictory understandings – from both an inside and an outside perspective – which surrounded their use of force in subduing suspects. In the case of sensitive topics, the intercalary role is particularly valuable, in Fielding's opinion, because it presents an opportunity to understand the issue of sensitivity from the point of view of the study participants, rather than simply from the perspective of the researcher. It is not clear, however, what the effects of an intercalary role are for those being studied, or for third parties. Does the researcher in effect become a kind of sociological conscience, or should the intercalary role have the kind of mediational character originally envisaged by Barnes?

Conclusion

Cassell (1988) has observed that issues of motive, method and morality are inextricably intertwined in field research. Entering and understanding social and cultural worlds other methodologies cannot reach may make field research a method of choice. Researchers who use field methods, however, must face the contradictions which inhere in the commitment to naturalistic understanding. The appreciative stance implicit in naturalism sits uneasily alongside the indignation which fuels the investigative paradigm and conflict research. A method which relies on intensive contact and the development of an ongoing personal relationship between researcher and researched cannot easily accommodate the deception at the heart of covert research. The desire to understand the perspective of the deviant groups and to work alongside the disadvantaged can lapse into a romanticized identification with the underdog (Gouldner, 1968). None of these contradictions is easy to resolve.

Notes

1. The distinction between overt and covert research may at times be relative. Those studied may sometimes forget that a researcher is present, and it is not always possible to apprise people of the research role (Thorne, 1983).

2. The call for researchers to make more use of data generated by the legal process has one ironic feature. In the United States the involvement of researchers in the courts has grown dramatically in recent years. However, rather than researchers using the law, the law has used researchers as expert witnesses (see, e.g., Rosen, 1977; R.M. Lee, 1989). Sociologists in the United States have been involved in litigation surrounding a number of controversial racial issues, such as those to do with school desegregation, racial imbalances in the use of the death penalty, or involving the custody of mixed race children. Anthropologists have testified extensively in cases involving American Indians, including disputes over aboriginal land titles, the identification of Indian tribes and the nature of treaties. Despite this involvement accounts by social scientists who have testified as expert witnesses do not suggest a use of the courts in the manner suggested by Lehmann and Young. On the contrary, much sociological writing in this area laments that 'incompatibilities between the non-adversarial academic sphere and the adversarial legal sphere inevitably create conflict for scholar-expert witnesses' (Kalmuss, 1981, 214) .

3. Unlike other aspects of the radical critique which crossed the Atlantic, conflict methodology seems not to have made much impact on British sociology. This may have been because of the rather fugitive character of some of the writing (Christie, 1976), and because much of the controversy over the use of conflict methodology was fought out at an *organizational* level in the American Sociological Association. It may also be that some of the American scholars who were influential in Britain in the 1970s, like C. Wright Mills and Howard Becker, can be regarded in a number of respects as methodological conservatives.

4. Although Marx points in each case to the underlying social processes involved, the terms he uses are slightly too broad to be helpful. The term 'coercion', for instance, leaves open the question of who is coercing whom. Moreover, the contingencies of which Marx speaks do not need to be uncontrollable for disclosure to take place. They need only to be *uncontrolled*. It is preferable, therefore, to speak

instead of unwitting disclosure, enforced disclosure, volunteered disclosure and uncontrolled contingencies.

5. Interestingly, one use of the FOIA has been to uncover evidence of FBI surveillance of sociologists beginning in the 1930s and continuing into the period of the Cold War (Keen, 1992).

9

Handling Sensitive Data

Attention paid to confidentiality helps to legitimate the research process (see Kelman, 1972). It convinces potential respondents that researchers are to be trusted, and presumably encourages accurate reporting. Indeed, even the perception that a researcher has violated the confidentiality of research participants can have negative consequences for the research (Zich and Temoshok, 1986). Most researchers probably rely on good housekeeping and physical security to protect against the 'leakage' of confidential information in their possession. However, the identity of research participants can sometimes be deduced from published material if insufficient care is taken to preserve confidentiality. Neither is it unknown for data to be examined surreptitiously by those who regard themselves as having an interest in it. Broadhead (1984, 117) discovered, for example, while acting as a consultant for a mental health centre, that the data he had been collecting was being read clandestinely by the centre's administrators (see also A.H. Barton, 1983). Robust techniques for preserving confidentiality are, therefore, indispensable to research on sensitive topics. They help to protect against the unexpected, as when data are lost, compromised or subject to legal intervention. While instances where confidentiality is breached are probably rare, researchers in recent years have also increasingly had to deal with attempts by the courts to compel researchers to disclose data deemed relevant to the litigation process. This chapter looks in the first instance at some of the issues raised by legal threats to data. It then goes on to discuss ways in which researchers can preserve the confidentiality of both quantitative and qualitative data.

Legal threats to data

Legal intervention in the research process has largely been a problem for researchers in the United States.[1] Subpoenas have been served there on researchers in a number of disciplines. Most often, the recipients have been sociologists, but subpoenas have also been received by economists, political scientists, social policy researchers and sex researchers (Knerr, 1982, 193–5). One example of such a case is that involving Mario Brajuha (Brajuha and Hallowell, 1986).

As a graduate student, Brajuha undertook a participant observation study of work processes in the restaurant which employed him as a waiter. Such a study seems hardly to be a 'sensitive' one. However, when the restaurant was destroyed, possibly by arson, Brajuha was served with a subpoena requiring him to hand over his fieldnotes. In addition to the Brajuha case it is possible to identify at least 13 earlier cases in the United States (Knerr, 1982) in which subpoenas have been served on researchers. Among the tactics apparently used by prosecutors are 'creeping subpoenas', where compliance with one subpoena brings forth another seeking more information, and so on (Kershaw and Small, 1972; see also Nejelski and Finsterbusch, 1973). It also seems that prosecutors frequently seek to obtain *all* of the researcher's materials, giving rise to the suspicion that researchers might be seen as appropriate for 'fishing expeditions'. In the Brajuha case, the researcher was also coerced to do some investigative work for detectives on the case. (Some further instances of pressures to disclose data falling short of a subpoena are cited in Bond, 1978.)

Although Knerr provides only a basic outline of each case, what is striking about them is their heterogeneity. Perhaps the most celebrated is the litigation which surrounded the 'Pentagon Papers'. A researcher, Samuel Popkin, was required by a grand jury to reveal the sources of confidential information he had obtained during research undertaken at the time when confidential documents relating to the Vietnam war were being leaked. Popkin refused and was briefly imprisoned (Boruch and Cecil, 1979). Other cases where researchers have been called to testify involve allegations of police brutality (Van Maanen, 1983), juvenile crime, drug abuse (Yablonsky, 1968) and murder. As the Brajuha case makes clear, however, legal difficulties can arise, even in a relatively innocuous study. Researchers studying corporate decision-making processes have been subpoenaed to disclose research materials in a civil case against the public utility company they had been studying (Knerr, 1982).

As far as one can judge, the source of subpoenas has been fairly evenly balanced between investigative committees of various sorts, local prosecutors and litigants. Taking the 13 cases described by Knerr together with the Brajuha case, the outcomes of cases in which subpoenas have been served on social researchers are shown in Table 9.1. (The table refers to cases in which subpoenas were issued and not to individual researchers served with them.)

In a majority of cases the proceedings were terminated or legal pressure ceased and the issue was not pressed to a final determination. Subpoenas were quashed in two cases. In one case, coded as

Table 9.1   *Outcome of subpoenas*

Outcome	No. of cases
Cessation of legal pressure	1
Proceedings terminated	4
Subpoena quashed	2
Researcher took Fifth Amendment	1
Files disclosed/researcher testified	3
Researcher imprisoned	2
Other	1
Total	14

Sources: Yablonsky, 1968; Knerr, 1982; Brajuha and Hallowell, 1986

'other' in the table, the sponsors of a negative income tax experiment were ordered to compensate the state for instances where participants in the study were illegally claiming welfare benefits while receiving support from the experiment. A researcher in one case took the Fifth Amendment when asked about a defendant's use of illegal drugs (Yablonsky, 1968). In three cases the requested materials were turned over or the researcher testified, while in a further two cases, researchers were imprisoned.

Knerr (1982) has usefully reviewed the legal protections available in the United States to researchers and their data. He notes that the law recognizes a 'testimonial privilege' which exists in the case of certain relationships. In other words, individuals standing in a particular relation to one another – the most common are those between husband and wife and between lawyer and client – are not required to divulge what has passed between them. In some fairly limited instances, according to Knerr, testimonial privilege may be extended to the relationship between a researcher and a respondent or informant who has supplied information under a guarantee of confidentiality. There are, for example, a variety of 'shield' laws at state level which might permit researchers to claim testimonial privilege, though scarcely any have been fully tested in the courts.[2] Researchers studying drug abuse are protected in a relatively large number of states from being forced to disclose the identity of research participants. In rather fewer states those involved in psychological research or in studies of mental health are also protected. In some states, laws to protect journalistic sources from disclosure might also be applicable to researchers.

At least one attempt has so far been made in a civil case in the United Kingdom to compel the disclosure to the courts of data held by a social scientist. The matter was not, however, pressed to a final conclusion.[3] There have also apparently been some instances of interest by the security services in the data of researchers looking at repressive aspects of the state apparatus (P. Cohen, 1979). In these cases data have not been subpoenaed, but seemingly examined surreptitiously. In criminal cases in the United Kingdom research materials of the kind collected by social scientists fall under the scope of the Police and Criminal Evidence Act, 1984. (For a useful summary and analysis of the Act, see Hargreaves and Levenson, 1985, 39–42. See also J. Williams, 1985, and, for a brief comment on the Act by the then President of the British Sociological Association, Brown, 1984.) Under the Act, police officers seeking evidence in connection with a 'serious arrestable offence' can gain access to 'personal records' held in confidence. If an assurance of complete anonymity has been given, the material is regarded as 'special procedure material'. To obtain such material, the police must apply to a circuit judge for a 'production order' or warrant. For the order to be granted the judge must be satisfied that the material sought is likely to be both of 'substantial value' to the investigation and 'relevant' in the sense of being potentially admissible in court.

Medical and counselling records, and, under some circumstances, 'journalistic material' which is held subject to an undertaking to hold it in confidence, are protected from seizure by the police (Robertson and Nicol, 1984, 127). Although the matter has never been put to the test, it seems unlikely that this exclusion could be extended to material collected by social scientists.[4] The experience of journalists and social workers in Britain also suggests that there are other circumstances where researchers would be potentially vulnerable to legal demands to reveal sources. In Britain, as Pearce (1988, 10–11) points out, the House of Lords has ruled that a promise of confidentiality does not of itself make information privileged. Private promises of confidentiality need to be weighed against the public interest. Journalists in Britain who have refused to disclose their sources have on occasion been heavily fined (Tan, 1988).

A number of researchers in the United States have attempted to resist subpoenas by invoking the First Amendment of the US Constitution which protects the free flow of information to the public (Knerr, 1982, 202; Nejelski and Finsterbusch, 1973). According to Knerr, First Amendment provisions have been successfully used against subpoenas by journalists and researchers involved in *civil* litigation. The situation in *criminal* cases is, however, quite different. In a number of cases, including the Pentagon Papers trial and cases involving journalists, First Amendment protections have not been supported in criminal cases. Although the First Amendment cannot be used to protect research data, Knerr (1982) points out that there are some limited protections available in a variety of Federal statutes. Researchers affiliated to the Bureau of the Census and the Social Security Administration are protected by statutes relating to the confidentiality of Census and Social Security records. Knerr also lists a number of Federal statutes which authorize researchers to protect the privacy of research subjects and protect data from forced disclosure. The degree of privilege allowed to researchers is, however, limited to those involved in certain kinds of research, relating mainly to drug abuse, mental health and law enforcement. Moreover, the provisions vary somewhat depending on the statute, and depend in some cases on administrative discretion (see also Reynolds, 1982, 119–20). In some instances, protection is only afforded to researchers holding grants or contracts from a particular agency.

A number of writers have expressed reservations about relying on shield laws. One argument is that, given the relatively small number of cases, the problem is actually an exaggerated one (see, e.g., Pattullo, 1978). Sagarin and Moneymaker (1979) have pointed to a potential danger in a blanket immunity for social scientists. Their point is a simple one. There may be occasions when a social scientist becomes privy to information about a serious crime in which harm will be caused to an innocent victim. A claim to protect confidentiality in this situation would be tantamount, in their view, to aiding and abetting the crime, something that would be morally, legally and professionally dubious. Van Maanen (1983) takes a slightly different position, arguing that the issues involved are moral rather than legal. Field researchers especially often discover much about deviance that those within a research setting would rather keep hidden. Even where no explicit guarantee of confidentiality is given, the researcher makes a 'behavioural bargain' with the researched by choosing not to avoid guilty knowledge. However, because the issue is a moral rather than a legal one, Van Maanen concedes that the extent of one's complicity need not be absolute. It is also bound partly by the nature of the relationship to those within the setting, and partly by the nature of the offence. Thus, although Van Maanen would not testify about his observation of the beating of a suspect in police custody, he was less sure that he could, morally, have withheld co-operation had the man been killed.

Some writers have argued that attempts to obtain legal protection for research data are evidence of the extent to which social researchers have become bureaucratically incorporated (J. D.

Douglas, 1978; Klockars, 1978; Pattullo, 1978). According to Jack Douglas the situation is no different from that faced by anyone threatened by the power of large scale bureaucracy. Rather than accepting that power the researcher faced with a subpoena should resist by the most forceful means possible. Or, as he puts it (1978, 158), 'let me suggest two steps. First, tell them – 'Nuts!' If that doesn't stop them – Fight like hell!' This is to underestimate, however, the personal costs which researchers face when they decide to fight a subpoena, and the extent to which grants of confidentiality do provide some protection from those costs.

Brajuha and Hallowell (1986) have graphically described some of the costs of being involved in litigation, and the impact legal intrusion can have on fieldwork roles. They point out that litigation is 'greedy'. It is time-consuming and expensive, and it engulfs personal and professional life. In Brajuha's case, relations with family, friends and academic colleagues were all pushed to breaking point. The case drained the Brajuhas' financial resources, putting a strain on family relationships. Friends and colleagues sometimes came to resent demands made on them for emotional and social support; demands which, when they were not met, induced a downward spiral of alienation and distrust between Brajuha and those around him. Further pressures arose, too, when it became clear that criminal elements were interested in what the fieldnotes might contain. Fearful for his physical safety, Brajuha had to hide his fieldnotes, while threatening to turn them over to the District Attorney if anything happened to him. In addition, not only did the case disrupt the research in terms of the demands it made on time and emotional resources, but also Brajuha had extreme difficulty in following his original research design. Because of his prior experience as a restaurant worker, Brajuha had been trusted by the co-workers he studied, and had gained a substantial degree of rapport with them. After the fire his role in the research setting changed considerably when, for a variety of reasons, formerly helpful informants ceased to co-operate with him.

There is some evidence that the availability of legal protection from subpoena does, in fact, reduce the personal and social costs to researchers of legal or judicial interest in their data. Nelson and Hedrick (1983) carried out a small survey of researchers who had received grants of confidentiality from the US Drug Enforcement Administration. A number of the researchers sampled reported attempts by law enforcement officials to obtain confidential information. In almost all cases, however, these attempts were abandoned once the grant of confidentiality became known. Grants of confidentiality seem to have allowed research to have been under-taken which might not have been otherwise. A quarter of all respondents said they would not have carried out the research if the grant of confidentiality had not been available (Nelson and Hedrick, 1983, Table 11.1, 226). In addition, research gatekeepers were more willing to co-operate when informed of the grant of confidentiality. Researchers who worked with populations facing high risk from disclosure, for example, drug dealers, were most likely to find the grant of confidentiality useful. At the same time, despite the grant, close to 90 per cent of respondents took additional precautions to protect the confidentiality of their materials, mostly by keeping identifiers separate from the data. Two respondents kept the master lists of respondent identifiers in another country to forestall the possibility of their being subpoenaed. On the negative side, Nelson and Hedrick record that knowledge of the process of obtaining grants was not well-known. Moreover, researchers seemed to exaggerate the protection offered to them. There are grounds for thinking that the scope of the grant is limited only to identifying information, and that other records associated with a research project could still be subpoenaed (Nelson and Hedrick, 1983, 221–2).

It can be argued that there are good reasons for complying with a subpoena. Social scientists seem generally to subscribe to a utili-tarian calculus which places a special premium on society's right to knowledge. There are times, however, when this right must be set beside the general good of upholding the law. In addition, the moral impetus to protect subjects might sometimes have to be weighed against the possibility of harm to a third party. However, as Garber (1979) points out, if researchers give guarantees of confidentiality they have to be prepared to deliver on their promises. A final option, therefore, is to refuse to hand over data and accept the consequences. Not to hand over data may bring with it the possibility of prison. No doubt some inveterate participant observers might be able to turn the experience of incarceration to good use, but the experience is likely to be an unpleasant one for all that. The most obvious lesson for those who fear legal intrusion into their research is to be rigorous and scrupulous about stripping identifying material from their data, particularly where their research relates to a 'sensitive' topic. Some researchers may wish to set the time and energy required to do this against the likely sensitivity of their data, although Mario Brajuha's experience remains a powerful caution against assuming that one's data must inevitably be innocuous.

Techniques for preserving the confidentiality of research data

By the late 1970s researchers faced pressures from three sources over privacy and the confidentiality of data – public concern about the ability of computers to hold and process personal information (Cope, 1979), the threat in some countries of forced disclosure to the courts or law enforcement agencies (Boruch and Cecil, 1979), and the urgings of national data protection authorities (Flaherty, 1979). As Caplan (1982) has noted, one consequence of these concerns was to fuel technical innovation in the form of imaginative methodological advances. As a result, in a number of countries (see, e.g., Boruch and Cecil, 1979; Campbell et al., 1977; Dalenius and Klevmarken, 1974; Newman, 1979), attempts have been made to develop technical means which would allow, at one and the same time, the 'maximization of research opportunity and minimization of privacy risks' (Caplan, 1982, 323). Detailed accounts of a range of strategies for preserving the confidentiality of research data can be found in Boruch and Cecil (1979; see also Boruch, 1979; Campbell et al., 1977). The various methods will be sketched here only in broad outline. In fact, the risk that confidentiality will be breached in research is rather low; the threat of disclosure posed by research has frequently been exaggerated, or based on rumour and misunderstanding (Cope, 1979; Boruch and Cecil, 1979, chap. 3).

One obvious solution to the problems of confidentiality is to obtain data which are anonymous at the point of collection or which are made so soon afterwards (Boruch and Cecil, 1979, chap. 4). To this end, data can be collected by means of anonymous self-completion questionnaires. In other situations, identifiers can be removed and destroyed at the completion of data collection.[5] A further possibility is to use an intermediary to administer questionnaires in the absence of the researcher and/or forward the responses obtained. As an earlier chapter made clear it is also possible to use a range of 'dejeopardizing techniques', such as randomized response, in which information on sensitive topics can be collected in ways which do not allow responses to be tied to specific identifiable individuals.

There are a number of situations in which these strategies are unhelpful. Special problems arise when, not just data, but the identity of research participants is in itself sensitive information; an example might be the identity of respondents in a study of psychiatric patients. In longitudinal studies disidentification is self-defeating. Tracking respondents obviously requires knowledge of who has appeared on a previous wave of interviewing. Similar problems may arise in a variety of other situations: where researchers use multiple methods or record linkage techniques, where there is a need to re-interview respondents to ensure quality control, or in situations where funding agencies build auditing procedures into their evaluations of research. In other cases, particularly where data are made available for secondary analysis or in the production of published statistical tables, simply disidentifying responses is insufficient. In these situations there may be a problem of 'deductive disclosure' (Boruch and Cecil, 1979); that is, users of the data may be able to infer the identity of an individual from some particular and distinctive combination of attributes.

Where it is necessary to disguise the fact that particular individuals are members of a sample, coded sample lists can be used. (For an example, see Barker, 1984, 262.) In addition, Boruch and Cecil (1979, 122) suggest that if there is a fear that a list might be stolen, two strategies can be used to make life difficult for the person who has obtained it. One is to pad the list with false names, thus adding to the burden of whoever might attempt to use it illicitly. The other is to use trace identifiers. The names of associates can be included, for example, in the hope that they may be able to give warning if signs appear that the list has been misappropriated.

In longitudinal research, aliases and/or list brokers can be employed to protect confidentiality. The use of aliases is self-explanatory. Respondents are given, or give themselves, a false name or numerical designation. Aliases can be generated by computer or from packs of cards containing arbitrary names or numbers. Respondents can also be presented with an algorithm for calculating identification numbers based on information likely to be known only to them, say the birth date of a close relative. Since aliases need to be used consistently, there must be some assurance that they will be remembered by respondents. Each alias must also be unique to only one individual. Boruch and Cecil (1979) have suggested that the difficulty of ensuring both uniqueness and recall may limit the use of aliases to relatively small samples and to research which, despite its longitudinal character, covers only a relatively short period of time. More recently, however, Kearney et al. (1984) have suggested that self-generated aliases can be used effectively. In their study they asked respondents to generate an identification code containing seven elements: the respondent's middle initial, the first letter of each parent's name, codes based on the respondent's sex, birth month, racial origin and number of siblings. Data were collected again after a month, and then again after a year. At first sight the results were disappointing. After one month only two-thirds of the codes matched exactly, while after a year the proportion of matched cases was only 46 per cent. Kearney et al. found, however, that when they included codes in which only one out of the seven elements was different, the number of matches rose to 92 per cent over one month and 78 per cent over a year.

Aliases, of course, need to be decipherable so that respondents can be re-contacted on subsequent waves of interviewing. Sometimes it will be sufficient simply to keep the key to the aliases in a separate and secure place. In situations of extreme sensitivity or where there is a possibility of external threat to the data, say from a subpoena, one might go further than this. The purpose of a list broker is to provide, through the medium of a third party, ways of managing data and identifiers so that the two are insulated from one another. Boruch and Cecil (1979, 106–12) provide specific details of a variety of means by which list brokers can be used, ranging from the simple to the very complex. For present purposes, an example of one of the more commonly used procedures, known as the 'link file' system, is probably sufficient. (See Figure 9.1.)

The link file system appears to have been discovered independently by a number of researchers (Manniche and Hayes, 1957; Steinberg, 1970; Astin and Boruch, 1970). Data from the first wave of a longitudinal survey are collected in the normal way with the information from each respondent being identifiable. Three files are then prepared. The first file contains material on each respondent but is identified only by an arbitrary code number, the actual identifiers having been stripped from the data. The second file contains a list of respondents. Associated with each entry on this list is a second arbitrary code number different from that attached to the data file. A third file contains the information necessary to link the arbitrary data identifiers on the first file with the arbitrary respondent identifiers on the second file. This third file is not retained by the researcher but is kept by a broker. At the appropriate time the researcher then collects the next wave of data. Again, identifiers are stripped off and replaced by the arbitrary respondent codes. The data are sent to the broker, who matches the arbitrary respondent identifiers with the arbitrary data identifiers and returns the data file with the arbitrary data identifiers attached. The Wave 1 and Wave 2 data sets are then merged using the arbitrary data identifiers. Subsequent waves of data can also be collected using the same basic procedures.

Depending on the circumstances, the use made of list brokers can be made more complicated in order to enhance confidentiality. In some cases the list broker may have an extra-jurisdictional location. For example, Astin and Boruch's (1970) study of student activists in the United States took place during a time in which there was

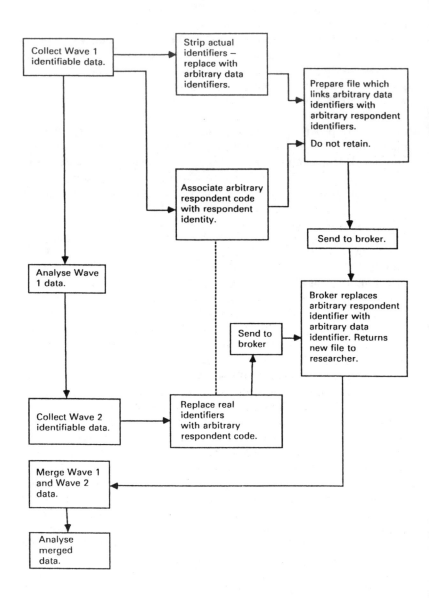

Figure 9.1   *Flow chart of link file system*

considerable suspicion of official information-gathering and surveillance. Accordingly, the list broker for the study was based in Canada to avoid the possibility of a subpoena being issued for the data.[6] A further variant of the link file system is also conceivable in which more than one outside agency is used, each separately generating only one part of the respondent alias. (For more detail, see Boruch and Cecil, 1979, 110–12.)

Deductive disclosure

Under some circumstances it might be possible to deduce the identity of individuals from published tables or from data made available for secondary analysis. (To state this as a possibility is not, of course, to imply that it has happened.) To forestall the possibility of deductive disclosure, raw data have sometimes been retained by the originator, or secondary analysis has been carried out only in-house. Census microdata (i.e. anonymized data on a sample of individuals, households or families) have only recently been released for secondary analysis in Britain. Previously such data had been held back because, according to Hakim,

> unlike the United States with a much larger population, the release of microdata does not by itself adequately prevent the disclosure of information about identifiable individuals. (1979, 145)

In a similar way secondary analysis of the OPCS Longitudinal Survey, which links data for a 1 per cent sample of the 1971 British Census with material from the 1981 Census and a variety of other public records, is only done in-house because of difficulties in ensuring adequate anonymization (Dale et al., 1988).

Even if data are released, special care may need to be taken where one is dealing with what Campbell et al. (1977) call 'public variables'. These are variables for which identifying information can be found elsewhere; for example, data on occupational and professional groups or organizations which appear in registers of various kinds. The availability of such records may be greater than at first appears. Webb et al. (1981, 84), speaking of the United States, point out that even such apparently innocuous records as driving licence applications and commercial registration records contain quite large amounts of personal information. For Britain, Rogers (1986) lists in some detail over 40 publicly available sources of information about individuals (not all of which, it must be said, permit unrestricted access). In these situations the relevant variables may simply have to be deleted from the released data.

Where data are published or can be made available for secondary analysis, the likelihood of deductive disclosure can be minimized by using a variety of strategies for introducing indeterminacy into the data. These include: 'broad banding', releasing results on only random sub-samples of the data, microaggregation, error inoculation, and mutually insulated file linkage. (For a more detailed review than is possible here, see Campbell et al., 1977.) As might be expected, because these strategies use imprecision to cloak identity, their use involves certain penalties since the reliability of the data is degraded. It is also, ironically, the case that data which have been treated in these ways may fall foul of data protection laws in some countries which insist that only accurate data be held (Akeroyd, 1988).

Data which are broad banded are categorized into crude rather than finely detailed report categories, so reducing the visibility of specific data entries. In surveys of employers, for example, the identity of a particular firm can often be deduced from information such as its size and industrial classification (Hedges, 1987, 282). Care must therefore be taken in reporting such data to ensure that the report categories used are crude enough to preclude the identification of individual firms. Inevitably, of course, broad banding means a loss of information. Boruch and Cecil (1979, 212–13) point out that if one has a large number of cases the possibility of disclosure can be forestalled by reporting, or releasing for secondary analysis, not the complete data set but only a random sample of cases. In this way there is no guarantee that a given individual is actually present in the data. Even here, though, it might be possible to identify some distinctive individual if the information refers to a small or relatively closed population, such as a prison, and a number of sufficiently detailed analyses are carried out. In this situation it may become necessary to go so far as to construct different tables based on independently generated random sub-samples of the data. This is done so that any given individual who appears in one table will not necessarily appear in another.

To preserve confidentiality, data are often aggregated to higher level naturally occurring units. For example, census data for enumeration districts might be aggregated to ward level or beyond. The principle here is that the less sharp the 'resolution' of the data, the more difficult it is to identify individual responses. The technique known as 'microaggregation' works in a slightly different way by merging data for similar individuals to produce synthetic rather than 'natural' aggregates. The strategy was originally proposed by Feige and Watt (1970) to permit the secondary analysis of data in cases where even anonymized individual records cannot be released. Synthetic cases are constructed, comprised of small, carefully designed clusters of individual sample units. Provided these composite cases are generated properly, useful analyses can be carried out without compromising the identity of individual cases. Sample size is, of course, reduced when microaggregation is used and there is a loss of statistical efficiency, although, according to Feige and Watt, the estimates obtained are not necessarily biased.[7] Campbell et al. (1977) point out that microaggregation procedures need to be carefully thought out in relation to the data concerned. In particular the variables used as the basis for aggregation need to be selected so as to be independent of sampling variation.

Dewdney (1983) describes the strategies used to maintain confidentiality in the British Census. Published reports generally present few problems since the areas to which they refer are for the most part well populated. Difficulty does arise, however, with the Small Area Statistics (SAS), sets of standard tables produced for areas such as enumeration districts, electoral wards (postcode sectors in Scotland), and local government districts. In the SAS tables two procedures are used to maintain confidentiality: 'suppression' and 'modification'. Thus, the Census Office follows a set of rules for suppressing tables where the identification of individuals might be easy. Specifically, SAS tables are not released for areas where the number of persons or households falls below a certain level (Dewdney, 1983). The modification procedure works as follows. Except for two cross-tabulations in each set, showing total numbers of persons and households, individual cells in SAS tables are modified by randomly adding a value of 1, 0 or −1. The level of error introduced into the data by this procedure is small but adjusted cell entries cannot be attached with any degree of certainty to specific individuals. Totals for each table are based on the adjusted cells. Overall, however, differences between actual and adjusted totals have been shown to be small (Newman, 1979).

The procedure used to modify cell entries in published SAS tables is a form of error inoculation. It uses small, deliberately induced changes to actual values in the data to prevent deductive disclosure. Campbell et al. (1977) recommend that slightly different forms of inoculation be used for different kinds of data. Where one has continuous variables, age or income for example, random error can be introduced. Each individual value on a given variable has added to it a random error which has a mean of zero and a variance which is small. Since a majority of individual values is changed by this procedure the likelihood of identifying individuals is reduced. However, one must be prepared to accept some minor statistical cost in using this procedure. The overall variance is increased and statistical relationships in the data are somewhat attenuated. For non-continuous data, it is preferable to use 'random score substitution'. A suitable level of error is chosen, say 5 per cent. Five per cent of values on a given non-continuous variable are then chosen at random, and for each of these values another randomly chosen value is substituted. Obviously, in selecting the substituted values it is necessary to ensure that the overall distribution of the original variable is maintained. (Again, more detail can be found in Campbell et al., 1977, and in Boruch and Cecil, 1979.)

Sometimes it is useful to link archival records from two different sources without compromising confidentiality. One common way to do this is to use a procedure known as 'mutually insulated file linkage' (Campbell et al., 1977). In brief, the procedure works in the following way. Lists of individuals are grouped according to some statistical criterion, say socio-economic level. Each sub-list formed in this way is randomly allocated a code name, and the lists are sent to the second archive. There, records on the individuals named on each sub-list are consulted and summary statistics are computed for the sub-list as a whole. (In some cases, to introduce further indeterminacy, one individual may be deleted at random from each sub-list.) The summary data for each sub-list are then returned to the first agency who reassemble the data according to the original scheme for grouping the sub-lists. Using this procedure, confidentiality is preserved since neither archive has access to information held on identifiable individuals held by the other archive.

It was noted earlier that procedures for maintaining confidentiality often depend on creating imprecision in the data. By their nature these procedures also make it difficult to assess the reliability of the underlying data. This is a major disadvantage of the techniques described above, although, as Boruch and Cecil (1979, 99–100, 115–16) point out, the problem is not an entirely insurmountable one. The data collected can at least be inspected for internal consistency. In approaches which use the link file method of preserving confidentiality, there is a brief period when identifiable data are held and which may provide an opportunity for carrying out reliability checks. Even in surveys where those sampled respond anonymously, some checks are possible using the common device of having respondents return separately a postcard containing an identifier.

A further disadvantage of many of these procedures is that they bring with them increases in the cost of research, and in the time taken to complete data collection and analysis. In general, the more care is taken to prevent deductive disclosure, the more cumbersome the procedures which have to be adopted. Demands on time and resources are, in consequence, pushed even further. Furthermore, many of the techniques have had only limited field testing. As a result, there is a limit to the extent to which they can be used 'off the shelf' without time spent in careful pre-testing or in the absence of specialized training or statistical assistance (Caplan, 1982). (This is something, incidentally, which probably inhibits the wider diffusion of the methods.) Finally, procedures for ensuring that confidentiality is maintained are well-developed in research based on quantitative methods, and on administrative data. Their wider applicability to less structured methods and data sources remains limited.

Protecting the confidentiality of qualitative data

Qualitative researchers face mounting pressures to protect the confidentiality of their data. One source of this pressure is the growth of field research in applied settings where there may be a greater likelihood of legal intervention (Broadhead, 1984). Another is that computer programs for the analysis of qualitative data have become common in the last few years. (For reviews of developments in this area, see Tesch, 1988; Lee and Fielding, 1991; Hinze, 1987, 440.) This rapid advance has come about, however, at a time when national data protection laws are becoming increasingly common (Akeroyd, 1988).[8] Despite these developments, field research has remained largely untouched by concerns about the misuse of computers and database technology. The efforts of quantitative researchers to design ways of maintaining the confidentiality of data have not been matched by qualitative researchers (Akeroyd, 1988; 1991; Boruch and Cecil, 1979, 204). One reason for this is that qualitative data are much less amenable than quantitative data to technical solutions to confidentiality problems. Depersonalizing quantitative data is relatively easy. Although the data files produced by quantitative researchers can be arranged in a number of more or less complicated ways (Dale et al., 1988), at heart, quantitative data-sets are usually organized on a 'case-wise' basis. That is, for each individual respondent a computer record exists in which a range of information about that individual is arrayed in the form (usually) of numerical variables. Both the organization of the data in this way and its numerical form, which permit the data to be transformed by the use of mathematical operations, facilitate the use of techniques such as broad banding or microaggregation. Moreover, although they vary in their complexity, these procedures can be performed systematically on computer records as a series of technical operations.

In the case of qualitative data, however, it is much less easy to ensure that the link between the data held and the individual to which it refers has been broken. Qualitative researchers gather textual data which, because it comprises words rather than numbers, cannot be mechanically transformed. In many instances, the data which qualitative researchers collect will not form a set of discrete cases. Instead, field research often produces an 'assemblage' of data. This assemblage is typically multi-stranded, comes from multiple sources, and may have multiple forms: transcripts, fieldnotes, documents and so on. Information about particular individuals may be spread across a range of records. Moreover, specific items of information are not usually recorded in a standardized way, and may be of varying quality, ranging from first person or eye-witness accounts to rumour and hearsay. Qualitative research also depends on an interactive relationship to the data. The analyst, in other words, moves back and forth from the field to the data to the analysis. Thus even the simple expedient of removing real names from field material can prove problematic while the researcher is still in the field since retaining real identities aids navigation through the material and prevents confusion (Broadhead, 1984, 116). All this might not matter too much if it were not for the fact that qualitative researchers, whatever the topic of their research, often cannot help discovering secret, discrediting or sensitive information. It is likely, moreover, that such material will be preserved in some form or another since field researchers typically record assiduously while in the field. In addition they are encouraged by their professional training to express in their fieldnotes thoughts, observations and judgements that they might be reticent to express in public (Kirk and Miller, 1986, 56).

The difficulties involved in anonymizing field data which may contain large amounts of collateral information, together with the power of computer software to retrieve personal data, may combine to produce what Akeroyd (1988) speaks of as the 'worst possible case' scenario. In this prognosis, qualitative researchers will face insuperable problems in complying with data protection legislation. Akeroyd's intention in painting this gloomy picture is explicitly to provoke discussion. The difficulties she points to, however, are real ones, even if in some respects her assessment may be too pessimistic. Presumably, the ability to protect identities is easier where the data are organized in a case-wise manner as a set of unstructured interviews with individuals, say, rather than as unstructured fieldnotes. Other things being equal, it is also likely that a small data-set will be easier to anonymize than a large one, unless the amount of data collected is large enough to have made some standardized data collection possible. The 'texture' of the data may be changed in some instances through the substitution of personal characteristics: males can be turned into females and so on. There are, of course, limits on how far one can go in this way. In any case, as Akeroyd (1988) indicates, such procedures are less acceptable in some disciplines – such as anthropology (see Ellen, 1984) – than in others.

In terms of anonymizing textual data, dedicated computer programs for analysing qualitative data can have some advantages. Before embarking on the substantive coding of transcripts or fieldnotes, it is possible to do a 'meta-coding'. Areas of text which are problematic from the point of view of confidentiality could be marked, retrieved and modified before proceeding to a full analysis. One problem here, though, is that while qualitative analysis programs typically allow one to modify codes associated with the text, it is usually not possible to change the text itself from within the program. Having identified segments of text which need to be changed, it is necessary to go back into a word processor to make the changes.

It is also true, however, that the designers of dedicated programs have given little thought to security, for example, by building in password protection or encryption facilities.[9] A further troubling development is that, increasingly, qualitative analysis programs allow one to do quasi-statistical analysis in terms of simple counts and cross-tabulations (Seidel, 1991). Given the small numbers of respondents typical of qualitative research, strategies such as the broad banding of data to preserve confidentiality are ineffective. In the longer term, it is possible that the development of 'expert systems' (see, e.g., Weber, 1985; Gerson, 1984) will help analysts detect patterns in textual data. Eventually such systems might not only be used for analysis. One potential application could be for them to alert researchers to areas of text which might permit deductive disclosure, or perhaps, even, to suggest ways of anonymizing the data.

Akeroyd (1988; 1991) stresses the need which arises to discuss the issues surrounding data protection and qualitative research. There are some reasons why that discussion may be muted. As has been seen, not only are the technical difficulties of anonymizing qualitative data formidable, but also there is much less of a tradition in qualitative research of the kind of 'instrumentalism' (Øyen and Olaussen, 1985; see also McCracken, 1988, 12–13) which has encouraged methodological innovation in quantitative research. In Akeroyd's view (1988; 1991) some researchers may prefer to opt out, either by not using computers at all, or simply by ignoring data protection laws. However, one of the dangers of regulatory systems such as that found in Britain is that evidence of abuse may only emerge by the time it has already reached substantial proportions. In this situation it can be difficult to resist calls for sharply restrictive legislation.

Conclusion

Encounters between the law and the research process involve a triangular power relation between the researcher, the researched and the state. Where legal intervention is involved the researcher usually has relatively little power to affect the outcome. This is so in the case of a subpoena, where the power of the state is high relative to both the researcher *and* the researched, and the need to protect research participants constrains further the researcher's ability to influence events. Not only is the researcher relatively powerless when the law intervenes in the research process, but also legal intervention, when it arises, frequently does so unexpectedly. Its consequences are often personally devastating, draining resources and disrupting research. Faced with action in the courts, researchers for the most part must confront the unpalatable choice between compliance and penalty. Where legal protections to particular problems have emerged, such as the grants of confidentiality available to some American researchers, their scope has been limited. As a result, it has become necessary to put faith in technical and procedural methods (Boruch, 1979) rather than legal means to forestall a number of the problems arising out of legal intervention.

Notes

1. At least one researcher in the United Kingdom has faced the possibility of a subpoena, although the matter was not pressed to a final determination. As an aside, it seems that in the UK one cannot rely on the provisions of the Data Protection Act in cases where data are sought by the courts. Among the exemptions under the Act is one which permits data users to disclose data for the prevention of crime or for taxation purposes. Data users are also required to disclose if ordered to do so by a court (Data Protection Registrar, 1987). There has been some suggestion that researchers in the Nordic countries can honour guarantees of confidentiality aided by their data protection laws (Marøy, 1988; Janson, 1979). There are doubts, however, as to whether this is actually the case (Jon Bing, Norwegian Research Centre for Computers and Law, personal communication, 1989).

2. The use of such a law was one of the strategies used in the Brajuha case. In that case a motion to quash the subpoena was filed on First Amendment grounds and on the basis of the New York state law which protects privileged communications by persons engaged in the dissemination of knowledge to the public. On appeal, the

judges in the case declared themselves willing to listen to constitutional claims about the applicability of scholar's privilege. In the event no ruling was made. Two of the central figures involved died and the case was dropped. As a result, no valid precedent was set (Brajuha and Hallowell, 1986).

3. It is not clear why legal intervention in the research process should be much more common in the United States than in Britain. Possibly, the American political and legal system allows a greater scope than does the British to investigation through, for example, legislative committees and grand juries. A further factor is likely to be that the volume of social research in the United Kingdom is less extensive than in the United States (Bulmer, 1987, 4). Social researchers in Britain are simply much less visible than their American counterparts. Added to this, because of the introduction of Constitutional considerations and the national publicity given to some cases, local prosecutors in the United States may have a greater degree of awareness of the possible usefulness of research materials and of their ability to compel disclosure (though see Nejelski and Finsterbusch, 1973).

4. Robertson and Nicol (1984, 14) have noted the growing use of injunctions to prevent publication in the United Kingdom in recent years. Although they have so far been confined to journalistic writing, conceivably they could also be used against researchers.

5. For this reason it is common practice in survey organizations to put identifiable information such as the name and address of the respondent on a separate cover sheet which can be torn off and destroyed on receipt of the questionnaire (Survey Research Center, 1976, 116–17).

6. Note, however, that in Europe such an arrangement might be hindered by national data protection laws relating to transborder data flows. See Akeroyd, 1988; Dale et al., 1988, 49–50.

7. Data from the New Earnings Survey carried out in the United Kingdom by the Department of Employment are microaggregated for release to secondary analysts (Thompson, 1987).

8. A draft directive designed to strengthen and harmonize data protection in the European Community has recently been introduced (European Commission, 1990).

9. One exception here is the program TEXTBASE ALPHA (Renata Tesch, personal communication). It is perhaps no coincidence that this program originated in one of the Nordic countries, Denmark.

10

Disclosure and Dissemination in Research on Sensitive Topics

Conflicts over publication are likely to be particularly stark where topics of a 'sensitive' kind are involved (Fichter and Kolb, 1953). Social scientists, when they publish, address themselves to a variety of audiences: research participants, sponsors, funders, publishers, other social scientists and the wider society. Each of these audiences has its own distinct expectations and interests (Fichter and Kolb, 1953; Becker, 1964; Barnes, 1979; C.G. Johnson, 1982), and, frequently, the interests and expectations of one audience collide with those of another. For example, as Barnes (1979) points out, social scientists prefer to maximize the amount of material that is published. Funders, gatekeepers or research participants do not always regard unrestricted publication as in their interest. The short-term interests of these groups need to be balanced against not just the short-term interests of the researcher but also the longer term societal interest of ensuring the open dissemination of knowledge.

The issues thrown up by conflicts over publication take a number of different forms depending on whether they take place before, during or after the reporting of research. Pre-emptive issues have to do with factors affecting publication which arise during the course of the study itself. Some of these issues have already been discussed; for example, the possibility that innocuous material is published because researchers deliberately study non-controversial topics, gatekeepers veto, inspect or control what is written, or potential research subjects either hoodwink the researcher or decline to participate in the research (Becker, 1964; Barnes, 1979). Anticipatory issues concern procedures and decisions which govern how information about research participants is disclosed during writing up. In some cases, as has already been seen, what finds its way into a written report may already be constrained by steps taken to protect raw data by technical means from unauthorized disclosure or legal intervention. However, implications for the content of reports also follow from assessments of how far the research site is likely to be identified, and the possible negative effect of publication on those concerned. Consequential issues relate to what happens after publication. Having found their way into the public realm, research findings may rebound on the author in various ways. Going into print can induce libel actions or embroil the writer in outright controversy. This chapter looks at both anticipatory and consequential issues.

The politics of disclosure in sociological writing

'What should be disclosed?' is a central anticipatory issue when the results of research on sensitive topics are to be published. Implicit in this broad question are two more specific questions (W.F. Whyte, 1958). First, should individuals be identified in published work? Second, if individuals are to be identified, what – if anything – should be done to avoid harming them? Although ethical standards vary over time (C.G. Johnson, 1982) and may be subject to fads and fashions which push researchers towards or away from reticence or revelation (Adler and Adler, 1989), pseudonyms have long been used in published reports to disguise research sites and research participants (Barnes, 1979, 136–7). Anonymity protects the privacy of those studied. It is also assumed that where research participants cannot be identified they cannot be harmed by information about them appearing in the public realm. The use of pseudonyms and disguised research sites has also been seen as indispensable to ensuring co-operation in research on deviance or in situations of social conflict (Jenkins, 1984).

Some writers have been meticulous about disguising those they have studied. (See, e.g., Sullivan and Cornfield, 1982; R.G. Burgess, 1984, 206.) Other writers, however, have dissented from the practice of using pseudonyms or challenged its universal applicability. Colvard (1967) has argued that full disclosure of information is a scientific norm which aids critical assessment and possible replication. In his view, therefore, the onus is on the researcher to demonstrate that the use of pseudonyms is actually essential. Spector (1980) argues that the convention of using pseudonyms can be set aside where those studied have been chosen precisely because of their uniqueness or visibility. Public figures, for example, often assume that, unless they request otherwise, they will be quoted 'on the record' and their statements attributed to them. Dispensing with anonymity has also sometimes been seen by research participants as protecting them against the possibility of falsehood or carelessness on the part of the researcher (Fielding, 1982). This is because statements attributed to named individuals can be checked against material in the public record.

Sometimes, of course, disguise is impractical. For example, few studies of factory closure or large-scale redundancy conceal the plant involved since in many cases its location and identity are self-evident. In some cases the use of pseudonyms has been rendered ineffectual by respondents' own self-advertisement (Plummer, 1983). The resolve of Klockars (1977) to go to prison, if need be, rather than reveal the identity of the professional fence 'Vincent' was undercut by Vincent's own campaign to publicize Klockars' (1975) book about him. Even without such 'assistance' the use of pseudonyms has not always been effective and disguises have frequently been penetrated (Boruch and Cecil, 1979, 205). Journalists found the family described in Oscar Lewis's book *Children of Sanchez* (Diener and Crandall, 1978, 103) and the factory Morgan (1972) studied. The variety of information produced, particularly by qualitative research, often means that identities can be deduced from descriptions of people's roles, their relations to others, and even, simply, from the overall 'texture' of the data. In other words, the detailed description of events, places or people may produce a sufficient accumulation of incidental detail to lead to deductive disclosure. For example, Carol Warren in a study of male homosexuals (1977) took strenuous efforts to maintain the anonymity of her data. She never labelled tape recordings of interviews but relied on being able to identify respondents by their voices. Tapes were erased immediately after transcription, and only pseudonyms were used in fieldnotes. The master-list which linked real names to pseudonyms was destroyed once the material had been written up. Even so, she records that:

> One subject-member pointed out a serious error I had made in the protection of his anonymity. When I visited him, after the book had been published, I noticed he had completely changed his home decor. Later he said, sarcastically, 'You gave a perfect description of my house in that book.' (1977, 99)

Other writers – perhaps more careless than Warren – have inadvertently made possible the identification of research sites. There are at least two books on Northern Ireland, for instance, where, despite disguises being used, the actual locales in which the research was carried out are readily discernible from the text. In one case, a document is quoted which contains the name of the Roman Catholic parish for the area *en clair*. In the other, official reports, local government documents and the like bearing the actual names of the areas concerned are cited in the bibliography. Indeed in one or two cases the pseudonym in the text is directly followed by a citation giving the actual name.

Barnes (1979) has argued that because pseudonyms are usually transparent to those within the research setting itself, they have a largely symbolic function. Their importance lies, according to Barnes (1979), in the illusion they give to those studied that possibly unflattering portrayals of themselves are hidden from outsiders. In his view this transparency is acceptable as long as respondents believe there is sufficient ambiguity to protect them. In fact, Barnes goes further than this to suggest that attempts at complete disguise are misguided. Changing too many details, in his view, runs the risk of distorting the data. It is not entirely clear, however, where the boundary between disguise and distortion lies, especially in the study of sensitive topics. In many instances, there may be 'immediate and tangible reasons or persons who demand to be protected from the potentially threatening disclosures that researchers can make' (Adler and Adler, 1989, 45). In such cases, many researchers have not only relied on disguise but have also often set aside their interest in maximizing publicly available information by exercising self-censorship.

Self-censorship

Self-censorship takes a number of forms. At one extreme, it might involve not publishing at all. Jahoda (1981) recounts, for example, that there were eight separate instances in the course of her career where she decided not to publish the results of a study. Sometimes material is published only in certain forms. Because of the sensitivity of some aspects of their research on collegiate sports, the Adlers, for example, held back on media interviews, and published their results in the less visible forum of journal articles rather than a book which might have attracted more attention (Adler and Adler, 1989). More commonly, researchers engage in partial self-censorship by deliberately choosing to omit specific items of sensitive information from published reports.

Adler and Adler (1989; 1992) point to a number of factors which lead to the suppression of information in published reports. A common source of self-censorship, they contend, derives from the development of personal loyalty to those involved in the study. In their case, their respect and admiration for the coach who had granted them access to the basketball team they studied made them unwilling to publish material which would be distressing to him. A similar factor seems to have been at work in Jahoda's (1981) decision not to publish a report on a scheme to aid unemployed Welsh miners originally undertaken in the 1930s but only fully reported many years later (Jahoda, 1987). A sponsor of the scheme helped her by going to Vienna to contact her family after the

Anschluß had put them, as Jews, at risk. When presented with evidence that the scheme was not working, Jahoda's benefactor told her that his life's work had been destroyed. She decided therefore not to publish.

Publication may be inhibited by an ongoing involvement in the research site. The researcher who wants to stay in the setting after the completion of the research or who wishes the research site to remain reusable may feel constrained not to publish potentially negative findings. Fetterman (1989) did not at the time disclose details of an incident at a school he was studying involving sexual relations between a school counsellor and a student. He felt that the incident was isolated and correctly handled by the school principal. According to Fetterman, disclosure would have had serious repercussions for the school and from the point of view of continued presence in the setting 'would have represented methodological suicide' (1989, 13).

As the Adlers note (1992), the problem of maintaining research access can be acute in 'opportunistic' studies where the researcher has capitalized on membership of a particular group in order to obtain access. They were loath to publish negative material about the university basketball team they studied for fear of jeopardizing their continued presence in the setting. The Adlers were additionally cautious about publishing material on the team for fear of 'biting the hand that fed them'. The university derived revenue from university sports. Given the strict regulatory regime surrounding such sports, revealing evidence of deviance, if it existed, could have had substantial negative consequences both for the team and the university.

Self-censorship may be necessary to *protect* those who have been studied. Klockars (1977) suppressed the fact that the professional fence he studied had been a police informer in order to protect him from retaliation. As Jenkins (1984) notes, this kind of self-censorship is particularly important in conflict situations. Accordingly, he did not use 'sensitive' information – implicitly about involvement in paramilitary activity – gleaned during his study of working-class youth lifestyles in Belfast (1984, 154). In other instances the researcher may feel a duty not to exacerbate a fraught social situation. Jahoda (1981), for example, decided not to publish a study concerning the resettlement in Britain of Asian families who had been expelled from Uganda. This study contained evidence of racial prejudice among the Asians themselves which she felt would not have facilitated their acceptance in Britain.

Related to situations of this kind are those in which researchers censor their own work to avoid reprisals against themselves or their families. For example, according to the Adlers (1992), publication of Parsa's (1988) study of the Iranian revolution was fraught with difficulty. Parsa knew his work was unlikely to find favour with the revolutionary government in Iran because pro-Khomeni demonstrators in the United States had disrupted talks he had given on his research. Moreover, he felt vulnerable because back in Iran his father had been placed on a government death list. Matters were further complicated by the death threat issued against Salman Rushdie. In the wake of the Rushdie affair, publication of Parsa's book was delayed while he tried to expunge from it further potentially sensitive information.

Self-censorship is also sometimes used by researchers to hold back evidence of their own activities in the field. Humphreys in his published work (1970), for example, successfully hid evidence of his participation in the 'tearooms' he studied (Warren, 1988; Adler and Adler, 1989). Such reticence often arises either out of embarrassment or because the researcher fears disapproval or sanction.

The examples given by Adler and Adler (1989; 1992) suggest that the intentional omission of information from published work is fairly common, and that, broadly speaking, the practice has two main functions. One of these is the maintenance of good personal or field relationships. The other is to protect those studied from harm. A third function of self-censorship unremarked by the Adlers is its use to avoid embroilment in contentious entanglements of various kinds, notably those of a legal nature or which promote controversy or disapproval by fellow professionals. (In both these cases, of course, self-censorship is only one of a number of relevant issues.) The Adlers note that the social science community loses out through being 'duped, deceived or misled' by the practice of self-censorship. They suggest that researchers should take greater steps to ensure free dissemination of information. In particular, it is important to assess how far self-censorship has to be a necessary outcome of the kinds of situation already described and whether possible alternatives to it can be found.

Self-censorship and field relations
What Adler and Adler call the 'classic Chicago school type of self-censorship' (1989, 39) typically arises from an implicit research bargain. Access to research participants and continued contact with them is exchanged for discretion on the part of the researcher. It is not clear that such situations need inevitably lead to self-censorship. It is true that publication beyond the bounds of discretion can often seem to those studied like betrayal. This may be, however, because the research bargain in fact hides conflicting expectations about the

research. If research participants are unfamiliar with social research they may feel uncomfortable with the 'abstract, relativistic, generalizing' approach of the social scientist in which 'something precious to them is treated as merely an instance of a class' (Becker, 1964, 273). They may also have difficulty with situations in which a researcher, while respecting personal secrets, reveals 'community secrets': negative aspects of social life, which, while common knowledge, are rarely articulated publicly (Scheper-Hughes, 1981). In these instances an obvious solution is to strive for clarification. Thus, as an alternative to self-censorship, Becker (1964) has suggested conducting seminars with those studied. In these, the researcher tries to educate research participants about social science research, and researcher and researched explore together the possible consequences publication might have. Carole Johnson (1982) argues that the 'tone' of social science writing is also important (see also Rainwater and Yancey, 1967, 160–2). Ways of expressing ideas can usually be found in her view which do no violence to the analytic point being made, but which minimize possible feelings of betrayal. For example, according to Johnson, describing specific cases in order to make a general point about private or unflattering behaviour may make those described feel singled out. It is usually less threatening to make general statements first before going on to discuss specific instances. What to the writer is a 'neutral' or 'objective' account may carry unfortunate overtones from the point of view of those studied. Reviewing the Springdale case (see below), Johnson notes, for example, that Vidich and Bensman's (1958) term 'invisible government' carried connotations of illegitimate authority which were offensive to Springdale's inhabitants (see also W.F. Whyte, 1958), even though it was not the authors' intention that the phrase should be interpreted in this way.

Implicit research bargains may also reflect varying levels of identification with those studied. At one extreme this can extend to 'going native', the taking on, root and branch, of the perspective of those studied. As Adler and Adler (1992) point out, this degree of identification with research participants represents an extreme form of self-censorship if, as a result, research findings are lost to the social science community. More commonly, processes of social alignment develop during the research which serve to muffle sociological expression. Publication of Vidich's study of 'Springdale', a small town in upper New York state (Vidich and Bensman, 1958), was greeted by a hostile response from townspeople and provoked sharp disagreements between Vidich and members of the wider research project of which his study had formed part. Vidich and Bensman (1964) contend that, by not resorting to self-censorship in their study, they had dismayed an alliance of 'academic bureaucrats and sensitive town people'. According to Vidich and Bensman, the bureaucratic organization of the wider research project and the social relations which developed between its members and the local élite fostered an 'optimistic' view of the town's social organization in line with Springdale's public image of itself. Identification with (as opposed to identification of) those studied encouraged researchers involved in the wider project to compromise their scientific objectivity by accepting and promoting a sanitized view of the town's political structure and organization. Vidich and Bensman (1964) note that patterns of this kind promote sociology's propensity to focus on the powerless. Since the powerful and articulate are most likely to express negative reactions to publication, self-censorship reinforces a tendency to mask upper level impropriety while the lower levels of society remain open to scrutiny.

Self-censorship to protect research participants
A number of harms may result to research participants from publication (C.G. Johnson, 1982). These include: (a) feelings of upset at how they have been portrayed in research reports by those able to identify themselves; (b) the attraction of unwanted publicity to research sites and those within them; and (c) disclosure of information about individuals which may permit others to treat them in an exploitative way. The more contentious or sensitive a particular topic is, the more likely it is that self-censorship will protect those involved from such harms (Barnes, 1984; Jahoda, 1981). Such situations, however, are also more likely to be those in which there is a clear and urgent social interest in accurate reporting (Fichter and Kolb, 1953). A number of writers (Barnes, 1979; Becker, 1964; Fichter and Kolb, 1953) have, therefore, cautioned against an overly 'sentimental' approach in which the harm publication may do is assumed rather than assessed. Becker argues that one should avoid publishing information or conclusions that would 'cause suffering out of proportion to the scientific gain of making them public' (1964, 284). He acknowledges that this rule is inherently ambiguous. What constitutes 'suffering' or 'out of proportion' is left undefined or unspecified. However, Becker's formulation implies that before self-censorship is considered one has studied the situation in sufficient detail to be aware of the possible consequences of publication. One should also be clear that potential harm which might arise is likely to be direct and tangible.

In a similar vein, Carole Johnson has advocated a comprehensive but rather cautious approach to assessing material for publication based around what she calls the 'ethical proofreading' of manuscripts. In preparing manuscripts for publication, researchers should assume that the identities of individuals and the location of the study will be uncovered. While identification in itself may not necessarily lead to harm, it makes it difficult to have control over subsequent and possible harmful uses to which published information might be put. What is to be reported therefore should be evaluated in an explicit manner. Questions should be asked about what is to be revealed, the possible positive and negative uses to which findings can be put, and whether the revelations made are worth the possible consequences. Again, as does Becker, Johnson (1982) argues that, if need be, what is to be included in published work should be discussed with research participants, forewarning them where necessary about the possible impact of dissemination.

Self-censorship seems most justifiable where publication is likely to produce violence or coercion directed towards the researcher, or towards those studied. As Diches (1986, 11) points out, a number of factors combine to make threats of violence compelling. Violence can easily be perpetrated because it requires little specialized equipment or esoteric knowledge for its deployment. It is also highly visible, and usually unmistakable in its impact. In most cases, therefore, and especially where publication threatens those studied, discretion is probably the better part of valour. Even so, threats of this kind can in theory be deflected in various ways. One possibility is counterthreat: the promise to make an even fuller and more damaging disclosure if action is taken against the researcher. (For the use of this strategy in a somewhat different context, see Brajuha and Hallowell, 1986.) Alternatively, evasion or attempts at mediation might be adopted. The author, in other words, can avoid trouble by hiding or making an exit from the field or by finding someone to mediate with those who have been offended. Although the parallel is not an exact one, strategies of this kind seem to have been used (albeit unsuccessfully) in the Rushdie affair. In academic contexts evasion may be helped by the lengthy periods which often elapse between research and publication and by the ability of researchers sometimes to put social and geographical distance between themselves and those they have studied.

Writers like Johnson and the Adlers tend to assume that the effects of publication are immediate, direct, individual and psychic. However, reactions to publication may be delayed or indirect. The negative effects of publication on those studied may be collective as well as individual in character. Research findings entering the public domain may also expose those studied to a variety of hazards, such as legal intervention, discrimination or violence. Although in many cases those potentially harmed by publication are individuals, the publication of research findings can also harm the collective interests of particular social groups, especially those which are relatively powerless; for example, by encouraging victim blaming or the development of disadvantageous social policies (Finch, 1984; Kelman, 1972). One alternative to self-censorship in these situations is to transform the research issue. Finch (1984) notes, for example, that some interpretations of her findings could have been used to justify social policies detrimental to the women she studied, an outcome she would have found undesirable. Interestingly, however, Finch does not suggest self-censorship as a solution to this problem. She notes instead that she resolved matters analytically. Considering the potential harm that might result from her research forced Finch to push her research questions further. Instead of focusing on individual patterns of behaviour which might be characterized by readers as pathological, she began to consider more fully the structural arrangements surrounding the lives of those she studied. It is not clear, however, how far Finch had to sacrifice ethnographic detail in order to reorient her research.

Felson (1991) argues that the kind of strategy Finch adopts is a recurrent one in sociology. The difficulty is, he argues, that in trying to avoid blaming the victim researchers ignore what he terms proximate variables and mediating processes. Instead, they typically prefer structural explanations based on the analysis of exogenous variables. Conventional sociological analysis, according to Felson, therefore exhibits an ambivalent attitude towards explanations which invoke socialization. It emphasizes, by contrast, constraints which affect the lives of subordinate group members as well as their mistreatment at the hands of the powerful. Felson is probably correct to attack what has sometimes seemed like a rather glib sociologizing of social problems but there seems no reason why disciplines like sociology should not provide a corrective to views based on cultural or psychological determinism, and which are already well-entrenched in the wider society. Furthermore, by proximate variables Felson seems to mean variables of an essentially psychologistic kind. It is true that such variables have, by and large, been ignored by sociologists. This is because, more often, they have preferred to explore the proximate bases of behaviour in a dynamic way through case-based methods, ethnography or community study. It is these methods, rather than theoretical predelictions alone, which have frequently demonstrated very clearly how structural factors are massively implicated in everyday life.

The publication of research on sensitive topics has sometimes produced an almost immediate response. Bond (1978) gives several examples of attempts to subpoena data or otherwise pressure researchers to provide information to law enforcement agencies prompted by the publication of research reports. At the same time, studies in benign contexts suggest that the direct and immediate utilization of social research is unusual (Weiss and Bucuvalas, 1980). There is no reason to suppose that harmful uses of social science knowledge should follow hard on the heels of publication. For example, a study of an undisguised Montagnard village in the Central Highlands of Vietnam undertaken in the 1950s (Condominas, 1977) was some years later translated without permission and distributed to US Special Forces at the time of the Vietnam war (Barnes, 1979). Barnes (1979) notes that, with foresight, the village might have been disguised or the study not published at all but suggests that unusual prescience would have been required to foresee the village's destruction in the war. As he puts it:

> caution cannot be relied upon to eliminate all cases of injustice and exploitation facilitated by ethnographic information. The recipe for eliminating injustice and exploitation, if one exists, must be sought elsewhere. The goal will not be brought nearer by refusing to publish anything at all. (1979, 156)

Instead, other means need to be found for dealing with the possible misuse of research findings. Diener and Crandall (1978) suggest that researchers may need to speak out against the misuse of research, organize themselves collectively to communicate the issues involved more forcefully, and seek to influence policies which are based on research or concerned with its use (see also Reynolds, 1982).

Social science research and the mass media

There are three broad reasons for attempting to have one's research reach a wider audience: responsibility to the public-at-large, the credibility of social science and the possible impact on élite audiences (Roberts, 1984; see also Stocking and Dunwoody, 1982). Research is often funded from public funds and members of the public frequently act as research participants. As Roberts puts it, 'Why should they [the public] not have the opportunity to hear more about the research, to find out what was found out, and if they wish to, to comment or criticize?' (1984, 210). It is conceivable that social science is held in poor public regard because its methods, findings and procedures are not widely understood. In this situation dissemination may enhance the credibility of social research. Popular understanding of social research may also alert potential respondents to the procedures used by social scientists as well as the ethical difficulties researchers face (Stocking and Dunwoody, 1982). Finally, media accounts of social research may help to shape the perceptions of potential users, policy-makers and political élites (Mazur, 1987; Stocking and Dunwoody, 1982).

Although there are benefits to wider dissemination, researchers have not always welcomed media coverage of their research. As Sieber and Stanley point out, 'sensitive research topics are more likely to have applications in the "real" world that society will enthusiastically embrace, irrespective of the validity of the application' (1988, 53). Those engaged in 'sensitive' research may therefore need to consider carefully the possible implications which may arise from media coverage of their work. A number of writers have complained that their work has been trivialized or sensationalized by journalists (Morgan, 1972; Roberts, 1984; see also Stocking and Dunwoody, 1982). To take one – far from extreme – example, research on the social and religious consequences of attendance at Roman Catholic schools in England and Wales (Hornsby-Smith and Lee, 1979) was unaccountably transformed in one newspaper report into a study of the sexual fantasies of convent schoolgirls! Complaints have also been made that media coverage of controversial social issues has been superficial, misleading and sometimes inflammatory (Weigel and Pappas, 1981).

Despite these concerns, Weiss and Singer's (1988) systematic study of social science reporting in the US media suggests that social scientists may have less to fear from media reporting than might at first appear. As they observe, 'Research doesn't happen in places routinely covered by the press' (1988, 25). Social science research is ignored because the work social scientists do is not regularly 'patrolled' by the media. Despite this, stories with a social science content have increasingly appeared in US news reports in recent years. However, even where research comes to the attention of editors and journalists, it competes for attention with a large and varied pool of other possible stories. Unless it is defined as newsworthy within the framework of journalistic values, research may not readily find its way into the public realm (see also Orfield, 1978).

Weiss and Singer have also argued that sensationalist treatments of social research are less common than is sometimes assumed. Social scientists they interviewed about media coverage of their work had few complaints about sensationalization. They rated media stories about their research as being generally accurate, although coverage was also often regarded as lacking in detail. In a general sense, Weiss and Singer's study is reassuring. They may, though, overstate the degree of accurate reporting. Their analysis is based on news stories appearing in major national media. Research may be reported differently, and sometimes less accurately, elsewhere: in the local press, in the tabloids or in specialist outlets (Walum, 1975; Peterson, 1991; Zich and Temoshok, 1986). Furthermore, even where stories are reported accurately, distorted impressions of their content can be conveyed through the use of eye-catching layouts or titles (L. Richardson, 1990; Frisch and Watts, 1980). Weiss and Singer also looked across a wide range of topics. As a result they were unable to examine in detail how particular areas of research are covered. Eleanor Singer's later study (1990) of news reports concerning research on a variety of medical, social and environmental hazards suggests that inaccurate stories, while still relatively uncommon, can arise out of journalistic attempts to dramatize particular issues.

Research is often used for dramatic effect where claims are being advanced in the media that a particular phenomenon should be recognized as a social problem. Journalists produce their reports within interpretive structures or 'story frames', to use Weiss and Singer's phrase (1988, 144). Through the use of story frames, journalists make their reports intelligible by giving them a narrative form. These narratives, moreover, are shaped by institutional imperatives to produce newsworthiness through devices such as immediacy, personification, simplification and so on (Chibnall, 1977). Alongside these elements journalists use sources to lend authority and authenticity to their stories. In the context of social problem claims, research findings and expert opinion provide an apparently authoritative mapping of the situation. Bury and Gabe (1990) have explored how expert opinion is embedded within popular television programme formats in ways which lend weight to claims that a social problem, in their case tranquillizer dependence, is worthy of concern (see also Gabe and Bury, 1988; Gabe et al., 1991). According to Bury and Gabe, magazine programmes which mix light entertainment with coverage of topical issues make relatively little use of experts in order to maintain a relatively 'light' tone. Current affairs programmes use opposing experts to provide a sense of 'balanced' coverage. However, programmes having an exposé format in which the 'main aim is exposure and advocacy rather than providing information and debate' (Bury and Gabe, 1990, 89) often rely on experts. Bury and Gabe argue that the exposé format is particularly prone to sensationalization. Central to it are dramatic devices, such as the use of vignettes describing individuals who are suffering in some way, which make the programme's point in a stark and striking way. Within this framework expert opinion is inserted into a narrative structure which links individual problems to interpretations and assessments of the scale of the problem in ways which imply the need for action of some kind. More specifically, experts are usually used to provide evidence on the extent and seriousness of the problem as opposed, say, to its wider social context or the variability of its impact.

It is important to note in all this that the account given of an expert's research may be factually accurate. The dramatization of research findings derives partly from their selective character. Journalists often rely on a relatively small pool of experts, who are known for their overall eminence rather than for their particular expertise in a given area (Weiss and Singer, 1988), or for their well-defined and ardent views concerning a particular topic (Gabe and Bury, 1988). Journalists also tend to select modes of explanation for social phenomena which are congruent with journalistic and lay conceptions of the problem to hand. A number of writers have pointed out that attempts to promote and legitimize particular issues as worthy of public concern are often advanced in relation to areas of social life where moral ambiguities surround questions of personal autonomy, responsibility and performance (Bury and Gabe, 1990; Beckford, 1985, 98–101). In dealing, if only implicitly, with such issues, the media seem to prefer expert definitions which are of a medical or psychological rather than a sociological kind. For example, James Richardson, a leading scholar of new religious movements, records that he was frequently approached by the media for comment following the Jonestown tragedy in Guyana in 1978 in which hundreds of members of the People's Temple sect died by murder or suicide. He notes, however, that he 'experienced difficulty getting most to adopt anything but [a] psychologized view that used concepts like "brainwashing" and "mind control"' (1980, 240), ideas strongly at variance with those of sociologists and others who have studied the internal dynamics of the movements. Commenting on their experiences of writing an article on the unemployed in Buffalo, New York, for the *New York Times*, Frisch and Watts (1980) have also provided evidence that journalists prefer accounts of how people respond emotionally to difficult situations while disfavouring evidence that individuals can rationally appreciate and articulate the wider social and class contexts surrounding their predicament.

Social research, while effectively marginalized in some contexts, remains of interest to journalists and editors as a source of human interest stories. (On editorial preferences in the reporting of science and social science research, see Dunwoody, 1986.) Human interest stories can be found throughout the media, on radio and television, in the 'quality' press as well as in the tabloids. Such stories are, however, a particular feature of the tabloid press. Unlike 'quality' papers, which rely on advertising revenue, tabloids must maximize their sales income to survive (Curran et al., 1980). One particular kind of human interest story is that which turns on the relationship between researcher and researched.[1] Following a conference report on his study of a factory employing a large number of women workers, Morgan's (1972) research received widespread newspaper coverage. In the popular press reports carried headlines such as 'A factory girl's dream of romance' and ' "What a giggle": When a man tells the secrets of life among the girls'. In many respects the stories seem to have traded in a rather prurient way on Morgan's anomalous position as a man studying a predominantly female workforce. Morgan notes that responses to the reports by the workers themselves were not uniformly hostile. They varied in ways which reflected existing patterns of social organization and conflict. These variable responses in turn provided a useful and additional perspective on social relations in the workplace. Nevertheless, media stories of this kind can cause hurt to those studied. They may also cause dismay and embarrassment to the researcher. The Adlers, for example, do not hide the fact that their own recreational drug use was a condition of their continued involvement with the drug dealers and smugglers they studied. They found, however, that journalists who reported on their research were particularly prone to mention this aspect of the study at the expense of other findings. One effect of this was that their daughter was badgered at school after a local newspaper report on their research mentioned their drug use (Adler and Adler, 1992).

It should be clear that trivialization of this kind is most likely to affect qualitative researchers or those whose topics or methods are unusual or sensitive in some way. This in part explains Peterson's (1991) otherwise rather unusual finding that cultural anthropologists feature more frequently in stories in the US tabloid press than they do in 'quality' newspapers. Their attraction for the tabloids is as a source of stories about 'bizarre tribes' indulging in extraordinary practices which can only be brought to light through the efforts of intrepid or 'whacky' researchers. Treating the activities of researchers in this way can encourage a negative image for social research as a whole. This in turn can have wider political consequences. During a period in Britain when the Conservative government was trying to cut funding for social science research, the allegedly trivial and bizarre character of some kinds of sociological research formed a basis for 'petty sniping' (Flather, 1987) at the social sciences in some segments of the popular press. The existence of conflict is often regarded as newsworthy. As Goodell, commenting on press coverage of the natural sciences observes, 'although much of science receives little media coverage, controversy within science receives a great deal' (1987, 587). The situation appears not to be very different in the social sciences (Dunwoody, 1986). Journalists often report social science research in ways which heighten its apparently controversial character. Thus, early coverage of the controversy over James Coleman's work on 'white flight' focused primarily on Coleman's apparent repudiation of his earlier views supporting school desegregation (Weigel and Pappas, 1981). This kind of reporting may be particularly apparent where research findings appear timely, or attract attention from columnists, leader writers or politicians. According to Rainwater and Yancey, for example, controversy over the 'Moynihan Report' owed much to a syndicated column by Evans and Novak (reproduced in Rainwater and Yancey, 1967, 375–77). This linked the report in an apparently knowing way to bureaucratic infighting in the US government over appropriate responses to urban rioting. Rainwater and Yancey also point out that in situations of this kind pressures exist for findings to enter prematurely into the public domain. Leaks and unattributable briefings ensured that the 'Moynihan Report' came to public attention while it was still technically an internal government document. Coleman's work arguing for a relationship between 'white flight' and school desegregation (Coleman et al., 1975) emerged via press conferences and interviews while analysis was still in progress (Weigel and Pappas, 1981; Pettigrew and Green, 1976). In both cases a more considered view might have emerged had material been made public at a later stage.

Media treatments of controversies in social science have themselves become controversial. In particular, the issue of how the media deal with research on controversial topics has formed part of a neo-conservative critique of the assumed liberal bias of academics and journalists. Snyderman and Rothman (1990) have argued, for example, that a lack of attention to substantive findings, an absence of technical detail and the citing of authorities rather than key players in the dispute itself are all features of media coverage of the controversy over intelligence testing. Comparing media treatment of the testing debate with the results of a survey showing, in their view, a broad consensus of expert opinion in favour of tests, Snyderman and Rothman suggest that the media have reported the controversy over intelligence testing in a misleading way. Reflecting what they perceive as a liberal bias in the US media, journalists, according to Snyderman and Rothman, have bolstered only one side in the controversy by underemphasizing crucial information.

There are some rather obvious difficulties with Snyderman and Rothman's analysis. One is that in controversies the nature of expertise is in itself problematic. Harwood (1976; 1977) points out that scientific controversies often take the form of boundary disputes between disciplines. In examining the debate on intelligence testing, Snyder and Rothman have in effect allowed the controversy to disappear by restricting their sample to experts of only one kind. A second problem with Snyderman and Rothman's approach is that one cannot assess media coverage of a specific controversy without reference to the way in which the media in general report scientific controversies. Snyderman and Rothman (1990), from a conservative standpoint, have detected a liberal bias in the media. Writers like Weigel and Pappas (1981), on the other hand, starting from a broadly liberal perspective, have used similar evidence, in this case relating to media coverage of the 'white flight' controversy, to assert that journalists report social issues in ways which reflect conservative values. In fact, as Goodell (1987) points out, the shift of coverage away from the reporting of substantive research findings, and towards coverage of the controversy itself, is very common in media treatments of scientific controversies. Professionals regard technical or methodological detail as crucial to the understanding and evaluation of the arguments involved. Journalists, however, usually avoid information of this kind, seeing it as being of little interest to the general reader. Instead, opinions are sought from recognized or visible scientific authorities. Even if they have little direct knowledge of or involvement in the specific issues under contention, they are often thought to produce apparently authoritative judgements understandable to lay people. In Goodell's view, the media, as a result of the practices she describes, play a largely non-adversarial role in the reporting of scientific controversies. One paradoxical outcome of this kind of treatment of scientific controversy may be, however, to sharpen the adversarial relations between contending parties to the dispute. In their study, Weiss and Singer (1988) found little evidence to support accusations of either a conservative or a liberal bias in the reporting of social science research. Clearly, however, a perception that the media are biased will often serve to amplify a controversy still further.

Shunning media interest may be one way of avoiding the inappropriate reception of research findings. The pressures which lead to self-censorship in academic writing also discourage some writers from making their work available to wider audiences. The

Adlers' (1992) decision, mentioned earlier, to report findings on deviance in sport only in academic journals where they would attract less attention is but one example of this kind of social scientific gatekeeping.[2] Some commentators have suggested that social scientists should take greater responsibility for the way in which their work is reported (see, e.g., Stocking and Dunwoody, 1982). In particular, it is suggested, social scientists should become more proactive by using press releases and by being more directive in interviews with journalists. Laurel Richardson (1990) has argued, on the basis of her experiences of writing for a popular audience, that researchers should not hesitate to present themselves as an authority on their topic when writing for mass-circulation outlets. This, she argues, allows writers to maintain control over the content of their writing and enhances their bargaining power with editors. For researchers engaged on qualitative or exploratory work this may be difficult. Some researchers at least may still need to be cautious in their dealings with journalists.

Research and the fear of libel

Examples of the difficulties which libel laws can cause are provided by Braithwaite's (1984) study of corporate crime in the pharmaceutical industry and Cavendish's (1982) study of a factory employing women workers. The publication of Braithwaite's book was delayed for two years while lawyers queried up to 300 statements made in it (Braithwaite, 1985). To forestall the possibility of libel action, Cavendish (who published under a pseudonym) was obliged to disguise not only the name of the firm she had worked in but its location and even the product it made. In a similar way, Bell and Newby's attempt to produce what they describe (1977, 11) as a British version of Hammond's (1964) *Sociologists at Work* was fraught with difficulty. One chapter, which should have formed part of this collection of first-person accounts of the research process, did not appear for fear of legal action. Bell and Newby comment that 'it is not even clear to us that we can safely discuss it or the reasons for its removal' (1977, 172).[3] Other accounts were accompanied, of necessity, by comments from writers other than the author presenting alternative points of view.

In English law, someone who feels they have been libelled must demonstrate that the material complained of has been published, that the person it refers to is identifiable and that it damages that person's reputation, for example, by lowering social esteem or inducing contempt (Evans and Whitaker, 1988; Robertson and Nicol, 1984). It is possible to libel not only individuals but also groups or corporate bodies, such as business firms. Even if one uses pseudonyms or disguises the identity of someone in a published work, there is no guarantee that one is protected from a libel suit. As Robertson and Nicol put it: 'Asterisks, blanks, initials and general descriptions will not avail, if evidence proves that readers have solved the puzzle correctly' (1984, 35). Since the effect on a person's public reputation is the principal criterion by which libel is judged, it follows that libel can be committed unintentionally. It is, therefore, possible to defame someone previously unknown to the author (Hooper, 1984).

There are a number of defences to libel in English law. Some are rather technical and rarely used, and some, like the privilege extended to judicial and parliamentary proceedings, are narrow in their scope (Evans and Whitaker, 1988). A libel action can success-fully be defended if it can be shown that the statement complained of is true, or is a matter of genuinely held opinion. In this last case, however, the comment also has to have been made in good faith, without malice and on a matter which is in the public interest. In most instances, the balance of advantage in libel cases would appear to be against the author and with the plaintiff. The requirements for showing that a statement is not libellous are fairly stringent. Litigation in libel cases is expensive and in civil libel cases in the United Kingdom legal aid is not available to the defendant. Potential damages can be considerable. It also seems to be a generally held view that juries can be unpredictable, especially as far as the size of damages is concerned.

In comparison with other countries British libel laws are rather stringent. In the United States, for example, it is for the plaintiff to prove the falsity of the libel rather than for the defendant to prove its truth, as in the English system (R. Adler, 1986). It is also the case that statements made about 'public figures' will not be construed as libellous if they refer to public rather than private conduct, although the remarks in question may not be based on a knowing lie or on a 'reckless disregard' for the truth (Phelps and Hamilton, 1966, 173).[4]

It is actually rather difficult to discuss particular cases involving the possibility of libel. It is not only the original author who is at risk; anyone who republishes the original libel may be open to action. Second, because discussion must be couched in very careful language, it is often difficult to know without inside knowledge what caused the difficulty. From accounts which have been published of the difficulties faced by researchers, it seems that there are two particular situations which render researchers vulnerable to accu-sations of libel. One is where the research takes place within a wider context of conflict, hostility or controversy. Robert Miller submitted an article to a social policy journal on the events surrounding his work as a consultant on a Fair Employment Agency (FEA) study of the promotion prospects for Roman Catholics in the Northern Ireland Civil Service. The chairman of the FEA threatened legal action, claiming the article was libellous. While the editorial board of the journal was prepared for the article to be published, the company which publishes the journal was not (R.L. Miller, 1988). In conflict situations, as Wallis points out, certain groups may come to see the researcher as 'a potential legitimator or defender of their public image, or as a threat to it' (1977, 164). This may be particularly so where a group defines itself in a very positive light but feels surrounded by detractors. Thus, in the face of widespread negative perceptions of new religious movements in the 1970s, a number of the movements had recourse to the threat of litigation. Both Wallis and at least one other British researcher who has written about new religious movements faced potential libel actions, although in both cases matters were eventually settled without a court case.

The other area where problems arise is when researchers discuss in print each other's conduct. One example of this is Bell's own (1977) contribution to the Bell and Newby collection describing a team research project in which he was involved. Bell's account of the research project, which involved a restudy of the town of Banbury in Oxfordshire, is an extremely contested one. It did not find favour with his former colleagues who were not prepared to waive their rights under English libel law. In consequence, the article is a rather blander document than it might otherwise have been.

Faced with the possibility of libel action there are a number of options open to an author. Neither of the two extremes of not publishing at all or of publishing and risking whatever consequences may arise seems very satisfactory. Not publishing hardly constitutes a viable option, especially for a younger researcher dependent on publications in order to obtain tenure. As Punch (1986, 67) indicates, on the basis of his own experience, the choice may be between superiors stressing the need to 'publish *or* perish', and those being researched whose message is 'publish *and* perish'. Outside the context of academic research, for example, in the media, risking the consequences of publishing a potentially libellous statement might have some attractions. Newspapers and broadcasting organizations presumably keep funds in reserve to meet potential damages. In addition, they may benefit indirectly from the publicity generated by the case, or by the reputation they gain for crusading zeal (Hooper, 1984; R. Adler, 1986). Academic researchers, on the other hand, normally have neither the resources nor the incentive to risk a suit.

Wallis (1977), discussing some of the difficulties he had in publishing material from a study on the Church of Scientology, points to some of the ways in which researchers are vulnerable in the face of a possible action. His publisher was covered by libel insurance under the terms of which Wallis was required to warrant that his manuscript was not libellous. A standard provision in publishing contracts, this places the burden firmly on the shoulders of the author, the person normally least able to command the necessary resources to fight the case. As Wallis puts it, 'Publishers and insurers have a common interest in minimizing legal conflict and therefore have an interest in eliminating controversial material' (1977, 166). This may be a little too sweeping. Punch (1986), for instance, notes that in a difficult legal situation his publisher, a university press, 'threw its weight and reputation into the struggle' in defence of what it regarded as a matter of principle. In commercial academic publishing, however, where profit margins are slim, the interests of the publisher are more often likely to lie in removing the book rather than fighting an action.

Bell and Newby (1977) remark that they thought briefly of leaving blank spaces in the text to show where material had been omitted. This, of course, is a strategy which has been used by the press under totalitarian regimes. However, it seems over-dramatic in the case of an academic book. In addition, it is likely to be ineffectual. Even in totalitarian situations the press deals with events about which there may be a good deal of public knowledge through rumour or clandestine discussion. The strategy of leaving blank spaces presumably works in part because people can 'read' the spaces, as it were, by putting in for themselves at least some of what is missing. It seems highly unlikely that one could read a research report in this way.

Having prepared a manuscript on the basis of his research into the Church of Scientology, Wallis (1976) gave sight of it to officials of the Church. Wallis notes that while he felt a responsibility not to harm those he studied or to misrepresent them, he was also motivated in his dealings with Scientology by the fear of litigation.[5] On the basis of comments produced by the Scientologists, and in the light of a legal opinion obtained by them, Wallis made changes to his manuscript where he felt his remarks had been injudicious, or where his comments were potentially libellous.

One aspect of the fear of libel, which emerges from Wallis's account, is that the author is encouraged not to make assertions without very firm evidence (see also Fielding, 1982). Insofar as this encourages good practice, it may in fact be a positive outcome. However, the difficulty with self-censorship, as Bell and Newby (1977) argue strongly, is that it inevitably produces anodyne accounts. Important and relevant material has to be left out, or couched in euphemistic and circumlocutory language. Thus, Newby, commenting on Bell's article on the Banbury restudy, points out that had it not been for the fear of libel it would have been possible for 'a more personally authentic, but also more vituperative and offensive account to be published' (Newby, 1977, 64).

An alternative strategy might be to give those commented on a right to set the record straight. Wallis does this both in his book on the Church of Scientology (1976) as well as in the article in the Bell and Newby collection (1977) which describes the events surrounding its publication. In each case the Scientologists were given a right of reply by being allowed to contribute an appendix containing – mostly negative – comments on Wallis's research. In situations where neither side actually wants to go through with costly legal action, this may provide an acceptable compromise. There are, however, constraints. Newby in his appendix to Bell's article argues that it was not economically feasible to produce a series of separate accounts of the Banbury restudy from Bell's former co-workers. Newby, therefore, summarized their criticisms of Bell's report.

One feature of a number of these cases is that it would be difficult to disguise those being discussed. In the case of Scientology, for instance, the organization was topical and controversial. Wallis could hardly fail to discuss its rather distinctive beliefs and practices. In a similar way, Bell could not have disguised the study he described or the colleagues whose work he discussed. Warren (1988, 63), has noted the development of a more 'confessional' style of field reporting in recent years. This openness may cause further difficulties in the future, not least between colleagues. However, because sociologists are relatively disinterested in individuals as opposed to social patterns and because it is often possible to disguise individuals and research sites, there is some protection from libel in the institutionalized practices of sociology.[6] The difficulty comes when one is dealing with corporate bodies whose activities may be controversial in some way, and whose activities are open to legitimate public interest. These bodies are difficult to disguise, and often have the resources and the will to use the libel laws pre-emptively. In other words, whatever the merits of an individual case, on balance, the libel laws in Britain provide a way for the powerful, or at least the affluent, to suppress unflattering depictions of themselves. In this respect, as in a number of others, the law of libel is clearly inequitable. To date, however, it has resisted reform (Hooper, 1984; Robertson and Nicol, 1984).

Conclusion

When they write up their research, researchers must walk a tightrope; careful neither to conceal too much, nor to disclose too little. Very often, however, what may be disclosed only becomes an issue once the research has been completed. Perhaps what is needed is for researchers to follow the suggestion made by Channels (1992) that 'throughout our research, including in the initial design and planning, we should make our methodological decisions with the intended audience and uses of information firmly in mind'. What Channels seems to have in mind here is that, as design and analysis proceed, researchers should think through the potential results of their work. In so doing they should anticipate potential distortions and misinterpretations and consider ways of presenting analytic complexities. All of this, she argues, helps to avoid oversimplifying research findings to meet the needs of lay audiences, on the one hand, and encourages researchers to make quite clear the contributions social scientists make to the understanding of pressing social issues, on the other.

Notes

1. One suspects this particular approach is not unique to media coverage of social research. It appears in stories dealing with medical researchers working with the incurably ill and biological scientists researching large furry animals or small slimy ones.

2. Such strategies are not always successful, it should be said. Against his advice, the publisher of Brewer's (1990b) book on the police in Northern Ireland serialized it in a popular Sunday newspaper.

3. An account of the research upon which this chapter was apparently based has eventually appeared, together with some rather critical comments on Bell and Newby's role as editors (Punch, 1986, 67–8).

4. Interestingly, the US Supreme Court has ruled that researchers are not public figures in a suit brought by Robert Hutchinson against Senator William Proxmire. Proxmire offered what he called a 'Golden Fleece Award' for publicly funded research which he felt wasteful of the taxpayers' money.

5. Beckford (1985) points out that Scientology for a time explicitly pursued a policy of litigiousness. He adds, however, that the policy was 'officially and publicly regretted and abandoned in 1983' (1985, 248).

6. Fielding's (1982) experience with the National Front is presumably unusual. The NF insisted that he use real names rather than pseudonyms in the book (Fielding, 1981), apparently as a protection against invention.

11

Conclusion

A number of implicit themes run through this book. One is that sensitive topics tax the ingenuity of researchers. To reiterate a point made in Chapter 1, the problems involved in researching sensitive topics encourage researchers to innovate. Methodological innovation has its dangers, notably in an absorption with the technical fix. For example, the considerable effort which has gone into the development of statistically intricate variants of the randomized response technique over the years has not been matched, relatively speaking, by rigorous attempts at validation or research into the practical administration of the method (Umesh and Peterson, 1991). On the other hand, one can observe more positively that the difficulties which surround research on sensitive topics promote potentially useful borrowings from other disciplines and sub-fields. The turning to the work of population ecologists by drug researchers interested in non-agency populations is an obvious example.

One might take this further and suggest, tentatively at least, that researching sensitive topics requires an imaginative cast of mind. Technical competence in research skills, even of the highest quality, is leavened by imagination. Without imagination, as many writers have pointed out, technical solutions risk being applied to research problems in mechanical and inappropriate ways (Mills, 1959; Lieberson, 1985; Webb et al., 1966; 1981; Webb and Weick, 1983; Abrams, 1981; R.G. Burgess, 1990). This point can be put more strongly. To paraphrase Webb and Weick (1983), foolishness is functional in research. This is not, as might seem at first sight, an invitation to make crass decisions. What Webb and Weick have in mind is that the ability to reflect in an imaginative, playful, even fanciful, way is helpful when faced with a difficult research situation. Such reflection serves, as they put it, to 'generate novel inputs and permit people to recognize and break the singular focus toward a problem in which they had persisted' (Webb and Weick, 1983, 213). Breaking the 'singular focus' can mean being open to a variety of research strategies. In the case of sensitive topics this makes at least pragmatic sense. Since routes to sensitive data are often blocked, alternative or multiple methods of reaching one's destination often have to be found. (For this reason, both quantitative and qualitative methods have been treated here in a relatively even-handed manner.) Looked at in this light, methodological invention may also betoken a refusal to be daunted by the obstacles which sensitive topics place in the path of the researcher. Again there are dangers in this, in particular the cutting of ethical corners. One does not, however, have to endorse the ethics of *Tearoom Trade* (Humphreys, 1970), for example, to recognize the indomitable character of its author's overall research strategy.

A second theme running through this book concerns the role of trust in the data collection process. In ideal typical terms, three distinct, but often implicit, conceptions of trust can be found in discussions of research on sensitive topics. A minority view, but one that has been strongly argued, is that what should define the research relationship is not trust but *distrust*. People, especially the powerful, are assumed as a matter of course to have the motive, means and opportunity to conceal information from researchers. To lack suspicion, therefore, is to collude with one's own deception. A second conception sees trust in procedural and consequential terms. Research participants, from this point of view, trust researchers, and therefore disclose to them, if mechanisms or procedures are in place to block possible negative repercussions from involvement in the research. Finally, trust is seen from a third viewpoint as having an emergent character. The establishment of trustful relations depends on the quality of the interpersonal engagement between researcher and researched and the building over the course of the research relationship of increasing levels of fellowship, mutual self-disclosure and reciprocity.

These competing conceptions of trust flow, of course, from sharply differing epistemological, ethical and political assumptions about the character of society and the nature of social research. Each, however, shares an assumption that, in the face of the threat posed by an investigator's interest, research participants mask aspects of their lives and will only drop those masks when they feel it safe to do so. What might be called the sceptical view of trust has not found widespread favour among researchers. Its critics have argued that it has a corrosive potential. A research stance based on distrust undermines the ethical sensitivity of researchers and impairs the relationship both between researcher and researched and between the research community and the wider public. Procedural trust technologies have become strongly embedded in survey research practice. It is clear, however, that they are only partially successful in encouraging research participants to disclose information about sensitive topics. Presumably, such strategies are always vulnerable to a calculation by those who fear incrimination that non-disclosure and non-co-operation, having a fail-safe character, are always potentially better protective strategies. By contrast, growing and deepening levels of disclosure are fostered by the trust which emerges out of an ongoing research relationship. This in turn, however, can increase the potential vulnerability of the discloser. Sustained trustful relations between researcher and researched add to both the volume and the quality of data produced, but in so doing increase the probability of holding sensitive information. In addition, the expressive character of the relationship between researcher and researched means that the dissemination of such information can be problematic. What is made publicly available, and how, may need to be carefully judged if the researcher is not to stand accused of betrayal.

A third theme found in the book is that the context of research is changing. Marsh (1985) has traced how researchers' conceptions of research participants have changed over time. In nineteenth-century social inquiry, and to a lesser extent in the work of the Chicago school of sociology, researchers gathered data from other professionals (Marsh, 1985; Bulmer, 1984). Proxy information about, usually, lower-class or deviant populations was sought from informants because underlying conceptions of social pathology encouraged researchers to devalue direct accounts from respondents in favour of those mediated by officials (see, e.g. Matza, 1969). Over time, however, informant interviewing slowly gave way to respondent interviewing. It was clear that reliable and valid data could be collected directly from research populations, a process which, Marsh points out, both encouraged and was encouraged by methodological developments such as standardized interviewing and random sampling. Marsh goes on to argue that since the Second World War researchers have increasingly developed a conception of the research participant as citizen. As she puts it, 'The subjects of research are increasingly accorded equality of status, and with it a *right* to speak, to have their views heeded' (1985, 218).

Marsh sees this increasing enfranchisement, rather narrowly, in terms of how public opinion, as expressed through polls and surveys, increasingly informs the political process. Seen in a broader context, however, the change represents a shift in the relative power of researchers and research participants. Increasingly, research participants have enhanced legal rights *vis-à-vis* researchers. In itself this is not an unwelcome change. As pointed out in an earlier chapter, however, existing attempts to provide a legal framework for the regulation of social research contain two lessons. One is that often social scientists have had imposed on them inappropriate regulatory frameworks designed to curb abuses by biomedical researchers or commercial interests. The second is that such regimes can unnecessarily hinder research on sensitive topics in ways which arguably run counter to the spirit of the regulatory frameworks which inspired them. Collectively, therefore, social scientists may need to pay sympathetic but critical heed in the future to changing legislative developments on matters such as privacy law, data protection and informed consent.

There is a further sense in which the 'subjects' of research are increasingly having their views heeded. Researchers now often enter collaborative relationships with and for powerless and marginalized groups, and through such relationships provide them with a vehicle for voicing their concerns and aspirations. It is clear that relationships of this kind are not immune to tensions or pressures towards co-option (Lawson, 1991). As Barnes (1984) points out, researchers feel commitments to their discipline which often make them less attached to the views of those they study than research participants would like. The social scientist, as he puts it, is a 'half-hearted, and therefore unreliable, partisan' who is 'necessarily a disappointment to the people he or she studies' (1984, 103). Nevertheless, as community-based AIDS researchers, in particular, have shown, workable models for collaborative relationships can be found (V. Merton, 1990). Perhaps the task for the future is to understand more clearly what makes them viable.

Researching sensitive topics makes substantial demands on researchers. They require skill, tenacity and imagination if they are successfully to confront the problems and issues which arise when research in various ways poses a threat to those who are studied. While this can seem like a daunting enterprise (Lee and Renzetti, 1990), it is also a challenging one.

References

Abrams, Philip 1981 'Visionaries and virtuosi: competence and purpose in the education of sociologists', *Sociology*, 15: 530–8.

Abu-Ela, A.A., B.G. Greenberg and D.G. Horvitz 1967 'A multi-proportions randomized response model', *Journal of the American Statistical Association*, 62: 990–1008.

Adler, Patricia A. 1985 *Wheeling and Dealing: An Ethnography of an Upper-Level Drug Dealing and Smuggling Community*. New York: Columbia University Press.

Adler, Patricia A. and Peter Adler 1987 *Membership Roles in Field Research*. Newbury Park, CA: Sage.

Adler, Patricia A. and Peter Adler 1989 'Self-censorship: the politics of presenting ethnographic data', *Arena Review*, 13: 37–48.

Adler, Patricia A. and Peter Adler 1992 'Ethical issues in self-censorship: ethnographic research on sensitive topics' in Claire M. Renzetti and Raymond M. Lee (eds), *Researching Sensitive Topics*. Newbury Park, CA: Sage.

Adler, Renata 1986 *Reckless Disregard: Westmorland v. CBS et al.; Sharon v. Time*. New York: Knopf.

Akeroyd, Anne V. 1988 'Ethnography, personal data and computers: the implications of data protection legislation for qualitative social research' in Robert G. Burgess (ed.), *Studies in Qualitative Methodology: Volume 1: Conducting Qualitative Research*. Greenwich, CT: JAI Press.

Akeroyd, Anne V. 1991 'Personal information and qualitative research data: some practical and ethical problems arising from data protection legislation' in Nigel G. Fielding and Raymond M. Lee (eds), *Using Computers in Qualitative Research*. London: Sage.

Akers, Ronald L., James Massey, William Clarke and Ronald M. Lauer 1983 'Are self-reports of adolescent deviance valid? Biochemical measures, randomized response, and the bogus pipeline in smoking behavior', *Social Forces*, 62: 234–51.

Alexander, C.S. and H.J. Becker 1978 'The use of vignettes in survey research', *Public Opinion Quarterly*, 42: 93–104.

Alves, W.M. and Peter H. Rossi 1978 'Who should get what? Fairness judgements of the distribution of incomes', *American Journal of Sociology*, 84: 541–64.

Anderson, Michael 1971 *Family Structure in Nineteenth Century Lancashire*. Cambridge: Cambridge University Press.

Anderson, Nels 1923 *The Hobo*. Chicago: Chicago University Press.

Anderson, Sandra C. and Deborah L. Mandell 1989 'The use of self-disclosure by professional social workers', *Social Casework*, 70: 259–67.

Argyris Chris. 1952 'Diagnosing defenses against the outsider', *Journal of Social Issues*, 8: 24–34.

Astin, A.W. and R.F. Boruch 1970 'A "link file system" for assuring confidentiality of research data in longitudinal studies', *American Educational Research Journal*, 7: 615–24.

Bailey, Kenneth D. 1988 'Ethical dilemmas in social problems research: a theoretical framework', *American Sociologist*, 19 :121–37.

Bakanic, Von, Clark McPhail and Rita J. Simon 1987 'The manuscript review and decision making process', *American Sociological Review*, 52: 631–42.

Bakanic, Von, Clark McPhail and Rita J. Simon 1989 'Mixed messages: referees' comments on the manuscripts they review', *Sociological Quarterly*, 30: 639–54.

Barker, Eileen 1984 *The Making of a Moonie: Choice or Brainwashing?* Oxford: Basil Blackwell.

Barnes, J.A. 1963 'Some ethical problems in modern fieldwork', *British Journal of Sociology*, 13: 118–34.

Barnes, J.A. 1979 *Who Should Know What?: Social Science, Privacy and Ethics.* Harmondsworth: Penguin.

Barnes. J.A. 1984 'Ethical and political compromises in social research', *The Wisconsin Sociologist*, 21: 100–10.

Bart, Pauline B. 1981 'A study of women who both were raped and avoided rape', *Journal of Social Issues*, 37: 123–37.

Barton, A.J. 1958 'Asking the embarrassing question', *Public Opinion Quarterly*, 22: 67–8.

Barton, Allen H. 1983 'The American leadership survey: issues, methods and ethics' in Robert B. Smith (ed.), *An Introduction to Social Research: Volume I of Handbook of Social Science Methods.* Cambridge, MA: Ballinger.

Bateson, Nicholas 1984 *Data Construction in Social Surveys*, London: Allen & Unwin.

Beauchamp Tom L., Ruth R. Faden, R. Jay Wallace, Jr and LeRoy Waters 1982 *Ethical Issues in Social Science Research.* Baltimore: Johns Hopkins University Press.

Beck, Bernard 1970 'Cooking welfare stew' in Robert W. Habenstein (ed.), *Pathways to Data.* Chicago: Aldine.

Becker, Howard S. 1963 *Outsiders: Studies in the Sociology of Deviance.* New York: Free Press.

Becker, Howard S. 1964 'Problems in the publication of field studies' in Arthur J. Vidich, Joseph Bensman and Maurice R. Stein (eds), *Reflections on Community Studies.* New York: Wiley.

Becker, Howard S. 1967 'Whose side are we on?', *Social Problems*, 14: 239–47.

Becker, Howard S. 1970 'Practitioners of vice and crime' in Robert W. Habenstein (ed.), *Pathways to Data.* Chicago: Aldine.

Becker, Howard and Irving Horowitz 1972 'Radical politics and sociological research: observations on methodology and ideology', *American Journal of Sociology*, 78: 48–66.

Beckford, James A. 1985 *Cult Controversies: The Societal Response to New Religious Movements.* London: Tavistock.

Beer, William R. 1983 *Househusbands: Men and Housework in American Families.* New York: Praeger.

Beer, William 1987 'Resolute ignorance: social science and affirmative action', *Society*, May/June: 63–9.

Beer, William 1988 'Sociology and the effects of affirmative action: a case of neglect', *American Sociologist*, 19: 218–31.

Beliaev, Edward and Pavel Butorin 1982 'The institutionalization of Soviet sociology: its social and political context', *Social Forces*, 61: 418–35.

Bell, Colin 1977 'Reflections on the Banbury restudy' in Colin Bell and Howard Newby (eds), *Doing Sociological Research*. London: Allen & Unwin.

Bell, Colin 1978 'Studying the locally powerful: personal reflections on a research career' in Colin Bell and Sol Encel (eds), *Inside the Whale*. Rushcutters Bay, NSW: Pergamon.

Bell, Colin 1984 'The SSRC: restructured and defended' in Colin Bell and Helen Roberts (eds), *Social Researching: Politics, Problems, Practice*. London: Routledge & Kegan Paul.

Bell, Colin and Sol Encel 1978 'Introduction' in Colin Bell and Sol Encel (eds),. *Inside the Whale*. Rushcutters Bay, NSW: Pergamon.

Bell, Colin and Howard Newby 1977 'Introduction: the rise of methodological pluralism' in Colin Bell and Howard Newby (eds), *Doing Sociological Research*. London: Allen & Unwin.

Bendix, Reinhard 1951 *Social Science and the Distrust of Reason*. Berkeley: University of California Press.

Bennett, Colin John 1986 'Regulating the Computer: A Comparative Study of Personal Data Protection Policy'. Unpublished PhD thesis, University of Illinois, Urbana Champaign.

Benson, Susan 1981 *Ambiguous Ethnicity*. Cambridge: Cambridge University Press.

Benton, Ted 1981 'Objective interests and the sociology of power', *Sociology*, 15: 161–84.

Ben-Tovim, Gideon, John Gabriel, Ian Law and Kathleen Stredder 1986 *The Local Politics of Race*. London: Macmillan.

Berardo, Felix M. and Constance L. Shehan 1984 'Family scholarship: a reflection of the changing family', *Journal of Family Issues*, 5: 577–98.

Berger, Peter L. and Hansfreid Kellner 1981 *Sociology Reinterpreted: An Essay on Method and Vocation*. Garden City, NY: Anchor Books.

Berk, Richard A. and Joseph M. Adams 1970 'Establishing rapport with deviant groups', *Social Problems*, 18: 102–17.

Best, Joel 1987 'Rhetoric in claims-making: constructing the missing children problem', *Social Problems*, 34: 101–21.

Best, Joel 1989 'Dark figures and child victims: statistical claims about missing children' in Joel Best (ed.), *Images of Issues: Typifying Contemporary Social Problems*. New York: Aldine de Gruyter.

Best, Joel and David Luckenbill 1980 'The social organization of deviants', *Social Problems*, 28: 14–31.

Beynon, Huw 1988 'Regulating research: politics and decision making in industrial organizations' in Alan Bryman (ed.), *Doing Research in Organizations*. London: Routledge.

Bibby, Reginald W. and Armand L. Mauss 1974 'Skidders and their servants: variable goals and functions of the Skid Road Rescue Mission', *Journal for the Scientific Study of Religion*, 13: 421–36.

Biderman, Albert D. and Albert J. Reiss, Jr 1967 'On exploring the "dark figure" of crime', *Annals of the American Academy of Political and Social Science*, 374: 1–15.

Biernacki, P. and D. Waldorf. 1981 'Snowball sampling: problems and techniques of chain referral sampling', *Sociological Methods and Research*, 10: 141–63.

Birkinshaw , Patrick 1988 *Freedom of Information: The Law, the Practice and the Ideal*. London: Weidenfeld & Nicolson.

Bittner, Egon 1973 'Objectivity and realism in sociology' in George Psathas (ed.), *Phenomenological Sociology: Issues and Applications*. New York: Wiley.

Blau, Peter M. 1955 *The Dynamics of Bureaucracy*. Chicago: Chicago University Press.

Blau, Peter M. 1964a 'The research process in the study of the dynamics of bureaucracy' in Phillip H. Hammond (ed.), *Sociologists at Work*. Boston: Basic Books.

Blau, Peter M. 1964b *Exchange and Power in Social Life*. New York: Wiley.

Blauner, Bob and David Wellman 1982 'The researcher and the researched: decolonizing social research' in Robert B. Smith and Peter K. Manning (eds) *A Handbook of Social Science Methods: Volume 2: Qualitative Methods*. Cambridge, MA: Ballinger.

Blower, J. Gordon, Laurence M. Cook and James A. Bishop 1981 *Estimating the Size of Animal Populations*. London: Allen & Unwin.

Blumberg, Herbert H. and B. Elizabeth Dronfield 1976 'Nomination techniques in the study of largely invisible groups: opiate users not at drug dependency clinics', *Social Science and Medicine*, 10: 415–22.

Boissevain, Jeremy 1974 *Friends of Friends: Networks, Manipulators and Coalitions*. Oxford: Basil Blackwell.

Bok, Sissela 1984 *Secrets: Concealment and Revelation*. Oxford: Oxford University Press.

Bond, Kathleen 1978 'Confidentiality and the protection of human subjects in social science research: a report on recent developments', *American Sociologist*, 13: 144–52.

Boruch, Robert F. 1979 'Methods of assuring personal integrity in social research: an introduction' in Martin Bulmer (ed.), *Censuses, Surveys and Privacy*. London: Macmillan.

Boruch Robert F. and Joe S. Cecil 1979 *Assuring the Confidentiality of Social Research Data*. Philadelphia: University of Pennsylvania Press.

Bossy, John 1975 'The social history of confession in the age before the Reformation', *Transactions of the Royal Historical Society (Fifth Series)*, 25: 21–38.

Bossy, John 1985 *Christianity in the West, 1400–1700*. Oxford: Oxford University Press.

Bouchard, Thomas J. 1976 'Unobtrusive measures: an inventory of uses', *Sociological Methods and Research*, 4: 267–300.

Bourgois, Phillipe 1989 'Crack in Spanish Harlem: culture and economy in the inner city', *Anthropology Today*, 5 (4): 6–11.

Bowser, Benjamin P. and Jean E. Sieber 1992 'AIDS prevention research: old problems and new solutions' in Claire M. Renzetti and Raymond M. Lee (eds), *Researching Sensitive Topics*. Newbury Park, CA: Sage.

Box, Steven 1981 *Deviance, Reality and Society* (2nd edn). London: Holt, Rienhart & Winston.

Bradburn, Norman M. 1983 'Response effects' in Peter H. Rossi, James D. Wright and Andy B. Anderson (eds), *Handbook of Survey Research*. New York: Academic Press.

Bradburn, Norman M. and Seymour Sudman 1979 *Improving Interview Method and Questionnaire Design*. San Francisco: Jossey-Bass.

Braithwaite, John 1984 *Corporate Crime in the Pharmaceutical Industry*. London: Routledge & Kegan Paul.

Braithwaite, John 1985 'Corporate crime research: why two interviewers are needed', *Sociology*, 19: 136–8.

Braithwaite, John, Brent Fisse and Gilbert Geis 1987 'Covert facilitation and crime: restoring the balance to the entrapment debate', *Journal of Social Issues*, 43: 5–42.

Brajuha, Mario and Lyle Hallowell 1986 'Legal intrusion and the politics of fieldwork: the impact of the Brajuha case', *Urban Life*, 14: 454–78.

Brannen, Julia 1988 'The study of sensitive subjects', *Sociological Review*, 36: 552–63.

Brenner, Michael 1978 'Interviewing: the social phenomenology of a research instrument' in Michael Brenner, Peter Marsh and Marilyn Brenner (eds), *The Social Contexts of Method*. London: Croom Helm.

Brewer, John D. 1990a 'Sensitivity as a problem in field research: a study of routine policing in Northern Ireland', *American Behavioral Scientist*, 33: 578–93.

Brewer, John D. 1990b *Inside the RUC: Routine Policing in a Divided Society*. Oxford: Oxford University Press.

Bridges, David 1989 'Ethics and the law: conducting case studies of policing' in Robert G. Burgess (ed.), *The Ethics of Educational Research*. London: Falmer Press.

Briggs, Charles L. 1987 *Learning How to Ask: A Sociolinguistic Appraisal of the Role of the Interview in Social Science Research*. Cambridge: Cambridge University Press.

Broadhead, Robert S. 1984 'Human rights and human subjects: ethics and strategies in social science research', *Sociological Inquiry*, 54: 107–23.

Broadhead, Robert S. and Ray C. Rist 1976 'Gatekeepers and the social control of social research', *Social Problems*, 23: 325–36.

Brown, C. and J. Ritchie 1981 *Focussed Enumeration: The Development of a Method of Sampling Ethnic Minority Groups*. London: Policy Studies Institute and Social and Community Planning Research.

Brown, Julia S. and Brian G. Gilmartin 1969 'Sociology today: lacunae, emphases and surfeits', *American Sociologist*, 4: 283–91.

Brown, Richard 1984 'For your eyes only' *Network: Newsletter of the British Sociological Association*, 30: 1.

Bruce, Steve 1987 'Gullible's travels: the native sociologist' in Neil P. McKegany and Sarah Cunningham-Burley (eds), *Enter the Sociologist: Reflections on the Practice of Sociology*. Aldershot: Avebury.

Bryan, James H. 1965 'Apprenticeships in prostitution', *Social Problems*, 12: 287–97.

Bryant, Christopher G.A. 1985 *Positivism in Social Theory and Research*. London: Macmillan.

Bryman, Alan 1988 *Quantity and Quality in Social Research*. London: Unwin Hyman.

Bulmer, Martin 1980 'Why don't sociologists make more use of official statistics?', *Sociology*, 14: 505–23.

Bulmer, Martin 1982a 'The merits and demerits of covert participant observation' in Martin Bulmer (ed.), *Social Research Ethics*. London: Macmillan.

Bulmer, Martin 1982b 'The research ethics of pseudo-patient studies: a new look at the merits of covert ethnographic methods', *Sociological Review*, 30: 628–48.

Bulmer, Martin 1984 *The Chicago School of Sociology: Institutionalization, Diversity and the Rise of Sociological Research*. Chicago: Chicago University Press.

Bulmer, Martin 1987 'Governments and social science: patterns of mutual influence' in Martin Bulmer (ed.), *Social Science Research and Government: Comparative Essays on Britain and the United States*. Cambridge: Cambridge University Press.

Burgess, Ernest 1932 'Discussion' in Clifford R. Shaw, *The Natural History of a Delinquent Career*. Chicago: University of Chicago Press.

Burgess, Robert G. 1984 *In the Field*. London: Allen & Unwin.

Burgess, Robert G. 1990 'Sociologists, training and research', *Sociology*, 24: 579–95.

Burstein, Paul 1991 '"Reverse discrimination" cases in the Federal courts: legal mobilization by a countermovement', *Sociological Quarterly*, 32: 511–28.

Burton, Frank, 1978 *The Politics of Legitimacy: Struggle in a Belfast Community*. London: Routledge & Kegan Paul.

Bury, Michael and Jonathan Gabe 1990 'Hooked? Media responses to tranquillizer dependence' in Pamela Abbott and Geoff Payne (eds), *New Directions in the Sociology of Health*. London: Falmer Press.

Button, K.J. 1984 'Regional variations in the irregular economy: a study of possible trends', *Regional Studies*, 18: 385–92.

Bytheway, Bill 1986 'Redundancy and the older worker' in Raymond M. Lee (ed.), *Redundancy, Lay-offs and Plant Closures: Their Causes, Character and Consequences*. Beckenham: Croom Helm.

Callender, Claire 1986 'Women and the redundancy process: a case study' in Raymond M. Lee (ed.), *Redundancy, Lay-offs and Plant Closures: Their Causes, Character and Consequences*. Beckenham: Croom Helm.

Campbell, Donald T., Robert F. Boruch, Richard D. Schwartz and Joseph Steinberg 1977 'Confidentiality-preserving modes of access to files and to interfile exchange for useful statistical analysis', *Evaluation Quarterly*, 1: 269–300.

Cannell, Charles F. 1985 'Overview: response bias and interviewer variability on surveys' in Terence W. Beed and Robert J. Stimson (eds), *Survey Interviewing: Theory and Techniques*. Sydney: Allen & Unwin.

Cannell, Charles F. and Robert L. Kahn 1968 'Interviewing' in Lindzey Gardner and Elliot Aronson (eds), *The Handbook of Social Psychology*. Reading, MA: Addison-Wesley.

Cannon, Sue 1989 'Social research in stressful settings: difficulties for the sociologist studying the treatment of breast cancer', *Sociology of Health and Illness*, 11: 62–77.

Cannon, Sue 1992 'Reflections on fieldwork in stressful situations' in Robert G. Burgess (ed.), *Studies in Qualitative Methodology: Volume 3: Learning about Fieldwork*. Greenwich, CT: JAI Press.

Caplan, Arthur L. 1982 'On privacy and confidentiality in social science research' in Tom L. Beauchamp, Ruth R. Faden, R. Jay Wallace, Jr and LeRoy Waters (eds), *Ethical Issues in Social Science Research*. Baltimore: Johns Hopkins University Press.

Carey, James T. 1972 'Problems of access and risk in observing drug scenes' in Jack D. Douglas (ed.), *Research on Deviance*. New York: Random House.

Carey, James T. 1975 *Sociology and Public Affairs: The Chicago School*. Beverly Hills: Sage.

Carter, Lewis F. 1987 'The "new renunciates" of the Bhagwan Shree Rajneesh: observations and identification of problems of interpreting new religious movements', *Journal for the Scientific Study of Religion*, 26: 148–72.

Cassell, Joan 1988 'The relationship of observer to observed when studying up' in Robert G. Burgess (ed.), *Studies in Qualitative Methodology: Volume 1: Conducting Qualitative Research*. Greenwich, CT: JAI Press.

Caudill, William 1958 *The Pyschiatric Hospital as a Small Society*. Cambridge, MA: Harvard University Press.

Cavan, Sherri 1966 *Liquor License*. Chicago: Aldine.

Cavendish, Ruth 1982 *Women on the Line*. London: Routledge & Kegan Paul.

Ceci, Stephen J., Douglas Peters and Jonathan Plotkin 1985 'Human subjects review, personal values and the regulation of social science research', *American Psychologist*, 40, 994–1002.

Channels, Noreen L. 1992 'Anticipating media coverage: methodological decisions in criminal justice research' in Claire M. Renzetti and Raymond M. Lee (eds), *Researching Sensitive Topics*. Newbury Park, CA: Sage.

Chesler, Mark A., Joseph Sanders and Debra S. Kalmuss 1988 *Social Science in Court: Mobilizing Experts in School Desegregation Cases*. Madison, WI: University of Wisconsin Press.

Chibnall, Steve 1977 *Law-and-Order News: An Analysis of Crime Reporting in the British Press*. London: Tavistock.

Christie, Robert M. 1976 'Comment on conflict methodology: a protagonist position', *Sociological Quarterly*, 17: 513–9.

Chubin, Daryl and James L. McCartney 1982 'Financing sociological research: a future only dimly perceived', *American Sociologist*, 17: 226–35.

Cicourel, Aaron V. 1964 *Method and Measurement in Sociology*. New York: Free Press.

Cisin, Ira H. and Judith Droitcourt Miller 1981 'New survey-based estimating techniques'. Paper presented to the Annual Meeting of the American Public Health Association, Los Angeles.

Clark, John P. and Larry L. Tifft 1966 'Polygraph and interview validation of self-reported deviant behavior', *American Sociological Review*, 31: 516–22.

Cohen, Phil 1979 'Turn out your pockets: some personal observations on the political science of police'. Unpublished MS, Institute of Education, University of London.

Cohen, Stanley 1972 *Folk Devils and Moral Panics: The Creation of the Mods and Rockers*. London: McGibbon & Kee.

Cohen, Stanley and Laurie Taylor 1977 'Talking about prison blues' in Colin Bell and Howard Newby (eds), *Doing Sociological Research*. London: Allen & Unwin.

Coleman, James S. 1958 'Relational analysis: the study of social organization with survey methods', *Human Organization*, 16: 28–36.

Coleman, James S. 1984 'Issues in the institutionalization of social policy' in Torsten Husén and Maurice Kogan (eds), *Educational Research and Policy: How Do They Relate?* Oxford: Pergamon Press.

Coleman, James S., Sara D. Kelly and John A. Moore 1975 'Recent trends in school integration'. Paper presented to the Annual Meeting of the American Educational Research Association, Washington DC.

Coleman, Kenneth M. and Lee Seligman 1988 'The 1985 USIA Central American Surveys', *Public Opinion Quarterly*, 52: 552–6.

Collins, H.M. and T.J. Pinch 1979 'The construction of the paranormal: nothing unscientific is happening' in Roy Wallis (ed.), *On the Margins of Science: The Social Construction of Rejected Knowledge*. Keele University: Sociological Review Monograph, No. 27.

Collins, Martin 1980 'Interviewer variability: a review of the problem', *Journal of the Market Research Society*, 22: 77–95.

Colvard, Richard 1967 'Interaction and identification in reporting field research: a critical reconsideration of protective procedures' in Gideon Sjoberg (ed.), *Ethics, Politics and Social Research*, London: Routledge & Kegan Paul.

218   *Doing Research on Sensitive Topics*

Condominas, Georges 1977 *We Have Eaten the Forest: The Story of a Montagnard Village in the Central Highlands of Vietnam*. London: Allen & Unwin.
Conrath, David W., Christopher A. Higgins and Ronald J. McClean 1983 'A comparison of the reliability of questionnaire versus diary data', *Social Networks*, 5: 315–22.
Converse, Jean M. 1987 *Survey Research in the United States: Roots and Emergence 1890–1960*. Berkeley: University of California Press.
Converse, Jean M. and Stanley Presser 1986 *Survey Questions: Handcrafting the Standardized Questionnaire*. Beverly Hills: Sage.
Cook, Karen S. and Richard M. Emerson 1978 'Power, equity and commitment in exchange networks', *American Sociological Review*, 43: 721–39.
Cook T.D. and Donald T. Campbell 1979 *Quasi-experimentation: Design and Analysis for Field Settings*. Chicago: Rand McNally.
Cope, David R. 1979 'Census-taking and the debate on privacy: a sociological view' in Martin Bulmer (ed.), *Censuses, Surveys and Privacy*. London: Macmillan.
Cornfield, Daniel B. 1986 'Ethnic inequality in layoff chances: the impact of unionization on layoff procedure' in Raymond M. Lee (ed.), *Redundancy, Layoffs and Plant Closures: Their Causes, Character and Consequences*. Beckenham: Croom Helm.
Council of Europe 1981 *Convention for the Protection of Individuals with Regard to the Automatic Processing of Personal Data*. Strasbourg: Council of Europe.
Cox, Eva, Fran Hausfield and Sue Wills 1978 'Taking the Queen's shilling: accepting social research consultancies in the 1970s' in Colin Bell and Sol Encel (eds), *Inside the Whale*. Rushcutters Bay, NSW: Pergamon.
Coxon, A.P.M. 1986 *Homosexual Sexual Behaviour*. University College Cardiff: Social Research Unit, Project SIGMA Working Paper, No. 9.
Coxon, Tony 1988 'Something sensational . . . The sexual diary as a tool for mapping detailed sexual behaviour', *Sociological Review*, 36: 353–67.
Cunningham-Burley, Sarah 1985 'Rules, roles and communicative performance in qualitative research interviews', *International Journal of Sociology and Social Policy*, 5: 67–77.
Curran, Daniel J. and Sandra Cook 1992 'Doing research in post-Tiananmen China' in Claire M. Renzetti and Raymond M. Lee (eds), *Researching Sensitive Topics*. Newbury Park, CA: Sage.
Curran, James, Angus Douglas and Gary Whannel 1980 'The political economy of the human-interest story' in Anthony Smith (ed.), *Newspapers and Democracy: Essays On a Changing Medium*. Cambridge, MA: MIT Press.
Dabbs, James M., Jr 1982 'Making things visible' in John Van Maanen, James M. Dabbs, Jr and Robert B. Faulkner (eds), *Varieties of Qualitative Research*. Beverly Hills: Sage.
Dale, Angela, Sara Arber and Michael Procter 1988 *Doing Secondary Analysis*. London: Unwin Hyman.
Dalenius, T. and A. Klevmarken 1974 *Personal Integrity and the Need for Data in the Social Sciences*. Stockholm: Swedish Council for Social Science Research.
Daniels, Arlene Kaplan 1967 'The low-caste stranger in social research' in Gideon Sjoberg (ed.), *Ethics, Politics and Social Research*. London: Routledge & Kegan Paul.
Data Protection Registrar 1987 *Data Protection Act: Guideline 6: The Exemptions*. Wilmslow, Cheshire.

Davies, P. M. 1986 *Some Problems in Defining and Sampling Non-heterosexual Males*. University College Cardiff: Social Research Unit Working Paper, No. 21.

Davis, Nannette 1982 'Researching an abortion market' in Robert B. Smith and Peter K. Manning (eds), *A Handbook of Social Science Methods. Volume 2: Qualitative Methods*. Cambridge, MA: Ballinger.

Day, K.J. 1985 'Perspectives on Privacy: A Sociological Analysis'. Unpublished PhD thesis, University of Edinburgh.

Dean, John P., Robert L. Eichhorn and Lois R. Dean 1969 'Fruitful informants for intensive interviewing' in George J. McCall and J.L. Simmons (eds), *Issues in Participant Observation: A Text and Reader*. Reading, MA: Addison-Wesley.

Dench, Geoff 1975 *The Maltese in London*. London: Routledge & Kegan Paul.

Denzin, Norman K. 1970 *The Research Act in Sociology*. London: Butterworths.

Dewdney, John C. 1983 'The 1981 Census and its results' in David Rhind (ed.), *A Census User's Handbook*. London: Methuen.

Diches, David 1986 'The phenomenon of violence' in David Diches (ed.), *The Anthropology of Violence*. Oxford: Basil Blackwell.

Diener, Edward and Rick Crandall 1978 *Ethics in Social and Behavioral Research*. Chicago: University of Chicago Press.

Dillman, Don A. 1978 *Mail and Telephone Surveys: The Total Design Method*. New York: Wiley.

Dilnot, A. and C.N. Morris 1981 'What do we know about the black economy?', *Fiscal Studies*, 2: 58–73.

Dingwall, Robert G. 1980 'Ethics and ethnography', *Sociological Review*, 28: 871–91.

Ditton, Jason 1977 *Part-time Crime*. London: Macmillan.

Ditton, Jason and R. Williams 1981 'The Fundable versus the Doable'. Glasgow: University of Glasgow, Department of Sociology, Occasional Paper.

Dobash, R. Emerson and Russell Dobash 1979 *Violence against Wives*. New York: Free Press.

Douglas, Dorothy 1972 'Managing fronts in observing deviance' in Jack D. Douglas (ed.), *Research on Deviance*. New York: Random House.

Douglas, Jack D. 1976 *Investigative Social Research*. Beverly Hills: Sage.

Douglas, Jack D. 1978 'Comment', *American Sociologist*, 13: 157–8.

Douglas, Mary 1985 *Risk Acceptability according to the Social Sciences*. London: Routledge & Kegan Paul.

Downes, David and Paul Rock 1988 *Understanding Deviance* (2nd edn). Oxford: Clarendon Press.

Duffy, John C. and Jennifer J. Waterton 1984 'Randomized response models for estimating the distribution function of a quantitative character', *International Statistical Review*, 52: 165–71.

Dunwoody, Sharon 1986 'When science writers cover the social sciences' in Jeffrey H. Goldstein (ed.), *Reporting Science: The Case of Aggression*. Hillsdale, NJ: Lawrence Erlbaum Associates.

Edgell, Stephen E., Samuel Himmelfarb and Karen L. Duchan 1982 'Validity of forced responses in a randomized response model', *Sociological Methods and Research*, 11: 89–100.

Eglin, Peter 1987 'The meaning and use of official statistics in the explanation of deviance' in R.J. Anderson, J.A. Hughes and W.W. Sharrock (eds), *Classic Disputes in Sociology*. London: Allen & Unwin.

220 *Doing Research on Sensitive Topics*

Eichler, Margit 1988 *Nonsexist Research Methods: A Practical Guide*. Boston: Allen & Unwin.

Ekker Knut, Greg Gifford, Sheila A. Leik and Robert A. Leik 1988 'Using microcomputer game-simulation experiments to study family response to the Mt St Helens eruptions', *Social Science Computer Review*, 6: 90–105.

Ellen, Roy 1984 'Data into text' in *Ethnographic Research: A Guide to General Conduct* (ASA Research Methods in Social Anthropology 1). London: Academic Press.

Emerson Richard M. 1962 'Power–dependence relations', *American Sociological Review*, 27: 31–40 .

Emerson, Robert M. 1981 'Observational field work', *Annual Review of Sociology*, 7: 351–78.

Erikson, Kai T. 1968 'A reply to Denzin', *Social Problems*, 15: 505–6.

European Commission 1990 *Proposal for a Council Directive Concerning the Protection of Individuals in Relation to the Processing of Personal Data*. Brussels, COM(90) 314 final.

Evans, James and Antony Whitaker 1988 'Libel', *Writers' and Artists' Yearbook*. London: Black.

Faden, Ruth R. and Tom L. Beauchamp 1986 *A History and Theory of Informed Consent*. New York: Oxford University Press.

Faraday, Annabel and Kenneth Plummer 1979 'Doing life histories', *Sociological Review*, 27: 773–98.

Farberow, Norman L. 1963 'Introduction' in Norman L. Farberow (ed.), *Taboo Topics*. New York: Atherton Press.

Feige, E.L. and H.W. Watt 1970 'Protection of privacy through microaggregation' in R.L. Biscoe (ed.), *Data Bases, Computers and the Social Sciences*. New York: Wiley.

Felson, Richard B. 1991 'Blame analysis: accounting for the behavior of protected groups', *American Sociologist*, 22: 5–23.

Fetterman, David E. 1989 *Ethnography: Step by Step*. Newbury Park, CA: Sage.

Fichter, Joseph and William L. Kolb 1953 'Ethical limitations on sociological reporting', *American Sociological Review*, 18: 544–50.

Fielding, Nigel G. 1981 *The National Front*. London: Routledge & Kegan Paul.

Fielding, Nigel G. 1982 'Observational research on the National Front' in Martin Bulmer (ed.), *Social Research Ethics*. London: Macmillan.

Fielding, Nigel G. 1990 'Mediating the message: affinity and hostility in research on sensitive topics', *American Behavioral Scientist*, 33: 608–20.

Finch, Janet 1984 '"It's great to have someone to talk to": the ethics and politics of interviewing women' in Colin Bell and Helen Roberts (eds), *Social Researching: Politics, Problems, Practice*. London: Routledge & Kegan Paul.

Finch, Janet 1986 *Research and Policy*. London: Falmer Press.

Finch, Janet 1987 'The vignette technique in survey research', *Sociology*, 21: 105–14.

Fineman, Stephen 1983 *White Collar Unemployment: Impact and Stress*. Chichester: Wiley.

Fishburne, Patricia 1980 'Survey Techniques for Studying Threatening Topics'. Unpublished PhD thesis, New York University.

Flaherty, David H. 1979 *Privacy and Government Data Banks: An International Comparison*. London: Mansell.

Flaherty, David H. 1984 'The need for an American Privacy Commission', *Government Information Quarterly*, 1: 235–58.

Flather , Paul 1987 '"Pulling through": conspiracies, counterplots and how the SSRC escaped the axe in 1982', in Martin Bulmer (ed.), *Social Science Research and Government: Comparative Essays on Britain and the United States*. Cambridge: Cambridge University Press.

Form, William H. 1971 'The sociology of social research' in Richard O'Toole (ed.), *The Organization, Management and Tactics of Social Research*. Cambridge, MA: Schenckman.

Form, William H. 1973 'Field problems in comparative research: the politics of distrust' in Michael Armer and Allen D. Grimshaw (eds), *Comparative Social Research: Methodological Problems and Strategies*. New York: Wiley.

Foucault, Michel 1981 *The History of Sexuality: Volume 1: An Introduction*. Harmondsworth: Penguin.

Fox, James Alan and Paul E. Tracy 1984 'Measuring associations with randomized response', *Social Science Research*, 13: 188–97.

Fox, James Alan and Paul E. Tracy 1986 *Randomized Response: A Method for Sensitive Surveys*. Beverly Hills: Sage.

Freese, Jan 1985 'Data regulations: the Swedish experience' in J.J.P. Kenney (ed.), *Data Privacy and Security: State of the Art Report*. Oxford: Pergamon Infotech.

Frey, B.S. and W.W. Pommerehne 1982 'Measuring the hidden economy: though this be madness, there is method in it' in Victor Tanzi (ed.), *The Underground Economy in the United States and Abroad*. Lexington, MA: D.C. Heath.

Frey B.S. and H. Weck 1983 'What produces a hidden economy? An international cross-section analysis', *Southern Economic Journal*, 49: 822–32.

Frisch, Michael and Dorothy L. Watts 1980 'Oral history and the presentation of class consciousness: the *New York Times* versus the Buffalo unemployed', *International Journal of Oral History*, 1: 88–110.

Fryer, Bob 1981 'State, redundancy and the law' in B. Fryer, A. Hunt, D. McBarnet and B. Moorehouse (eds), *Law, State and Society*. London: Croom Helm.

Fuller, Linda 1988 'Fieldwork in forbidden terrain: the US State and the case of Cuba', *American Sociologist*, 99–120.

Fulton, John F. 1975 'Intermarriage and the Irish clergy: a sociological study' in Michael Hurley (ed.), *Beyond Tolerance: The Challenge of Mixed Marriage*. London: Geoffrey Chapman.

Gabe, Jonathan and Michael Bury 1988 'Tranquillisers as a social problem', *Sociological Review*, 36: 320–52.

Gabe, Jonathan, Ulla Gustafsson and Michael Bury 1991 'Mediating illness: newspaper coverage of tranquilliser dependence', *Sociology of Health and Illness*, 13: 332–53.

Galliher, John F. 1973 'The protection of human subjects: a re-examination of the professional code of ethics', *American Sociologist*, 8: 93–100.

Galliher, John F. 1980 'Social scientists' ethical responsibilities to superordinates: looking upward meekly', *Social Problems*, 27: 298–308.

Galliher, John F. and James L. McCartney 1973 'The influence of funding agencies on juvenile delinquency research', *Social Problems*, 21: 77–90.

Galtung, Johan 1967 *Theory and Methods of Social Research*. London: Allen & Unwin.

Gans, Herbert J. 1962 *The Urban Villagers*. New York: Free Press.

Garber, Edith E. 1979 'Privacy and social research' in Murray L. Wax and Joan Cassell (eds), *Federal Regulations: Ethical Issues and Social Research*. Boulder,

CO: Westview Press and The American Association for the Advancement of Science.

Garfinkel, Harold 1967 *Studies in Ethnomethodology.* Englewood Cliffs, NJ: Prentice-Hall.

Gelles, Richard J. 1973 'Child abuse as psychopathology: a sociological critique and reformulation', *American Journal of Orthopsychiatry*, 43: 611–21.

Gelsthorpe, Loraine and Allison Morris 1988 'Feminism and criminology in Britain', *British Journal of Criminology*, 28: 93–110.

George, Alison 1983 '"You know . . ., you know . . .": the theoretical and methodological implications of what is not said in interviews'. Paper presented at British Sociological Association Conference, Cardiff.

Gerson, Elihu M. 1984 'Qualitative research and the computer', *Qualitative Sociology*, 7: 61–74.

Giddens, Anthony 1976 *New Rules of Sociological Method: A Positive Critique of Interpretative Sociologies.* London: Hutchinson.

Gillespie, Dair L. and Ann Leffler 1987 'The politics of research methodology in claims-making activities: social science and sexual harassment', *Social Problems*, 21: 77–90.

Gilmore, David D. 1991 'Subjectivity and subjugation: fieldwork in the stratified community', *Human Organization*, 50: 215–24.

Gladwin, Thomas 1972 'Comment on Hessler and New', *Human Organization*, 31: 452–4.

Glaser, Barney G. and Anselm L. Strauss 1967 *The Discovery of Grounded Theory.* Chicago: Aldine.

Glass, Gene V., Barry McGaw and Mary Lee Smith 1981 *Meta-analysis in Social Research.* Beverly Hills: Sage.

Goffman, Erving 1956 *The Presentation of Self in Everyday Life.* Edinburgh: Social Sciences Research Centre.

Goffman, Erving 1957 'Alienation from interaction', *Human Relations*, 10: 47–59.

Goffman, Erving 1961 *Asylums: Essays on the Social Situation of Mental Patients and Other Inmates.* New York: Doubleday Anchor.

Goffman, Erving 1963 *Stigma: Notes on the Management of Spoiled Identity.* Englewood Cliffs, NJ: Prentice-Hall.

Gold, Margaret 1977 'A crisis of identity: the case of medical sociology', *Journal of Health and Social Behavior*, 18: 160–8.

Golding, Peter and Sandra Middleton 1982 *Images of Welfare.* Oxford: Martin Robertson.

Goldstein, Michael S. 1984 'Creating and controlling a medical abortion market in Los Angeles after liberalization', *Social Problems*, 31: 514–29.

Goodell, Rae 1987 'The role of the mass media in scientific controversy' in H. Tristam Engelhardt, Jr and Arthur L. Caplan (eds), *Scientific Controversies: Case Studies in the Resolution and Closure of Disputes in Science and Technology.* Cambridge: Cambridge University Press.

Goodstadt, Michael S., Gaynoll Cook and Valerie Gruson 1978 'The validity of reported drug use: the randomized response technique', *International Journal of the Addictions*, 13: 359–67.

Gordon, Robert A. 1980 'Research on IQ, race and delinquency: taboo or not taboo' in Edward Sagarin (ed.), *Taboos in Criminology.* Beverly Hills: Sage.

Goudy, Willis J. and Robert O. Richards 1973 'On resistance to community surveys: who puts the bite on whom?', *Social Problems*, 20: 400–1.

Gouldner, Alvin W. 1954 *Patterns of Industrial Bureaucracy*. Glencoe, IL: Free Press.

Gouldner, Alvin W. 1962 'Anti-minotaur: the myth of value-free sociology', *Social Problems*, 9: 199–213.

Gouldner, Alvin W. 1968 'The sociologist as partisan', *American Sociologist*, 3: 103–16.

Gouldner, Alvin W. 1970 *The Coming Crisis in Sociology*. London: Heinemann.

Gouldner, Alvin W. 1973 *For Sociology: Renewal and Critique in Sociology Today*. Harmonsdworth: Penguin.

Goyder, John 1987 *The Silent Minority: Non-respondents on Sample Surveys*. Cambridge: Polity Press.

Graham, Hilary 1983 '"Do her answers fit his questions?": women and the survey method' in Eva Gamarnikow, David Morgan, June Purvis and Daphne Taylorson (eds), *The Public and the Private*. London: Heinemann.

Granovetter, Mark S. 1973 'The strength of weak ties', *American Journal of Sociology*, 78: 1360–80.

Granovetter, Mark S. 1974 *Getting a Job*. Cambridge, MA: Harvard University Press.

Gray, Bradford H. 1979 'Human subjects review committees and social research' in Murray L. Wax and Joan Cassell (eds), *Federal Regulations: Ethical Issues and Social Research*. Boulder, CO: Westview Press and The American Association for the Advancement of Science.

Gray, Bradford H. 1982 'The regulatory context of social and behavioral research' in Tom L. Beauchamp , Ruth R. Faden, R. Jay Wallace, Jr and LeRoy Waters (eds), *Ethical Issues in Social Science Research*. Baltimore: Johns Hopkins University Press.

Greenberg, B.G., A. Abu-Ela, W.R.Simmons and D.G. Horvitz 1969 'The unrelated question randomized response model: theoretical framework', *Journal of the American Statistical Association*, 64: 520–59.

Greenberg, B.G., R.R. Keubler, J.R. Abernethy and D.G. Horvitz 1971 'Application of the randomized response technique in obtaining quantitative data', *Journal of the American Statistical Association*, 66: 243–50.

Groves, Robert M. and Robert L. Kahn 1979 *Surveys by Telephone: A National Comparison with Personal Interviews*. New York: Academic Press.

Guillemin, Jeanne and Irving Louis Horowitz 1983 'Social research and political advocacy: new stages and old problems in integrating science and values' in Daniel Callahan and Bruce Jennings (eds), *Ethics, the Social Sciences and Policy Analysis*. New York: Plenum.

Gusfield, Joseph R. 1955 'Field work reciprocities in studying a social movement', *Human Organization*, 14: 29–34.

Hakim, Catherine 1979 'Census confidentiality in Britain' in Martin Bulmer (ed.), *Censuses, Surveys and Privacy*. London: Macmillan.

Hakim, Catherine 1985 *Employers' Use of Outwork: A Study Using the 1980 Workplace Industrial Relations Survey and the 1981 National Homeworking Survey*. London: Department of Employment Research Paper, No. 44.

Hakim, Catherine 1982 'Secondary analysis and the relationship between official and academic research', *Sociology*, 16: 12–28.

Hammar, T. 1976 'The political resocialization of immigrants project' in T. Dalenius and A. Klevmarken (eds), *Personal Integrity and the Need for Data in the Social Sciences*. Stockholm: Swedish Council for Social Research.

Hammersley, Martyn and Paul Atkinson 1983 *Ethnography: Principles in Practice*. London: Tavistock.

Hammond, Philip E. 1964 *Sociologists at Work*. Boston: Basic Books.

Hanmer, Jalna and Diana Leonard 1984 'Negotiating the problem: the DHSS and research on violence in marriage' in Colin Bell and Helen Roberts (eds), *Social Researching: Politics, Problems, Practice*. London: Routledge & Kegan Paul.

Harding, Philip and Richard Jenkins 1989 *The Myth of the Hidden Economy*. Milton Keynes: Open University Press.

Hardy, Cynthia 1985 *Managing Organizational Closure*. Farnborough: Gower.

Hargreaves, Fiona and Howard Levenson 1985 *A Practictioner's Guide to the Police and Criminal Evidence Act*. London: Legal Action Group.

Harris, C.C. and the Swansea Redundancy and Unemployment Research Group 1987 *Redundancy and Recession in South Wales*. Oxford: Basil Blackwell.

Hartnoll, Richard, Emmanuelle Daviaud, Roger Lewis and Martin Mitcheson 1985a *Drug Problems: Assessing Local Needs*. London: Drug Indicators Project, Birkbeck College, University of London.

Hartnoll, Richard, Martin Mitcheson, Roger Lewis and Susan Bryer 1985b 'Estimating the prevalence of opioid dependence', *The Lancet*, 26 January: 203–5.

Harvey, Lee 1987 *Myths of the Chicago School*. Aldershot: Avebury.

Harwood, Jonathan 1976 'The race–intelligence controversy: a sociological approach. I – professional factors', *Social Studies of Science*, 6: 369–94.

Harwood, Jonathan 1977 'The race–intelligence controversy: a sociological approach. II – external factors', *Social Studies of Science*, 7: 1–30.

Harwood, Jonathan 1982 'American academic opinion and social change: recent developments in the nature-nurture controversy', *Oxford Review of Education*, 8: 41–67.

Hedges, Barry 1987 'Survey research for government' in Martin Bulmer (ed.), *Social Science Research and Government: Comparative Essays on Britain and the United States*. Cambridge: Cambridge University Press.

Henslin, James M. 1972 'Studying deviance in four settings: research experiences with cabbies, suicides, drug users and abortionees' in Jack D. Douglas (ed.), *Research on Deviance*. New York: Random House.

Hepworth, Mike 1971 'Deviants in disguise: blackmail and social acceptance' in Stanley Cohen (ed.), *Images of Deviance*. Harmondsworth: Penguin.

Hepworth, Mike and Bryan S. Turner 1982 *Confession: Studies in Deviance and Religion*. London: Routledge & Kegan Paul.

Herrnstein, R.J. 1971 'IQ', *Atlantic Monthly*. September: 43–64.

Herrnstein, R.J. 1973 *IQ in the meritocracy*, Boston: Little-Brown.

Hertzberger, Sharon D. 1990 'The cyclical pattern of child abuse: a study in research methodology', *American Behavioral Scientist*, 33: 529–45.

Hessler, Richard M. and John F. Galliher 1983 'Institutional Review Boards and clandestine research: an experimental test', *Human Organization*, 42: 82–7.

Hessler, Richard M. and Peter Kong-Ming New 1972 'Toward a research commune?', *Human Organization*, 31: 449–51.

Hessler, Richard M., Peter Kong-Ming New and Jude Thomas May 1980 'Conflict, consensus and exchange', *Social Problems*, 27: 320–9.

Hill, Robert B. 1983 'Social problems research' in Robert B. Smith (ed.), *A Handbook of Social Science Methods: Volume 1: An Introduction to Social Research*. Cambridge, MA: Ballinger.

Himmelfarb, Harold S. 1974 'The Impact of Religious Schooling: The Effects of

Jewish Education Upon Adult Religious Involvement'. Unpublished PhD thesis, University of Chicago.

Himmelfarb, Harold S., R. Michael Loar and Susan H. Mott 1983 'Sampling by ethnic surnames: the case of American Jews', *Public Opinion Quarterly*, 47: 247–60.

Himmelfarb, Samuel and Stephen E. Edgell 1980 'Note on "The Randomized Response Approach": Addendum to Fox and Tracy', *Evaluation Review*, 6: 279–84.

Hinze, Kenneth 1987 'Computing in sociology: bringing back balance', *Social Science Microcomputer Review*, 5: 439–51.

Hoffman, Joan Eakin 1980 'Problems of access in the study of social élites and boards of directors' in William B. Shaffir, Robert A. Stebbins and Alan Turowetz (eds), *Fieldwork Experience: Qualitative Approaches to Social Research*. New York: St Martin's Press.

Hoinville, Gerald 1985 'Methodological research on sample surveys: a review of developments in Britain' in Martin Bulmer (ed.), *Essays on the History of British Sociological Research*. Cambridge: Cambridge University Press.

Hoinville, Gerald and Roger Jowell 1978 *Survey Research Practice*. London. Heinemann.

Holden, George W. 1988 'Investigating social relations with computer-presented social situations', *Social Science Computer Review*, 6: 108–10.

Homan, Roger 1978 'Interpersonal communication in Pentacostal meetings', *Sociological Review*, 26: 499–518.

Homan, Roger and Martin Bulmer 1982 'On the merits of covert methods: a dialogue' in Martin Bulmer (ed.), *Social Research Ethics*. London: Macmillan.

Hooper, David 1984 *Public Scandal, Odium and Contempt: An Investigation of Recent Libel Cases*. London: Secker & Warburg.

Hope, Emily, Mary Kennedy and Anne De Winter 1976 'Homeworkers in North London' in Diana Leonard Barker and Sheila Allen (eds), *Dependence and Exploitation in Work and Marriage*. London: Longman.

Hornsby-Smith, Michael P. and Raymond M. Lee 1979 *Roman Catholic Opinion: A Study of Roman Catholics in England and Wales in the 1970s*. Guildford: University of Surrey.

Hughes, John A. 1976 *Sociological Analysis: Methods of Discovery*. London: Thomas Nelson & Sons.

Humphreys, Laud 1970 *Tearoom Trade: A Study of Homosexual Encounters in Public Places*. London: Gerald Duckworth.

Hunt, Jennifer 1984 'The development of rapport through the negotiation of gender in fieldwork among police', *Human Organization*, 43: 283–96.

Hunt, Jennifer 1989 *Psychoanalytic Aspects of Fieldwork*. Newbury Park, CA: Sage.

Hunt, Morton 1985 *Profiles of Social Research: The Scientific Study of Human Interactions*. New York: Russell Sage Foundation.

Hyman, Herbert H. 1972 *Secondary Analysis of Sample Surveys*. New York: Wiley.

Irwin, John 1972 'Participant observation of criminals' in Jack D. Douglas (ed.), *Research on Deviance*. New York: Random House.

Jacob, Herbert 1984 *Using Public Data: Errors and Remedies*. Beverly Hills: Sage.

Jahoda, Marie 1981 'To publish or not to publish', *Journal of Social Issues*, 37: 208–20.

Jahoda, Marie 1987 'Unemployed men at work' in David Fryer and Philip Ullah (eds), *Unemployed People: Social and Psychological Perspectives*. Milton Keynes: Open University Press.

Janson, Carl-Gunnar 1979 'Privacy legislation and social research in Sweden' in E. Mochman and P.J. Mullaer (eds), *Data Protection and Social Science Research: Perspectives from Ten Countries*. Frankfurt: Campus Verlag.

Jasso, Guillermina and Peter H. Rossi 1977 'Distributive justice and earned income', *American Sociological Review*, 42: 639–51.

Jenkins, Richard 1983 *Lads, Citizens and Ordinary Kids*. London: Routledge & Kegan Paul.

Jenkins, Richard 1984 'Bringing it all back home: an anthropologist in Belfast' in Colin Bell and Helen Roberts (eds), *Social Researching: Politics, Problems, Practice*. London: Routledge & Kegan Paul.

Jenkins, Richard 1987 'Doing research on discrimination: problems of method, interpretation and ethics' in G. Clare Wenger (ed.), *The Research Relationship*. London: Allen & Unwin.

Jenkins, Richard, Alan Bryman, Janet Ford, Teresa Keil and Alan Beardsworth 1983 'Information in the labour market: the impact of the recession', *Sociology*, 17: 260–7.

Jensen, Arthur 1969 'How much can we boost IQ and scholastic achievement?' *Harvard Educational Review*, 39: 1–123.

Jensen, Arthur 1972 *Genetics in Education*. London: Methuen.

Johnson, Carole Gaar 1982 'Risks in the publication of fieldwork' in Joan E. Sieber (ed.), *The Ethics of Social Research: Volume 2: Fieldwork, Regulation and Publication*. New York: Springer-Verlag.

Johnson, John M. 1975 *Doing Field Research*. New York: Free Press.

Johnson, John M. 1989 'Horror stories and the construction of child abuse' in Joel Best (ed.), *Images of Issues: Typifying Contemporary Social Problems*. New York: Aldine de Gruyter.

Johnson, Loch K. 1989 *America's Secret Power: The CIA in a Democratic Society*. New York: Oxford University Press.

Johnson, Weldon T. and John D. Delamater 1976 'Response effects in sex surveys', *Public Opinion Quarterly*, 40: 165–81.

Jones, Delmos 1980 'Accountability and the politics of urban research', *Human Organization*, 39: 99–104.

Josephson, Eric 1970 'Resistance to community surveys', *Social Problems*, 18: 117–29.

Jowell, Roger and Julia Field 1989 'Peering through the keyhole', *Observer*, 17 September, 24.

Kalmuss, Debra 1981 'Scholars in the courtroom: two models of applied social science', *American Sociologist*, 16: 212–23.

Karmen, Andrew 1980 'Race, inferiority, crime and research taboos' in Edward Sagarin (ed.), *Taboos in Criminology*. Beverly Hills: Sage.

Kay, Helen 1989 'Can respondents give informed consent?', Paper given at Social Research Association Seminar, London, October.

Kearney, Kathleen, Ronald H. Hopkins, Armand L. Mauss and Ralph A. Weishert 1984 'Self-generated identification codes for anonymous collection of longitudinal research data', *Public Opinion Quarterly*, 48: 270–8.

Keen, Mike 1992 'The FBI and American Sociology', *ASA Footnotes*, 19 (19): 14.

Kelman, Herbert C. 1972 'The rights of the subject in social research: an analysis in terms of relative power and legitimacy', *American Psychologist*, 27: 989–1016.

Kennamer, J. David 1990 'Self-serving biases in perceiving the opinions of others: implications for the spiral of silence', *Communication Research*, 17: 393–404.

Kennedy-Bergen, Raquel 1992 'Interviewing survivors of marital rape: doing feminist research on sensitive topics' in Claire M. Renzetti and Raymond M. Lee (eds), *Researching Sensitive Topics*. Newbury Park, CA: Sage.

Kershaw, D.N. and J.C. Small 1972 'Data confidentiality and privacy: lessons from the New Jersey negative income tax experiment', *Public Policy*, 20: 257–80.

Keyfitz, Nathan 1987 'The social and political context of population forecasting' in William Alonso and Paul Starr (eds), *The Politics of Numbers*. New York: Russell Sage Foundation.

Killian, Lewis M. 1981 'Sociologists look at the cuckoo's nest: the misuse of ideal types', *American Sociologist*, 16: 230–9.

Kimmel, Allan J. 1988 *Ethics and Values in Applied Social Research*. Newbury Park, CA: Sage.

Kinsey, Alfred C., Wardell B. Pomeroy and Clyde E. Martin 1948 *Sexual Behavior in the Human Male*. Philadelphia: Saunders.

Kinsey, Alfred C., Wardell B. Pomeroy, Clyde E. Martin and Paul H. Bebhard 1953 *Sexual Behavior in the Human Female*. Philadelphia: Saunders.

Kirby, Richard and Jay Corzine 1981 'The contagion of stigma', *Qualitative Sociology*, 4: 3–20.

Kirk, Jerome and Marc L. Miller 1986 *Reliability and Validity in Qualitative Research*. Newbury Park, CA: Sage.

Kish, Leslie 1965 *Survey Sampling*. New York: Wiley.

Kitsuse, John I. and Aaron V. Cicourel 1963 'A note on the uses of official statistics', *Social Problems*, 2: 135–9.

Klatch, Rebecca E. 1988 'The methodological problems of studying a politically resistant community' in Robert G. Burgess (ed.), *Studies in Qualitative Methodology: Volume 1: Conducting Qualitative Research*. Greenwich, CT: JAI Press.

Klockars, Carl B. 1975 *The Professional Fence*. London: Tavistock.

Klockars, Carl B. 1977 'Field ethics for the life history' in Robert S. Weppner (ed.), *Street Ethnography*. Beverly Hills: Sage.

Klockars, Carl B. 1978 'Comment', *American Sociologist*, 13: 164–5.

Klockars, Carl B. 1979 'Dirty hands and deviant subjects' in Carl B. Klockars and Finbarr O'Connor (eds), *Deviance and Decency: The Ethics of Research with Human Subjects*. Beverly Hills: Sage.

Klockars, Carl B. and Finbarr O'Connor (eds) 1979 *Deviance and Decency: The Ethics of Research with Human Subjects*. Beverly Hills: Sage.

Knerr, Charles R. 1982 'What to do before and after a subpoena of data arrives' in Joan E. Seiber (ed.), *The Ethics of Social Research: Volume 1: Surveys and Experiments*. New York: Springer-Verlag.

Kollock, Peter and Philip Blumstein 1987 'A microsociology of close relationships: the case of friendship'. Paper presented at the 82nd Annual Meeting of the American Sociological Association, Chicago.

Kotarba, Joseph A. 1990 'Ethnography and AIDS: returning to the streets', *Journal of Contemporary Ethnography*, 19: 259–70.

Kraemar, Helena Chmura 1980 'Estimation and testing of bivariate association using data generated by the randomized response technique', *Psychological Bulletin*, 87: 304–8.

Krueger, Richard A. 1988 *Focus Groups: A Practical Guide for Applied Research*. Newbury Park, CA: Sage.

Kübler-Ross, Elisabeth 1970 *On Death and Dying*. London: Tavistock.
Ladd, Everett C. and Seymour Martin Lipset 1975 *The Divided Academy*. New York: McGraw-Hill.
La Fontaine, Jean 1990 *Child Sexual Abuse*. Cambridge: Polity Press.
Laslett, Barbara and Rhona Rapoport 1975 'Collaborative interviewing and interactive research', *Journal of Marriage and the Family*, 37: 968–77.
Lawson, Annette 1991 'Whose side are we on now? Ethical issues in social research and medical practice', *Social Science and Medicine*, 32: 591–9.
Lazarsfeld, Paul F. 1962 'The sociology of empirical social research', *American Sociological Review*, 27: 757–67.
Lee, Alfred McClung 1978 *Sociology for Whom?* New York: Oxford University Press.
Lee, John Alan 1979 'The gay connection', *Urban Life*, 8: 175–98.
Lee, Raymond M. 1981 'Interreligious Courtship and Marriage in Northern Ireland'. Unpublished PhD thesis, University of Edinburgh.
Lee, Raymond M. 1985a 'Patterns of Catholic–Protestant intermarriage in Northern Ireland', *International Journal of the Sociology of the Family*, 15: 27–34.
Lee, Raymond M. 1985b 'Redundancy, labour markets and informal relations', *Sociological Review*, 33: 469–94.
Lee, Raymond M. 1986a 'Introduction' in Raymond M. Lee (ed.), *Redundancy, Lay-offs and Plant Closures: Their Causes, Character and Consequences*. Beckenham: Croom Helm.
Lee, Raymond M. 1986b *Methodological Approaches to the Study of the 'Black' Economy*. Report to the Department of Employment.
Lee, Raymond M. 1987 'Problems in field research: some simple teaching techniques', *Teaching Sociology*, 15: 151–6.
Lee, Raymond M. 1988 'Using simulations for teaching social research methods' in Danny Saunders, Alan Coote and David Crookhall (eds), *Experiential Learning through Games and Simulations*. Loughborough: SAGSET.
Lee, Raymond M. 1989 'Expert witnesses and the legal conflict over new religious movements'. Unpublished MS.
Lee, Raymond M. 1992 ' "Nobody said it had to be easy": postgraduate field research in Northern Ireland' in Robert G. Burgess (ed.), *Studies in Qualitative Methodology: Volume 3: Learning about Fieldwork*. Greenwich, CT: JAI Press.
Lee, Raymond M. and Claire M. Renzetti 1990 'The problems of researching sensitive topics: an overview and introduction', *American Behavioral Scientist*, 33: 510–28.
Lee, Raymond M. and Nigel G. Fielding 1991 'Computing for qualitative analysis: options, problems, potential' in Nigel G. Fielding and Raymond M. Lee (eds), *Using Computers in Qualitative Research*. London: Sage.
Lehmann, Timothy and T. R. Young 1974 'From conflict theory to conflict methodology: an emerging paradigm for sociology', *Sociological Inquiry*, 44: 15–28.
Leifer, Eric M. 1988 'Interaction preludes to role setting: exploratory local action', *American Sociological Review*, 53: 865–78.
Liazos, Alexander 1972 'The poverty of the sociology of deviance: nuts, sluts and perverts', *Social Problems*, 20: 103–19.
Lieberson, Stanley 1985 *Making It Count*. Berkeley: University of California Press.
Lieberson, Stanley 1988 'Asking too much: expecting too little', *Sociological Perspectives*, 31: 379–97.

Liebow, Elliot 1967 *Tally's Corner: A Study of Negro Streetcorner Men.* Boston: Little, Brown & Co.

Livesley, Denise and Jennifer J. Waterton 1985 'Measuring individual attitude change' in Roger Jowell and Sharon Witherspoon (eds), *British Social Attitudes: The 1985 Report.* Aldershot: Gower.

Lofland, Lyn H. 1983 'Understanding urban life: the Chicago legacy', *Urban Life,* 11: 491–511.

Long, Gary L. and Dean S. Dorn 1983 'Sociologists' attitudes toward ethical issues: the management of an impression', *Sociology and Social Research,* 67: 288–300.

Lopata, Helen Znaniecki 1980 'Interviewing American widows' in William B. Shaffir, Robert A. Stebbins and Alan Turowetz (eds), *Fieldwork Experience: Qualitative Approaches to Social Research.* New York: St Martin's Press.

Luhmann, Niklas 1979 *Trust and Power.* New York: Wiley.

Lukes, Steven 1974 *Power: A Radical View.* London: Macmillan.

Lundman, Richard J. and Paul T. McFarlane 1976 'Conflict methodology: an introduction and preliminary assessment', *Sociological Quarterly,* 17: 503–12.

Lynch, Frederick R. 1989 *Invisible Victims: White Males and the Crisis of Affirmative Action.* New York: Greenwood Press.

McCarthy, John D. and Mayer N. Zald 1977 'Resource mobilization and social movements', *American Journal of Sociology,* 82: 1212–41.

McCracken, Grant 1988 *The Long Interview.* Newbury Park, CA: Sage.

McFarlane, Graham 1979 'Mixed marriages in Ballycuan, Northern Ireland', *Journal of Comparative Family Studies,* 10: 191–205.

McFarlane, Graham 1986 'Violence in rural Northern Ireland: social scientific models, folk explanations and local variation (?)' in David Diches (ed.), *The Anthropology of Violence.* Oxford: Basil Blackwell.

McFarlane, Paul T. 1971 'Simulation games as social psychological research sites: methodological advantages', *Simulation and Games,* 2: 149–62.

MacIntyre, Alasdair 1982 'Risk, harm and benefit assessments as instruments of moral evaluation' in Tom L. Beauchamp, Ruth R. Faden, R. Jay Wallace, Jr and LeRoy Waters (eds), *Ethical Issues in Social Science Research.* Baltimore: Johns Hopkins University Press.

Macintyre, Sally 1978 'Some notes on record taking and making in an antenatal clinic', *Sociological Review,* 26: 595–611.

McKee, Lorna and Margaret O'Brien 1983 'Interviewing men: taking gender seriously' in Eva Gamarnikow, David Morgan, June Purvis and Daphne Taylorson (eds), *The Public and the Private.* London: Heinemann.

MacKenzie, Donald 1990 *Inventing Accuracy: A Historical Sociology of Nuclear Missile Guidance.* Cambridge, MA: MIT Press.

McRae, Susan 1986 *Cross-class Families.* Oxford: Clarendon Press.

Madge, John 1953 *The Tools of Social Science.* London: Longmans.

Madge, John 1963 *The Origins of Scientific Sociology.* London: Tavistock.

Malsteed, Joanna 1987 'Straw men: a note on Ann Oakley's treatment of textbook prescriptions for interviewing', *Sociology,* 21: 629–31.

Manniche, Erik and Donald P. Hayes 1957 'Respondent anonymity and data matching', *Public Opinion Quarterly,* 21: 384–8.

Marøy, Terje 1988 'Data protection and data access'. Paper presented to the IFDO Conference, Cologne.

Marris, Peter 1958 *Widows and their Families.* London: Routledge & Kegan Paul.

Marsh, Catherine 1982 *The Survey Method.* London: Allen & Unwin.

Marsh, Catherine 1985 'Informants, respondents and citizens' in Martin Bulmer (ed.), *Essays on the History of British Sociological Research*. Cambridge: Cambridge University Press.

Martin, Elizabeth 1983 'Surveys as social indicators: problems in monitoring trends' in Peter H. Rossi, James D. Wright and Andy B. Anderson (eds), *Handbook of Survey Research*, New York: Academic Press.

Marx, Gary T. 1972 'Introduction' in Gary T. Marx (ed.), *Muckraking Sociology: Research as Social Criticism*. New Brunswick: Transaction Books.

Marx, Gary T. 1980 'The new police undercover work', *Urban Life*, 8: 399–446.

Marx, Gary T. 1984 'Notes on the discovery, collection and assessment of hidden and dirty data' in Joseph W. Schneider and John I. Kitsuse (eds), *Studies in the Sociology of Social Problems*. Norwood, NJ: Ablex Publishing Company.

Masterson, J.G. 1970 'Consanguinity in Ireland', *Human Heredity*, 20: 371–82.

Mattera, Philip 1985 *Off the Books: The Rise of the Underground Economy*. London: Pluto Press.

Matza, David 1969 *Becoming Deviant*. Englewood Cliffs, NJ: Prentice-Hall.

Maynard, Eileen 1974 'The growing negative image of the anthropologist among American Indians', *Human Organization*, 33: 402–4.

Mazur, Allan 1987 'Scientific disputes over policy' in H. Tristam Engelhardt, Jr and Arthur L. Caplan (eds), *Scientific Controversies: Case Studies in the Resolution and Closure of Disputes in Science and Technology*. Cambridge: Cambridge University Press.

Melton, Gary B. and Joni N. Gray 1988 'Ethical dilemmas in AIDS research: individual privacy and public health', *American Psychologist*, 43: 60–4.

Melton, Gary B., Robert J. Levine, Gerald P. Koocher, Robert Rosenthal and William C. Thompson 1988 'Community consultation in socially sensitive research: lessons from clinical trials for treatments of AIDS', *American Psychologist*, 43: 573–81.

Merton, Robert K. 1972 'Insiders and outsiders: a chapter in the sociology of knowledge', *American Journal of Sociology*, 77: 9–47.

Merton, Robert K. and Patricia Kendal 1946 'The focused interview', *American Sociological Review*, 51: 541–7.

Merton, Vanessa 1990 'Community-based AIDS research', *Evaluation Review*, 14: 502–37.

Midanik, Lorraine 1982 'The validity of self-reported alcohol consumption and alcohol problems: a literature review', *British Journal of Addiction*, 77: 357–82.

Migdal, Joel S. 1979 *Palestinian Society and Politics*. Princeton: Princeton University Press.

Miles, Ian and John Irvine 1979 'The critique of official statistics' in John Irvine, Ian Miles and Jeff Evans (eds), *Demystifying Social Statistics*. London: Pluto Press.

Miller, Judith Droitcourt 1984 'A New Survey Technique for Studying Deviant Behavior'. Unpublished PhD thesis, George Washington University.

Miller, Judith Droitcourt and Ira H. Cisin 1984 'The item-count/paired lists technique: an indirect method of surveying deviant behaviour'. Unpublished MS, George Washington University.

Miller, Peter V. and Robert M. Groves 1985 'Matching survey response to official records: an exploration of validity in victimization reporting', *Public Opinion Quarterly*, 49: 366–80.

Miller, Robert L. 1988 'Evaluation research "Ulster style": investigating equality of opportunity in Northern Ireland', *Network: Newsletter of the British Sociological Association*, 42, October: 4–7.

Miller, Roberta Balstead 1987 'Social science under siege: the political response, 1981–1984', in Martin Bulmer (ed.), *Social Science Research and Government: Comparative Essays on Britain and the United States*. Cambridge: Cambridge University Press.

Mills, C. Wright 1959 *The Sociological Imagination*. New York: Oxford University Press.

Mishler, Elliot G. 1986 *Research Interviewing: Context and Narrative*. Cambridge, MA: Harvard University Press.

Moe, Terry M. 1984 'The new economics of organizations', *American Journal of Political Science*, 28: 739–77.

Moltoch, Harvey and Marilyn Lester 1974 'News as purposive behavior: on the strategic use of routine events, accidents and scandals', *American Sociological Review*, 39: 101–12.

Moltoch, Harvey and Marilyn Lester 1975 'Accidental news: the Great Oil Spill as local occurrence and national event', *American Journal of Sociology*, 81: 235–60.

Moore, Joan W. 1967 'Political and ethical problems in a large-scale study of a minority population' in Gideon Sjoberg (ed.), *Ethics, Politics and Social Research*. London: Routledge & Kegan Paul.

Moore, Joan W. 1973 'Social constraints on sociological knowledge: academics and research concerning minorities', *Social Problems*, 21: 65–77.

Moore, Mark 1983 'Invisible offenses: a challenge to minimally intrusive law enforcement' in M. Caplan (ed.), *Abscam Ethics*. Washington, DC: The Police Foundation.

Morgan, D.H.J. 1972 'The British Association scandal: the effect of publicity on a sociological investigation', *Sociological Review*, 20: 185–206.

Morgenstern, Oskar 1963 *On the Accuracy of Economic Observations* (2nd edn). Princeton, NJ: Princeton University Press.

Moser, C. A. and G. Kalton 1971 *Survey Methods in Social Investigation*. London: Heinemann.

Mosteller, Frederick 1977 'Assessing unknown numbers: order of magnitude estimation' in William B. Fairley and Frederick Mosteller (eds), *Statistics and Public Policy*. Reading, MA: Addison-Wesley.

Moyser, George and Margaret Wagstaffe 1987 'Studying élites: theoretical and methodological issues' in George Moyser and Margaret Wagstaffe (eds), *Research Methods for Élite Studies*. London: Allen & Unwin.

Nader, Laura 1972 'Up the anthropologist: perspectives gained from studying up' in Dell Hymes (ed.), *Reinventing Anthropology*. New York: Pantheon.

Nejelski, Paul and Kurt Finsterbusch 1973 'The prosecutor and the researcher: present and prospective variations in the Supreme Court's *Branzburg* decision', *Social Problems*, 21: 3–20.

Nelkin, Dorothy and Judith P. Swazey 1981 'Science and social control: controversies over research on violence' in Willard Gaylin, Ruth Macklin and Tabitha M. Powledge (eds), *Violence and the Politics of Research*. New York: Plenum Press.

Nelson, Barbara J. 1984 *Making an Issue of Child Abuse: Political Agenda Setting for Social Problems*. Chicago: University of Chicago Press.

Nelson, Robert L. and Terry E. Hedrick 1983 'The statutory protection of confidential research data: synthesis and evaluation' in Robert F. Boruch and Joe

S. Cecil (eds), *Solutions to Ethical and Legal Problems in Social Research*. New York: Academic Press.

Newby, Howard 1977 'Editorial note' in Colin Bell and Howard Newby (eds), *Doing Sociological Research*. London: Allen & Unwin.

Newman, Dennis 1979 *Techniques for Ensuring the Confidentiality of Census Information in Great Britain*. Office of Population Censuses and Surveys, Occasional Paper No. 4.

Nicholson, Richard H. (ed.) 1986 *Medical Research and Children: Ethics, Law and Practice*. Oxford: Oxford University Press.

Nisbett, Richard and Lee Ross 1980 *Human Inference: Strategies and Shortcomings of Social Judgment*. Englewood Cliffs, NJ: Prentice-Hall.

Noelle-Neuman, Elizabeth 1984 *The Spiral of Silence: Our Social Skin*. Chicago: University of Chicago Press.

Oakley, Ann 1981 'Interviewing women: a contradiction in terms', in H. Roberts (ed.), *Doing Feminist Research*. London: Routledge & Kegan Paul.

Oakley, Ann 1987 'Comment on Malsteed', *Sociology*, 21: 63.

Oberschall, Anthony 1972 'Introduction: the sociological study of the history of social research' in Anthony Oberschall (ed.), *The Establishment of Empirical Sociology: Studies in Continuity, Discontinuity and Institutionalization*. New York: Harper & Row.

Olensen, Virginia 1979 'Federal regulations, Institutional Review Boards and qualitative social science research: comments on a problematic era' in Murray L, Wax and Joan Cassell (eds), *Federal Regulations: Ethical Issues and Social Research*. Boulder, CO: Westview Press and The American Association for the Advancement of Science.

Orfield, Gary 1978 'Research, politics and the antibusing debate', *Law and Contemporary Problems*, 42: 141–73.

Oromaner, Mark 1977 'The career of sociological literature: a diachronous study', *Social Studies of Science*, 7: 126–32.

Øyen, Ørjar 1974 'Social research and the protection of privacy: a review of the Norwegian development', *Acta Sociologica*, 19: 249–62.

Øyen, Ørjar and Thore Gaard Olaussen 1985 'Social science and data protection in Norway: a case of accommodation to conflicting goals'. Paper presented at the European Consortium for Political Research, Workshop on Confidentiality, Privacy and Data Protection, Barcelona.

Palmer, Vivian 1928 *Field Studies in Sociology: A Student's Manual*. Chicago: Chicago University Press.

Parsa, Misagh 1988 *Social Origins of the Iranian Revolution*. New Brunswick, NJ: Rutgers University Press.

Patton, Michael Quinn 1980 *Qualitative Evaluation Methods*. Beverly Hills: Sage.

Patton, Michael Quinn 1987 *How to Use Qualitative Methods in Evaluation*. Newbury Park, CA: Sage.

Pattullo, E. L. 1978 'Comment', *American Sociologist*, 13: 168–9.

Pattullo, E. L. 1982 'Modesty is the best policy: the Federal role in social research' in Tom L. Beauchamp, Ruth R. Faden, R. Jay Wallace, Jr and LeRoy Waters (eds), *Ethical Issues in Social Science Research*. Baltimore: Johns Hopkins University Press.

Payne, Geoff, Robert Dingwall, Judy Payne and Mick Carter 1980 *Sociology and Social Research*. London: Routledge & Kegan Paul.

Payne, Stanley 1951 *The Art of Asking Questions*. Princeton, NJ: Princeton University Press.

Pearce, Penelope 1988 'The Law' in Penelope Pearce, Phyllida Parsloe, Huw Francis, Alexander Macara and David Watson (eds), *Personal Data Protection in Health and Social Service*. London: Croom Helm.

Pelz, Donald C. 1978 'Some expanded perspectives on use of social science in public policy' in J. Milton Yinger and Stephen J. Cutler (eds), *Major Social Issues: A. Multidisciplinary View*. New York: Free Press.

Pendakur, Manjurath 1985 'Dynamics of cultural policy making: the US film industry in India', *Journal of Communication*, 35: 52–72.

Peritore, N. Patrick 1990 'Reflections on dangerous fieldwork', *American Sociologist*, 21: 359–72.

Peters, Stephanie Doyle, Gail Elizabeth Wyatt and David Finkelhor 1986 'Prevalence' in David Finkelhor (ed.), *A Sourcebook on Child Abuse*. Beverly Hills: Sage.

Peterson, Mark Allen 1991 'Aliens, ape men and whacky savages: the anthropologist in the tabloids', *Anthropology Today*, 7, (5): 4–7.

Pettigrew, Thomas F. and Robert L. Green 1976 'School desegregation in large cities: a critique of the Coleman "white flight" thesis', *Harvard Educational Review*, 46: 1–53.

Phelps, Robert H. and E. Douglas Hamilton 1966 *Libel: Rights, Risks, Responsibilities*. New York: Macmillan.

Platt, Jennifer 1976 *Realities of Social Research*. London: Sussex University Press.

Platt, Jennifer 1983 'The development of the "participant observation" in sociology', *Journal of the History of the Behavioral Sciences*, 19: 379–93.

Platt, Jennifer 1985 'Weber's *verstehen* and the history of qualitative research', *British Journal of Sociology*, 36: 448–66.

Platt, Jennifer 1992 'Case study in American methodological thought', *Current Sociology*, 40: 17–48.

Plummer, Ken 1981 'Researching into homosexualities' in K. Plummer (ed.), *The Making of the Modern Homosexual*. London: Hutchinson.

Plummer, Ken 1983 *Documents of Life: An Introduction to the Problems and Literature of a Humanistic Method*. London: Allen & Unwin.

Plummer, Kenneth 1975 *Sexual Stigma*. London: Routledge & Kegan Paul.

Pollner, Melvin and Robert M. Emerson 1983 'The dynamics of inclusion and distance in fieldwork relations' in Robert M. Emerson (ed.), *Contemporary Field Research: A Collection of Readings*. Boston: Little, Brown & Co.

Polsky, Ned 1971 *Hustlers, Beats and Others*. Harmondsworth: Penguin.

Power, Robert 1989 'Participant observation and its place in the study of illicit drug abuse', *British Journal of Addiction*, 84: 43–52.

Powledge, Tabitha M. 1981 'How not to study violence' in Willard Gaylin, Ruth Macklin and Tabitha M. Powledge (eds), *Violence and the Politics of Research*. New York: Plenum Press.

Powledge, Tabitha M. 1986 'What is "The Media" and why is it saying those terrible things about aggression research?' in Jeffrey H. Goldstein (ed.), *Reporting Science: The Case of Aggression*. Hillsdale, NJ: Lawrence Erlbaum Associates.

Presser, Stanley 1984 'The use of survey data in basic research in the social sciences' in Charles F. Turner and Elizabeth Martin (eds), *Surveying Subjective Phenomena: Volume 2*. New York: Russell Sage Foundation.

Price, Vincent and Scott Allen 1990 'Opinion spirals, silent and otherwise: applying small-group research to public opinion phenomena', *Communication Research*, 17: 369–92.

Punch, Maurice 1979 *Policing the Inner City: A Study of Amsterdam's Warmoesstraat*. London: Macmillan.

Punch, Maurice 1986 *The Politics and Ethics of Fieldwork*. Beverly Hills: Sage.

Punch, Maurice 1989 'Researching police deviance: a personal encounter with the limitations and liabilities of field-work', *British Journal of Sociology*, 40: 177–204.

Raab, Charles 1987 'Oral history as an instrument of research into Scottish educational policy making' in George Moyser and Margaret Wagstaffe (eds), *Research Methods for Élite Studies*. London: Allen & Unwin.

Rabow Jerome and Carole E. Neuman 1984 'Garbaeology as a method of cross-validating interviewer data on sensitive topics', *Sociology and Social Research*, 68: 480–97.

Rainwater, Lee and David J. Pittman 1967 'Ethical problems in studying a politically-sensitive and deviant community', *Social Problems*, 14: 357–66.

Rainwater, Lee and William L. Yancey 1967 *The Moynihan Report and the Politics of Controversy*. Cambridge, MA: MIT Press.

Rapoport A. and W.J. Horvath 1961 'A study of a large sociogram', *Behavioral Science*, 6: 279–91.

Record, Jane Cassels 1967 'The research institute and the pressure group' in Gideon Sjoberg (ed.), *Ethics, Politics and Social Research*. London: Routledge & Kegan Paul.

Reiss, Albert J. 1979 'Government regulation of scientific inquiry: some paradoxical consequences' in Carl B. Klockars and Finbarr W. O'Connor (eds), *Deviance and Decency: The Ethics of Research with Human Subjects*. Beverly Hills: Sage.

Relyea, Harold C. 1989 'Public access through the Freedom of Information and Privacy Acts' in Peter Hernon and Charles R. McClure (eds), *Federal Information Policies in the 1980s: Conflicts and Issues*. Norwood, NJ: Ablex Publishing Corporation.

Reuter, P. 1982 'The irregular economy and the quality of macroeconomic statistics' in Victor Tanzi (ed.), *The Underground Economy in the United States and Abroad*. Lexington, MA: D.C. Heath.

Reynolds, Paul Davidson 1982 *Ethics and Social Science Research*. Englewood Cliffs, NJ: Prentice-Hall.

Reynolds, Paul Davidson 1983 'Commentary on "Institutional Review Boards and Clandestine Research: An Experimental Test"', *Human Organization*, 42: 87–90.

Richardson, James T. 1980 'People's Temple and Jonestown: a corrective comparison and critique', *Journal for the Scientific Study of Religion*, 19: 239–55.

Richardson, Laurel 1990 *Writing Strategies: Reaching Diverse Audiences*. Newbury Park, CA: Sage.

Richardson, Stephen A., Barbara Snell Dohrenwend and David Klein 1965 *Interviewing: Its Forms and Functions*. New York: Basic Books.

Ricoeur, Paul 1970 *Freud and Philosophy: An Essay on Interpretation*. New Haven: Yale University Press.

Roadberg Alan 1980 'Breaking relationships with research subjects: some problems and suggestions', in William B. Shaffir, Robert A. Stebbins and Alan Turowetz (eds), *Fieldwork Experience: Qualitative Approaches to Social Research*. New York: St Martin's Press.

Roberts, Helen 1984 'Putting the show on the road: the dissemination of research findings' in Colin Bell and Helen Roberts (eds), *Social Researching: Politics, Problems, Practice*. London: Routledge & Kegan Paul.

Robertson, Geoffrey and Andrew G. L. Nicol 1984 *Media Law: The Rights of Journalists, Broadcasters and Publishers*. London: Sage.

Rock, Paul 1973 *Deviant Behaviour*. London: Hutchinson.

Rock, Paul 1979 *The Making of Symbolic Interactionism*. London: Macmillan.

Roethlisberger, F.J. and William J. Dickson 1939 *Management and the Worker*. Cambridge, MA: Harvard University Press.

Rogers, Colin D. 1986 *Tracing Missing Persons*. Manchester: Manchester University Press.

Rosen, Lawrence 1977 'The anthropologist as expert witness', *American Anthropologist*, 79: 555–78.

Rosenhan, D. L. 1973 'On being sane in insane places', *Science*, 179: 250–8.

Rosenthal, Robert and Ralph L. Rosnow 1984 'Applying Hamlet's question to the ethical conduct of research: a conceptual addendum', *American Psychologist*, 39: 561–3.

Rossi, Peter H. 1987 'No good applied social research goes unpunished', *Society*, 25: 73–80.

Rossi, Peter H. and Andy B. Anderson 1982 'The factorial survey approach: an introduction' in Peter H. Rossi and Steven L. Nock (eds), *The Factorial Survey Approach*. Beverly Hills: Sage.

Rossi, Peter H. and Howard E. Freeman 1982 *Evaluation: A Systematic Approach*. Beverly Hills: Sage.

Rossi Peter H. and Steven L. Nock 1982 *The Factorial Survey Approach*. Beverly Hills: Sage.

Rostocki, Andrzej 1986 'Sensitive questions in sociological survey', *Polish Sociological Bulletin*, 75: 27–32.

Roth, Julius A. 1966 'Hired-hand research', *American Sociologist*, 1: 190–6.

Rothbart, G.S., Michelle Fine and Seymour Sudman 1982 'On finding and interviewing the needles in the haystack: the use of multiplicity sampling', *Public Opinion Quarterly*, 46: 408–21.

Rothstein, Lawrence E. 1986 *Plant Closings: Power, Politics and Workers*. Dover, MA: Auburn House.

Sagarin, Edward and James Moneymaker 1979 'The dilemma of research immunity' in Carl B. Klockars and Finbarr W. O'Connor (eds), *Deviance and Decency: The Ethics of Research with Human Subjects*. Beverly Hills: Sage.

Sanders, Clinton R. 1980 'Rope burns: impediments to the achievement of basic comfort early in the field research experience' in William B. Shaffir, Robert A. Stebbins and Alan Turowetz (eds), *Fieldwork Experience: Qualitative Approaches to Social Research*. New York: St Martin's Press.

Saunders, Peter 1981 *Social Theory and the Urban Question*. London: Hutchinson.

Schatzmann, Leonard and Anselm L. Strauss 1973 *Field Research: Strategies for a Natural Sociology*. Englewood Cliffs, NJ: Prentice-Hall.

Scheff, Thomas J. 1988 'Shame and conformity: the deference-emotion system', *American Sociological Review*, 53: 395–406.

Schensul, Stephen L. 1980 'Anthropological fieldwork and sociopolitical change', *Social Problems*, 27: 309–19.

Scheper-Hughes, Nancy 1981 '*Cui bonum* – for whose good? A dialogue with Sir Raymond Firth', *Human Organization*, 40: 371–2.

Schuman, Howard 1982 'Artifacts are in the mind of the beholder', *American Sociologist*, 17: 21–8.

Schuman, Howard and Jean Converse 1971 'The effects of black and white interviewers on black responses in 1968', *Public Opinion Quarterly*, 35: 44–68.

Schur, Edwin M. 1965 *Crimes without Victims*. Englewood Cliffs, NJ: Prentice-Hall.

Scott, John 1990 *A Matter of Record: Documentary Sources in Social Research*. Cambridge: Polity Press.

Scott, W. Richard 1965 'Field methods in the study of organizations' in James G. March (ed.), *Handbook of Organizations*. Chicago: Rand McNally.

Sechrest, Lee and Melinda Phillips 1979 'Unobtrusive measures: an overview' in Lee Sechrest (ed.), *Unobtrusive Measurement Today*. San Francisco: Jossey-Bass.

Seidel, John 1991 'Method and madness in the application of computer technology to qualitative data analysis', in Nigel G. Fielding and Raymond M. Lee (eds), *Using Computers in Qualitative Research*. London: Sage.

Seiler, Laren H. and James M. Murtha 1980 'Federal regulation of social research using "human subjects": a critical assessment', *American Sociologist*, 15: 146–56.

Selltiz, Claire 1955 'The use of survey methods in a citizens' campaign against discrimination', *Human Organization*, 14: 19–25.

Shalin, Dimitri N. 1990 'Sociology for the *glasnost* era: institutional and substantive changes in recent Soviet sociology', *Social Forces*, 68: 1019–39.

Shapiro, Susan P. 1987 'The social control of impersonal trust', *American Journal of Sociology*, 93: 623–58.

Sheatsley, Paul B. 1983 'Questionnaire construction and item writing' in Peter H. Rossi, James D. Wright and Andy B. Anderson (eds), *Handbook of Survey Research*. New York: Academic Press.

Shils, Edward 1980 'Social science and social policy' in Edward Shils, *The Calling of Sociology and Other Essays on the Pursuit of Learning*. Chicago: Chicago University Press.

Shipman, Marten 1980 'A view from experience in local government' in Malcolm Cross (ed.), *Social Research and Public Policy: Three Perspectives*. London: Social Research Association.

Shlapentokh, Vladimir 1987 *The Politics of Sociology in the Soviet Union*. Boulder, CO: Westview Press.

Sieber Joan E. 1992 'The ethics and politics of sensitive research' in Claire M. Renzetti and Raymond M. Lee (eds), *Researching Sensitive Topics*. Newbury Park, CA: Sage.

Sieber Joan E. and Barbara Stanley 1988 'Ethical and professional dimensions of socially sensitive research', *American Psychologist*, 43: 49–55.

Siegel, Karolynn and Laurie J. Bauman 1986 'Methodological issues in AIDS-related research' in Douglas A. Feldman and Thomas M. Johnson (eds), *The Social Dimensions of AIDS*. New York: Praeger.

Silver, Roxanne, Cheryl Boon and Mary H. Stones 1983 'Searching for meaning in misfortune: making sense of incest', *Journal of Social Issues*, 39: 81–102.

Silverman, David 1989 'Making sense of a precipice: constituting identity in an HIV clinic' in Peter Appleton, Graham Hart and Peter Davies (eds), *AIDS: Social Representations and Practices*. London: Falmer Press.

Simitis, Spiros 1981 'Data protection and research: a case study of control', *American Journal of Comparative Law*, 29: 583–605.

Simon, Rita J., Von Bakanic and Clark McPhail 1986 'Who complains to journal editors and what happens', *Sociological Inquiry*, 56: 259–71.

Simpson, Richard L. 1961 'Expanding and declining fields in American sociology', *American Sociological Review*, 26: 458–66.

Singer, Eleanor 1978 'Informed consent: consequences for response rate and response quality in social surveys', *American Sociological Review*, 43: 144–62.

Singer, Eleanor 1983 'Informed consent procedures: some reasons for minimal effects on response' in Robert F. Boruch and Joe E. Cecil (eds), *Solutions to Ethical and Legal Problems in Social Research*. New York: Academic Press.

Singer, Eleanor 1990 'A question of accuracy: how journalists and scientists report research on hazards', *Journal of Communication Research*, 40: 102–16.

Singer, Merrill 1992 'AIDS and US ethnic minorities: the crisis and alternative anthropological approaches', *Human Organization*, 51: 89–95.

Sirken, Monroe G. 1974 'The counting rule strategy in sample surveys', *Proceedings of the American Statistical Association (Social Statistics Section)*: 119–23.

Sirken, M.G., G.P. Indefurth, C.E. Burnham and K.M. Danchik 1975 'Household sample surveys of diabetes: design effects of counting rules', *Proceedings of the American Statistical Association (Social Statistics Section)*: 659–63.

Sjoberg, Gideon and Roger Nett 1968 *A Methodology for Social Research*. New York: Harper & Row.

Sluka, Jeffrey A. 1990 'Participant observation in violent social contexts', *Human Organization*, 49: 114–26.

Smart, Carol 1984 *The Ties that Bind*. London: Routledge & Kegan Paul.

Smith David J. 1983 *Police and People in London: Volume 1: Survey of Londoners*. London: Policy Studies Institute.

Smith, Dennis 1988 *The Chicago School: A Liberal Critique of Capitalism*. London: Macmillan.

Smith, Linda L., Walter T. Federer and Damaraju Raghavarao 1974 'A comparison of three techniques for eliciting truthful answers to sensitive questions', *Proceedings of the American Statistical Association (Social Statistics Section)*: 447–52.

Snyderman, Mark and Stanley Rothman 1990 *The IQ Controversy, the Media and Public Controversy*. New Brunswick, NJ: Transaction Books.

Spector, Malcolm 1980 'Learning to study public figures' in William B. Shaffir, Robert A. Stebbins and Allan Turowetz (eds), *Fieldwork Experience: Qualitative Approaches to Social Research*. New York: St Martin's Press.

Spencer, Gary 1973 'Methodological issues in the study of bureaucratic élites: a case study of West Point', *Social Problems*, 21: 90–103.

Spradley, James P. 1979 *The Ethnographic Interview*. New York: Holt, Rinehart & Winston.

Spradley, James P. 1980 *Participant Observation*. New York: Holt, Rinehart & Winston.

Stanley, Barbara, Joan E. Sieber and Gary B. Melton 1987 'Empirical studies of ethical issues in research: a research agenda', *American Psychologist*, 42: 735–41.

Starn, Orin 1991 'Missing the revolution: anthropologists and the war in Peru', *Cultural Anthropology*, 6: 63–91.

Starr, Paul 1987 'The sociology of official statistics' in William Alonso and Paul Starr (eds), *The Politics of Numbers*. New York: Russell Sage Foundation.

Steinberg, J. 1970 'Data linkage problems and solutions' in R.L. Biscoe (ed.), *Data Bases, Computers and the Social Sciences*. New York: Wiley.

Stocking, S. Holly and Sharon L. Dunwoody 1982 'Social science in the mass media: images and evidence' in Joan E. Sieber (ed.), *The Ethics of Social Research: Fieldwork, Regulation and Publication*. New York: Springer-Verlag.

Sudman, Seymour 1983 'Applied Sampling' in Peter H. Rossi, James D. Wright and Andy B. Anderson (eds), *Handbook of Survey Research*. New York: Academic Press.

Sudman, Seymour and Norman Bradburn 1974 *Response Effects on Surveys: A Review and Synthesis*. Chicago: Aldine.

Sudman, Seymour and Norman M. Bradburn 1982 *Asking Questions: A Practical Guide to Questionnaire Design*. San Francisco: Jossey-Bass.

Sudman, Seymour and Graham Kalton 1986 'New developments in the sampling of special populations', *Annual Review of Sociology*, 12: 401–29.

Sudnow, David 1965 'Normal crimes: sociological features of the penal code', *Social Problems*, 12: 255–64.

Sullivan, Teresa A. and Daniel B. Cornfield 1982 'Gaining access to the large corporation for research'. Paper presented at the Convention of the Society for the Study of Social Problems, San Francisco.

Survey Research Center 1976 *Interviewer's Manual*. Ann Arbor: Institute for Social Research, University of Michigan.

Sykes, Wendy and Martin Collins 1988 'Effects of modes of interview: experiments in the UK', in Robert M. Groves, Paul P. Biemer, Lars E. Lyberg, James T. Massey, William L. Nicholls II and Joseph Waksberg (eds), *Telephone Survey Methodology*. New York: Wiley.

Sykes, Wendy and Gerald Hoinville 1985 *Telephone Interviewing on a Survey of Social Attitudes: A Comparison with Face-to-Face Procedures*. London: Social and Community Planning Research.

Tan, Ying Hui 1988 'Punishment for journalist's contempt', *The Independent*, 27 January: 24.

Tanur, Judith M. 1983–4 'Methods for large-scale surveys and experiments' in Samuel Leinhardt (ed.), *Sociological Methodology*. San Francisco: Jossey-Bass.

Tanzi, Victor 1982 'A second (and more skeptical) look at the underground economy in the United States' in Victor Tanzi (ed.), *The Underground Economy in the United States and Abroad*. Lexington, MA: D.C. Heath.

Taylor, D. Garth 1982 'Pluralistic ignorance and the spiral of silence: a formal analysis', *Public Opinion Quarterly*, 46: 311–35.

Taylor, Rupert 1988 'Social scientific research on the "troubles" in Northern Ireland', *Economic and Social Review*, 19: 123–45.

Taylor, Steve 1989 'How prevalent is it?' in Wendy Stainton Rogers, Denise Hevey and Elizabeth Ash (eds) *Child Abuse and Neglect: Facing the Challenge*. London: B.T. Batsford.

Tentler, Thomas N. 1977 *Sin and Confession on the Eve of the Reformation*. Princeton: Princeton University Press.

Tesch, Renata 1988 'Computer software and qualitative analysis: a reassessment' in G. Blank, J.L. McCartney and E. Brent (eds), *Sociology and New Technology*. · New Brunswick, NJ: Transaction.

Thomas, J.J. 1988 'The politics of the black economy', *Work, Employment and Society*, 2: 169–90.

Thomas, J.J. 1990 'Measuring the underground economy: a suitable case for interdisciplinary treatment?', *American Behavioral Scientist*, 33: 621–37.

Thomas, Rosamund M. 1991 *Espionage and Secrecy: The Official Secrets Acts 1911–1989 of the United Kingdom*. London: Routledge.

Thompson, Andrew 1987 'The New Earnings Survey', *ESRC Data Archive Bulletin*, 37, May: 7–8.

Thorne, Barrie 1983 'Political activist as participant observer: conflicts of commitment in a study of the draft resistance movement of the 1960s' in Robert M. Emerson (ed.), *Contemporary Field Research: A Collection of Readings*. Boston: Little, Brown & Co.

Thornes, Barbara and Jean Collard 1979 *Who Divorces?* London: Routledge & Kegan Paul.

Tibbitts, Helen G. 1962 'Research in the development of sociology: a pilot study in methodology', *American Sociological Review*, 27: 892–901.

Tourganeau, R. and A.W. Smith 1985 'Finding subgroups for surveys', *Public Opinion Quarterly*, 49: 351–65.

Tracy, Paul E. and James Alan Fox 1981 'The validity of randomized response for sensitive measurements', *American Sociological Review*, 46: 187–200.

Trew, Karen and R. Kilpatrick 1984 'The daily life of the unemployed: social and psychological dimensions'. Unpublished MS, Department of Psychology, Queen's University of Belfast.

Trimble, Joseph E. 1977 'The sojourner in the American Indian community: methodological issues and concerns', *Journal of Social Issues*, 33: 159–74.

Troiden, Richard R. 1987 'Walking the line: the personal and professional risks of sex education and research', *Teaching Sociology*, 15: 241–9.

Tropp, Richard 1982 'A regulatory perspective on social science research' in Tom L. Beauchamp, Ruth R. Faden, R. Jay Wallace, Jr and LeRoy Waters (eds), *Ethical Issues in Social Science Research*. Baltimore: Johns Hopkins University Press.

Ullah, Philip 1987 'Unemployed black youth in a northern city' in David Fryer and Philip Ullah (eds), *Unemployed People: Social and Psychological Perspectives*. Milton Keynes: Open University Press.

Umesh, U.N. and Robert A. Peterson 1991 'A critical evaluation of the randomized response method: applications, validation and research agenda', *Sociological Methods and Research*, 20: 104–38.

Van Maanen, John 1982 'Fieldwork on the beat' in John Van Maanen, James M. Dabbs, Jr and Robert R. Faulkner (eds), *Varieties of Qualitative Research*. Beverly Hills: Sage.

Van Maanen, John 1983 'On the ethics of fieldwork' in Robert B. Smith (ed.), *A Handbook of Social Science Methods: Volume 1: An Introduction to Social Research*. Cambridge, MA: Ballinger.

Van Maanen, John 1988 *Tales of the Field*. Chicago: Chicago University Press.

Vargus, Brian S. 1971 'On sociological exploitation: why the guinea pig sometimes bites', *Social Problems*, 19: 238–48.

Vidich, Arthur J. and Joseph Bensman 1958 *Small Town in Mass Society: Class Power and Religion in a Rural Community*. Princeton: Princeton University Press.

Vidich, Arthur J. and Joseph Bensman 1964 'The Springdale Case: academic bureaucrats and sensitive townspeople' in Arthur J. Vidich, Joseph Bensman and Maurice R. Stein (eds), *Reflections on Community Studies*. New York: Wiley.

Waksberg, J. 1978 'Sampling methods for random digit dialling', *Journal of the American Statistical Association*, 73: 40–6.

Walford, Geoffrey 1987 'Research role conflicts and compromises in public schools' in Geoffrey Walford (ed.), *Doing Sociology of Education*. London: Falmer Press.

Walker, Alan 1982 *Unqualified and Underemployed: Handicapped Young People and the Labour Market*. London: Macmillan.

Waller, Willard 1938 *The Family: A Dynamic Interpretation*. New York: Cordon Co.

Wallis, Roy 1976 *The Road to Total Freedom: A Sociological Analysis of Scientology*. London: Heinemann.

Wallis, Roy 1977 'The moral career of a research project' in Colin Bell and Howard Newby (eds), *Doing Sociological Research*. London: Allen & Unwin.

Walsh, Brendan M. 1971 *Religion and Demographic Behaviour in Ireland*. Dublin: Economic and Social Research Institute Paper, No. 55.

Walsh, James Leo 1972 'Comment on Hessler and New', *Human Organization*, 31: 451–2.

Walter, Sheryl L. and Allan R. Adler 1991 'Fees and fee waivers' in Allan Robert Adler (ed.), *Litigation Under the Federal Open Government Laws* (16th edn), Washington, DC: American Civil Liberties Union Foundation.

Walum, Laurel Richardson 1975 'Sociology and the mass media: some major problems and modest proposals', *American Sociologist*, 10: 28–32.

Warner, Stanley 1965 'Randomized response: a technique for eliminating evasive answer bias', *Journal of the American Statistical Association*, 60: 884–8.

Warren, Carol A.B. 1977 'Fieldwork in the gay world: issues in phenomenological research', *Journal of Social Issues*, 33: 93–107.

Warren, Carol A.B. 1984 'Toward a cooptive model of qualitative research', *Communication Quarterly*, 32: 104–12.

Warren, Carol A.B. 1987 *Madwives: Schizophrenic Women in the 1950s*. Rutgers, NJ: Rutgers University Press.

Warren, Carol A.B. 1988 *Gender Issues in Field Research*. Newbury Park, CA: Sage.

Waterman, Stanley and Barry Kosmin 1986 'Mapping an unenumerated ethnic population', *Ethnic and Racial Studies*, 9: 484–50.

Wax, Murray L. 1977 'On fieldworkers and those exposed to fieldwork: Federal Regulations and moral issues', *Human Organization*, 36: 321–8.

Wax, Murray L. 1980 'Paradoxes of "consent" to the practice of fieldwork', *Social Problems*, 27: 272–83.

Wax, Murray L. and Joan Cassell 1979a *Federal Regulations: Ethical Issues and Social Research*. Boulder, CO: Westview Press and The American Association for the Advancement of Science.

Wax, Murray L. and Joan Cassell 1979b 'Fieldwork, ethics and politics: the wider context' in Murray L. Wax and Joan Cassell (eds), *Federal Regulations: Ethical Issues and Social Research*. Boulder, CO: Westview Press and The American Association for the Advancement of Science.

Wax, Murray L. and Joan Cassell 1981 'From regulation to reflection: ethics in social research', *American Sociologist*, 16: 224–9.

Wax, Rosalie H. 1952 'Reciprocity as a field technique', *Human Organization*, 12: 11–21.

Wax, Rosalie H. 1971 *Doing Fieldwork: Warnings and Advice*. Chicago: University of Chicago Press.

Webb, Eugene J., Donald T. Campbell, Richard D. Schwartz and Lee Sechrest 1966 *Unobtrusive Measures: Nonreactive research in the Social Sciences*. Chicago: Rand McNally.

Webb, Eugene J., Donald T. Campbell, Richard D. Schwartz, Lee Sechrest and Janet Belew Grove 1981 *Nonreactive Measures in the Social Sciences*. Boston: Houghton Mifflin.

Webb, Eugene and Karl E. Weick 1983 'Unobtrusive measures in organization theory: a reminder' in John Van Maanen (ed.), *Qualitative Methodology*. Beverly Hills: Sage.

Webb, Norman and Robert Wybrow 1982 *The Gallup Report*. London: Sphere Books.

Weber, Robert Philip 1985 *Basic Content Analysis*. Beverly Hills: Sage.

Weigand, Bruce 1987 'Political considerations of studying tax compliance', *American Sociologist*, 18: 375–84.

Weigel, Russell H. and Jeffrey J. Pappas 1981 'Social science and the press: a case study and its implications', *American Psychologist*, 36: 480–7.

Weinberg, Elizabeth A. 1992 '*Perestroika* and Soviet sociology', *British Journal of Sociology*, 43: 1–10.

Weinberg, Martin and Colin J. Williams 1972 'Fieldwork among deviants: social relations with subjects and others' in Jack D. Douglas (ed.), *Research on Deviance*. New York: Random House.

Weiss, Carol H. and Michael J. Bucuvalas 1980 'Truth tests and utility tests: decision makers' frames of reference for social science research', *American Sociological Review*, 45: 302–13.

Weiss, Carol H. and Eleanor Singer 1988 *Reporting of Social Science in the National Media*. New York: Russell Sage Foundation.

Weppner, Robert S. 1976 'The complete participant: problems in participant observation in a therapeutic community', *Addicitive Diseases: An International Journal*, 2: 643–58.

West, Louis Jolyon 1986 'How not to publicize research: the UCLA violence center' in Jeffrey H. Goldstein (ed.), *Reporting Science: The Case of Aggression*. Hillsdale, NJ: Lawrence Erlbaum Associates.

West, W. Gordon 1980 'Access to adolescent deviants and deviance' in William B. Shaffir, Robert A. Stebbins and Alan Turowetz (eds), *Fieldwork Experience: Qualitative Approaches to Social Research*. New York: St Martin's Press.

Whyte, William Foote 1958 'Editorial – freedom and responsibility in research the "Springdale" Case', *Human Organization*, 17: 1–2.

Whyte, William H. 1955 *Street Corner Society*. Chicago: Chicago University Press.

Williams, J. Allen 1964 'Interviewer–respondent interaction: a study of bias in the information interview', *Sociometry*, 27: 338–52.

Williams, John 1985 'The Police and Criminal Evidence Act and the press' in John Baxter and Laurence Koffman (eds), *Police, the Constitution and the Community*. Abingdon: Professional Books.

Winckler, John 1987 'The fly on the wall of the inner sanctum: observing company directors at work' in George Moyser and Margaret Wagstaffe (eds), *Research Methods for Élite Studies*. London: Allen & Unwin.

Wise, Sue 1987 'A framework for discussing ethical issues in feminist research: a review of the literature', *Studies in Sexual Politics*, 19: 47–88.

Wiseman, F., M. Moriarty and M. Schafer 1976 'Estimating public opinion with the randomized response model', *Public Opinion Quarterly*, 40: 507–13.

Wolff, Kurt H. (ed.) 1950 *The Sociology of Georg Simmel*. New York: Free Press.

Wong, Siu-Lun 1975 'Social enquiries in the People's Republic of China', *Sociology*, 9: 459–76.

Wood, Stephen 1980 'Reactions to Redundancy'. Unpublished PhD thesis, University of Manchester.

Yablonsky, Lewis 1965 'Experiences with the criminal community' in Alvin W. Gouldner and S. M. Miller (eds), *Applied Sociology: Opportunities and Problems*. New York: Free Press.

Yablonsky, Lewis 1968 'On crime, violence, LSD, and legal immunity for social scientists', *American Sociologist*, 3: 148–9.

Yancey, William L. and Lee Rainwater 1970 'Problems in the ethnography of the urban underclasses' in Robert W. Habenstein (ed.), *Pathways to Data*. Chicago: Aldine.

Young, Jock 1971 'The role of the police as amplifiers of deviancy, negotiators of reality and translators of fantasy: some consequences of our present system of drug control as seen in Notting Hill' in Stanley Cohen (ed.), *Images of Deviance*. Harmondsworth: Penguin.

Young, Malcolm 1991 *An Inside Job: Policing and Police Culture in Britain*. Oxford: Clarendon Press.

Young, Penny 1986 'The survey respondent's experience of a structured interview'. Unpublished MS, Social and Community Planning Research, London.

Young, T. R. 1971 'The politics of sociology: Gouldner, Goffman, Garfinkel', *American Sociologist*, 6: 276–81.

Zaslavskaya, Tat'yana 1988 '*Perestrokia* and sociology', *Social Research*, 55: 267–76.

Zaslavsky, V and 'Z' 1981 'Adult political socialization in the USSR: a study of attitudes of Soviet workers to the invasion of Czechoslovakia', *Sociology*, 15: 407–23.

Zdep, S.M. and Isabelle N. Rhodes 1976 'Making the randomized response technique work', *Public Opinion Quarterly*, 40: 531–7.

Zdep, S.M., Isabelle N. Rhodes, R.M. Schwartz and M. Kilkenny 1979 'The validity of the randomized response technique', *Public Opinion Quarterly*, 43: 544–9.

Zich, Jane and Lydia Temoshok 1986 'Applied methodology: a primer on the pitfalls and opportunities in AIDS research' in Douglas A. Feldman and Thomas M. Johnson (eds), *The Social Dimensions of AIDS*. New York: Praeger.

Zimmerman, Don H. and D. Lawrence Weider 1982 'The diary–diary interview method' in Robert B. Smith and Peter K. Manning (eds), *A Handbook of Social Science Methods: Volume 2: Qualitative Methods*. Cambridge, MA: Ballinger.

Zuckerman, Harriet and Robert K. Merton 1971 'Patterns of evaluation in science: institutionalization, structure and functions of the referee system', *Minerva*, 9: 66–100.

Index